The Last of the Best

Los Angeles Times

To all of Jim Murray's fans
who read him and loved him

Los Angeles Times

Book Development Manager: Carla Lazzareschi

Editors: Bill Dwyre
Mike James
Steve Horn

Design and Typography: Michael Diehl

ISBN 1-883792-50-9

Published by the Los Angeles Times
Times Mirror Square, Los Angeles, California 90053
A Times Mirror Company

First printing November 1998

Printed in the U.S.A.

Table of Contents

Foreword

I was out of town that day in 1990 when I heard that Jim Murray had won the Pulitzer Prize. When I called home that night, it was the first thing my wife wanted to talk about. She was really excited.

She said that the first thing Jim had said, as he was being quoted in the press, was "I never thought you could win a Pulitzer Prize just for quoting Tommy Lasorda correctly." I remember thinking, "Wow, what an honor. I'm the first person he talked about."

We were such good friends. I loved just being around him, listening to him, learning from him. I grew up in the East, reading Jimmy Cannon and Red Smith. And then I came to California and started reading Jim Murray. And to my mind, he was the height of them all.

I remember when he used to come into the clubhouse, looking for a column. Back then, the players really knew him, knew who he was. He would walk in that clubhouse and things would change immediately. He'd ask me who would make a good column, and I'd suggest somebody. Then I'd go get the player and bring him into my office and close the door and say, "Here, this is Jim Murray. Use my office. Take all the time you want." Being interviewed by Jim Murray was like getting an audience with the Pope.

—Tommy Lasorda

Former Dodger manager and current executive vice president, who celebrates his 50th year with the Dodger organization in 1999.

Introduction

On September 26, 1998, the Los Angeles Times held a public memorial service for its longtime sports columnist Jim Murray.

Among the featured speakers was Jerry West, former pro basketball star and longtime team official with the Los Angeles Lakers.

Near the end of his speech to a crowd of nearly 3,000 in Dodger Stadium, West said his one wish that day was that the Times, or someone, put together a book that contains "every column Jim Murray ever wrote."

Well, this book is an effort in that direction. When West made his public request, The Last of the Best was already within days of going to press. It features Murray in the '90s, an era of his column writing that followed his 1990 Pulitzer Prize for commentary. Much of his previous work had been reprinted along the way, but nothing in the '90s. The truth is, some of his best work is represented here. Some would find a Pulitzer Prize as an ending to a fine career, with a giant exclamation point. Murray saw it as a confirmation of a fine career and a chance to just keep writing sentences.

Those sentences, of course, were like none other ever written in American sports journalism.

He told the Indy 500 people to begin their race with the call: "Gentlemen, start your coffins."

He speculated that the interminably slow progress on building the freeway outside the new stadium in Cincinnati was because "it was Kentucky's turn to use the cement mixer."

He profiled jockey Bill Shoemaker with a sentence that said it all: "Shoemaker was born 2 pounds 7 ounces and it was the only edge he ever needed in life."

And he went to a boxing weigh-in and gave the readers the real truth with his own quick jab: "Buster Douglas looked like something that should be floating over a Thanksgiving Day Parade."

Jim Murray's loss is tremendous because he won't be writing any new words. But his legacy is tremendous because he left us with so many wonderful old ones.

—Bill Dwyre

Sports Editor, Los Angeles Times
October 1, 1998

1990

• •

JANUARY 29, 1990

Broncos Again Play Clay Pigeons in the NFL's Biggest Skeet Shoot

NEW ORLEANS—What can I tell you?

Embarrassing, huh?

Look. There are certain things that shouldn't happen. You shouldn't be able to club baby seals on an ice floe in the St. Lawrence River. You shouldn't pick wings of butterflies. You shouldn't park a baby carriage on a slippery hill leading down to a river.

And, you shouldn't be allowed to play the Denver Broncos in the Super Bowl.

Where is the Humane Society when you need it? Where are those organizations against cruelty to dumb animals?

The Denver Broncos went to their fate like guys going to the electric chair. They didn't put up much of a fight. Cagney did it better. You should struggle a little.

It wasn't a game, it was an execution. It was the biggest mismatch since the Christians and the lions.

Come back, Bud Grant, wherever you are. Minnesota Vikings, you can come out now. The Super Bowl record for futility has been taken away from you. Denver has been in four Super Bowls now, and they get progressively worse. They lost the first one by 17 points, the second by 19, the third by 32 and Sunday by 45. They have allowed 163 points in four games. They are now the William Jennings Bryans, the Harold Stassens, Tom Deweys of football. The Denver Broncos lost a Super Bowl Sunday. And the Pope is Catholic and the earth is round and John Elway has buck teeth.

I won't say they are a municipal embarrassment around Denver these days, but if you happen to mention "Denver Broncos" on a sidewalk in the Rocky Mountains, you can expect the listener to say "Who?" The only orange in town for a while will be in fruit bins.

Chicago has its Cubs, Hardy had Laurel—and Denver has the Broncos. The community is trying to distance itself from this community embarrassment, but it should just treat the Broncos like backward children. They keep blundering into the Super Bowl. They apparently like the spotlight, the hoopla and just don't seem to comprehend they're making fools of themselves. It's kind of pathetic.

They should have a clause in their agreement with the league that they don't have to play any game under 5,000 feet.

And they shouldn't play the San Francisco 49ers anywhere.

Come to think of it, they haven't played the 49ers yet. You couldn't call what they did Sunday playing football. Chaplin was never funnier.

There wasn't much difference between the two teams. The 49ers were bigger, faster, smarter, tougher, and they looked better in their uniforms. Apart from that, it was a contest. The outcome was as foregone as a tidal wave. You would have been all right if you had the Broncos and 46 points, but don't let that lull you. The 49ers took their head executioner off the field with about 11 minutes left and the score already 55-10.

All right, so Joe Montana can walk on water. Bullets probably bounce off him. He may be the most effective throwing machine in the annals of football. His public humiliation of John Elway and the Denver Broncos was thorough, deadly, impersonal and total. Whoever in history may dispute Joe Montana's eminence as the top of the profession, John Elway ain't one of them. They used to say in Hollywood, "Never make a movie with a dog or Spencer Tracy." Well, you should never get in a Super Bowl with Joe Montana. He's now put away Dan Marino, Boomer Esiason, Ken Andersen and John Elway. The question is no longer whether he's better than his contemporaries, it's whether he's better than his ancestors.

He had help. Some commentator noted that giving Joe Montana

Jerry Rice and Roger Craig was like giving a lion horns.

He scored at will Sunday. If you liked this game you would love pictures of the German army going through Belgium or puppies sailing down a flood on a barn roof. Only people who stop to look at freeway accidents still had their sets on by the fourth quarter.

You expect to get beat by Joe Montana, Roger Craig and Jerry Rice when you play the 49ers, but when guys you never heard of start beating up on you, it's time to throw in the towel.

The chances are you never heard of a guy named Michael Walter. This guy with two first names is a right inside linebacker on the 49ers. This designates a position in which you take the strong side rush of the opposition. It's not a glamour position. You're in the boiler room of football. Your nose bleeds a lot and your ears ring.

You expect Jerry Rice, John Taylor, Roger Craig and even Tom Rathman to catch passes. You don't expect Michael Walter.

Walter became a receiver in the third quarter of the Super Bowl Sunday. It was his first catch of the season. On the face of it, it doesn't look as significant as the graceful receptions of Rice and Taylor and company, but the situation was this: San Francisco was ahead 27-3 as the third quarter opened and the Broncos unaccountably stopped the 49ers on their first series of downs. The Broncos had the ball on their own 24 and were ready to start their comeback drive. On first down, Elway went back to pass.

He threw a beautiful spiral. It had trajectory, fluidity and velocity. Michael Walter was open. He was open because he had seen this same pattern earlier in the game and he broke with the primary receiver. He faked the move again this time but drifted into the path he knew the football was going to take.

It was one of the few passes all day John Elway had right on target. It hit Walter right in the chest. It wasn't so much an interception as a reception. If he'd had the speed of, say, a Rice or a Taylor, he would have scored, too.

What he did was, he put a tombstone on the game for Denver. On the very next play, Joe Montana threw for a touchdown. Denver went quietly after that.

Walter is symptomatic of the kind of ho-hum perfection the 49ers bring to the game of football. You would not ordinarily expect a guy who was a defensive end at the University of Oregon to become a deft, Bill Walsh type of pro linebacker. You would not expect a guy who was cut loose by the Dallas Cowboys to become a Super Bowl receiver.

Michael Walter's picture will never make the cover of Sports Illustrated or the inside pages of the Sporting News. His name never appears in Herb Caen's column. But he leads the 49ers annually in tackles (103 this season, 97 last, and 94 the year before that.)

He made five tackles Sunday—and caught one pass. He's not Joe Montana but he gets Joe the ball.

The 49ers aren't a team, they're a scourge. A dynasty.

If all they had to play was the Denver Broncos, they'd be an empire.

Beating Denver is like being a fighter who goes on tour beating his chauffeur. Around a racetrack, when a horse overcomes this kind of company, they say "He beat nuthin'." Denver shouldn't count. You should have an asterisk after the victory. Denver in a Super Bowl is not a participant, just the scenery.

• •

February 4, 1990

Ben Hogan: The Man, The Myth and the New Tour

The time was 1931, the place, Brookside Golf Club in Pasadena.

Few people would have guessed they were looking at history when this skinny little youngster with the grim visage, hook swing and what was to become a trademark white cap took his stance on the first tee, teeth clenched, knuckles white.

If someone had told them they were looking at the man who would become the most mythic figure in the annals of golf, they would have laughed.

He was barely 5-feet-7, couldn't have weighed 125. His butt was so nonexistent his hip pockets ran together. His clubs had a remnant-barrel look, and his clothes, while neat, had a mail-order look about them.

The only thing that would give him away were the eyes. Gray-blue, they had a piercing quality. They were the eyes of a circling bird of prey: fearless, fierce, the pupil no more than a dot in their imperious center. They were not the eyes of a loser. They were the eyes of a guy who could play the hand.

The ball, when he struck it—with uncommon ferocity, as it turned out—took off in this little flat arc, a low, biting right-to-left trajectory of the classic smother hook.

You picture in the mind someone in the gallery frowning and peering at a pairing sheet. "Who in the world's that?" he will want to know. "Someone named W. Ben Hogan," comes the answer. "Never heard of him," is the response. "If he doesn't get rid of that hook, you never will," comes the retort.

Few ever had a tougher time breaking into golf than Ben Hogan. It is a story almost Dickensian. Or, at least, Horatio Alger.

Four times in the '30s, Hogan tried the golf tour. Four times, he had to pack up and go back to Ft. Worth and start cleaning other people's clubs for a living. His is the story of the most determined, dogged pursuit of a sport dream in history, a refusal to accept failure. Dempsey rode rods, Ruth came out of an orphanage, Knute Rockne was a postman, but no one chased his goal with the single-mindedness of William Ben Hogan.

In the first place, the country was in the grip of the Depression those years. Bread was only a nickel. But nobody had the nickel. You bought day-old loaves for a cent.

When Hogan played in the Pasadena Open, sponsors gave each

contestant a bag of oranges. Hogan lived off them for the week. When he arrived in Oakland for a tournament six years later, thieves jacked up his Model-A Ford and removed the wheels. He might still be there—he had nine cents in his pocket at the time—except he won $380 for finishing fifth in the tournament that week.

He went almost a decade without winning a tournament, but there was something about Hogan that uneased the competition. For one thing, he practiced. Oh, how he practiced! He stayed on the course until his hands bled or he had to putt by flashlight, then he went to his hotel room and propped a pillow in a chair and practiced hitting wedges into it until the guy in the next room complained. He putted grooves in the floor rugs. He broke a motel mirror once practicing his takeaway.

It was a hard time. Veterans on the tour did not help the newcomers the way they do today. They even hazed them. You never spoke to a rookie. He was after your money and there wasn't enough to go around.

Hogan didn't mind. I once asked him if his peers ever offered any advice on his game when he first came on tour. "I never asked them," said Hogan, coldly. "I didn't belong to the lodge."

In a way, he never did. There was always something about Hogan that set him apart. For one thing, he hit the ball 10 to 15 yards farther than anybody except for the tour gorilla, Jimmy Thomson. For another, there was a purposefulness about Ben Hogan on the course that made you shudder. It was almost as if he were extracting some frightful revenge from it. He didn't play a course, he stalked it.

He unnerved you. Even early in his career, other pros began an attitude of "Who is this guy?"

He studied his game. He studied your game. He studied the course. He was an agronomist, a geologist, engineer, surveyor. "I watched them fellows like a hawk," he admits. The other pros got the message. Hogan became "the Hawk" on the tour.

Others played a course. Hogan memorized it. He knew the salinity of the soil and its composition down to the core of the earth. He didn't just hit the ball, he controlled it. "You have to learn how to manage a round," he explains. "You can be the best player out there, but if you don't engineer the round you can't win."

When he finally licked the hook, it was all over. Hogan broke the logjam in his career, winning the North-South Open at Pinehurst, N.C., in 1940, and from then on, golf was his.

There are more myths about Hogan than there are about Lincoln. Golfers love to tell Hogan stories far into the night. Everyone has his favorite Hogan story. He's half-man, half-myth. He was a cult.

The funny part is, it was all true. No one ever struck a golf ball with the precision and authority of a Ben Hogan. Mike Souchak said it best. "Ben Hogan," he said, "just knows something about hitting a golf ball the rest of us don't know."

His record speaks for itself—62 tournaments won, many of them after he had his vena cava removed after his accident. In 1953, he entered seven tournaments and won five of them—the U.S. Open, the British Open, the Masters, the Colonial and the Pan American Open. When Hogan didn't win a tournament, he didn't miss the cut, he finished second.

He won a Portland Open once by 17 shots—over Byron Nelson, no less. He was 27 under par.

He has always been a man as careful with his name as he is with his drives. Many years ago, when a promoter came up with the idea of a chain of golf schools using the Hogan name, the real Hogan declined. He could not consider anyone a pupil unless he personally taught them, he explained.

Which makes it special and unique that the name Ben Hogan is going on the newest tour concept, a beefed-up, sanctioned mini-tour for the younger, non-exempt players of the tour, the Ben Hogans of tomorrow, if you will (or if there can be).

Ben has lent his name to this tour because he remembers what it was like to be the new kid on the block with a hook grip and big dreams.

The Ben Hogan Tour, which kicks off in Bakersfield this weekend, is a 30-event series of 54-hole tournaments in which the prize money is $100,000, but the even better news is that the top five finishers on the Ben Hogan Tour get their regular PGA Tour cards for next season.

It is a triple-A league of golf. Says Hogan: "I wish they had something like this when I was coming up."

I don't. Anything less than the crucible he went through and Hogan might not be Hogan. And wouldn't that be a terrible thing for golf! I mean, what would Lincoln be without the log cabin?

• • • • • • • • • • • • • • • • • • • •

FEBRUARY 20, 1990

She Doesn't Need the Kindness of Strangers

Hogan won here. So did Snead. Byron Nelson. Tommy Bolt won his first tournament here, Johnny Miller almost his last.

Nicklaus never won here. Neither did Palmer. But a Pat Fitzsimons did. So did a T.C. Chen. It was their only tour victories.

Riviera is a grande dame of American golf courses. A golf tournament at Riviera is like a World Series in Yankee Stadium, an opera at La Scala, a waltz in Vienna, a war in the Balkans. Fitting. The way it should be.

But the proposition before the house is, is she a fading old dowager living in the shadows of a glorious past, a scrapbook golf course? Today, they build golf courses with three-story traps, doglegs to nowhere, artificial lakes, railroad ties instead of real trees, man-made obstacle courses more suited to training a group of Marines than testing athletes, 18-hole Halls of Horror, as distorted as amusement park mirrors.

Riviera may be the last golf course they held a U.S. Open on that they didn't hopelessly try to trick up. In fact, it's the reason why they began to remanufacture Open courses. When Ben Hogan and two other players broke the old Open record here, the U.S. Golf Assn. vowed never to let that happen again even if it had to put quicksand in the traps.

The USGA was horrified, but the facts of the matter were, Hogan would have broken the Open record underwater that year.

But that was then. Now, Hogan's Riviera record (275) gets broken more often than the federal speed limit. Fitzsimons tied it in 1975. Hale Irwin broke it (272) the next year. Nine guys have broken the old Hogan mark in the past 14 years. Lanny Wadkins shot a 264 in 1985.

So, is Riviera yesterday's roses? Is it cowering in a corner with its hands over its head saying "Please don't hit me anymore!" as the world's best pros descend on it this week for the 1990 Nissan Los Angeles Open?

Hardly. Riviera is still one of the world's best pure tests of golf. It's a golf course, not a booby trap.

The test of a golf course is, if you play your shots right, you make birdie. If you don't, you make bogey. It's not a course, as Jack Nicklaus' Memorial was before they ironed it out, where your scorecard reads "4-4-3-11," or "3-4-9." It doesn't have blind shots, it doesn't have any water on it. It doesn't have unfair bounces. Its only eccentricity is a sand trap in the middle of one green. It's like a British Open course. It can be handled. But you better bring your A-game. No lucky bounces here.

They shoot low numbers at the Riv now because the equipment is better, the balls go farther, the competition is tougher. And the PGA is not interested in having one of its weekly tournaments look like a truck-drivers' flight at a municipal track in Terre Haute.

There were years when, in advance of the L.A. Open, the club would dutifully grow ankle-deep rough till the fairway driving area would be barely 22 yards wide. The members would struggle with it. Then, on the eve of play, the PGA's Jack Tuthill would arrive, take one look at the narrowing and order "Cut it back!"

Riviera is nobody's pitch-and-putt patch. Lanny Wadkins shot 264 here in 1985. But he shot an 84 in a third round only a few years earlier.

When the weather cooperates, Riviera can be rewarding. When the wind blows off the sea (or land), it can be as penal as Alcatraz.

Riviera is not some parvenu in the neighborhoods of the golf world. It is not a mass of insecurities like some resort course that feels it has to be just this side of a climb on Mt. Everest to command respect. Riviera knows what it is and where it belongs. Its ego is not bruised by 63s. Like the Brits, it can say, good on ya, mate!

So, what the golfers will face today is not some faded, jaded old belle, but a formidable adversary. There is not an easy shot on it. I said to Tom Weiskopf, the great player, one day, "Don't you like that tough finishing hole, 18?" and Weiskopf retorted, "There are 18 tough finishing holes out there!"

They are, in order:

No. 1—If there's an easy hole at Riv for the pros, this is it—501 yards to a big green from an elevated tee. You have to get your birdies here. If you don't get birdie or eagle on the last day, forget it. In one memorable L.A. Open duel, Hale Irwin and Tom Watson both eagled this hole on the last day. You'll hate to leave it. It's like saying goodbye to Kathleen Turner.

No. 2—The golf course starts here. A 460-yard par four that the members play as a five. Weiskopf was lying four in a fairway trap here one Open when he suddenly realized he had the flu. He must have. From the look on his face, his temperature must have been 104 and his blood pressure 220/90. This hole can give you the flu. This hole can give you schizophrenia.

No. 3—Looks easy. So did Buster Douglas.

No. 4—Hogan said it was the toughest par three in America when the wind was blowing. The wind is always blowing. I asked Snead what he used here one Open. "I cut a little driver in there," he said. "You either make two or five."

No. 5—You'll never believe it's only 426 yards when you play it. You know how they name holes at the Masters the "Flowering Crabapple" or the "White Dogwood"? They should name this hole "Help!"

No. 6—It has a trap in the middle of the green. I love it! Greatest invention since the thumbscrew. I'd give a week's pay to see Curtis Strange get in it.

No. 7—Hit it straight. Also, hit it left because everything slopes to the right. Don't hit it too far left or you'll have the ever-popular tree-root shot. Broken more clubs than Tommy Bolt.

No. 8—Looks boring. So did Lizzie Borden. Gary Player looked at it for the first time and said, "Where is the fairway?" There isn't any, Gary. It's all trees. Call this hole "Tarzan."

No. 9—You can spray off the tee. If your second shot is short, kiss your act goodbye. Uphill all the way and no green to speak of.

No. 10—Looks like a long par three (306 yards). It's evil. Try frontal assault and you can go back and forth across peninsula green till sun sets. Lew Worsham did in the '48 Open, and he was defending champion.

No. 11—At least it's a par five. If you can drive the ball through a keyhole, you're all right. Green is about the size of Rickey Henderson's strike zone. And you know what that is.

No. 12—Bogart used to sit under the tree that guards the left side of this green with a thermos full of something nourishing. It's like sitting next to a flooded-out railroad trestle and waiting for the trains to come. Ghoulish.

No. 13—Tom Watson hit two balls out of bounds here when he was leading one year. Call this hole "Jail." Hit it in the trees on the left and you'll need a court order to get out.

No. 14—A par three, it says here. Any more sand and you'd need a camel. Better make two here.

No. 15—This hole has the soul of a serial killer. It's long (450 yards), doglegs right and has more cleavage in the green than Dolly Parton. It's like putting in a bathtub where the hole is on the side.

No. 16—I once made a hole in one here. This hole should be ashamed of itself.

No. 17—Long, downwind, and you can play drivers off the fairway. But Fuzzy Zoeller once four-putted himself out of the tournament on this hole. You can be aggressive with this hole. You can kick a sleeping lion, too.

No. 18—Ah! The Enforcer! The keeper of the keys, defender of the faith. If Jack Nicklaus could have just parred this hole four days, he would have won two tournaments—including the PGA. It's a fortress. The fairway sits above the tee 50 yards. If you need a three here to win, bring a rosary.

Well, that's Riviera as it looks from here. Shoot to kill. The old girl hates to be patronized.

MARCH 13, 1990

The Most Unwelcome Spectator

The time you won your town the race
We chaired you through the market place;
Man and boy stood cheering by
And home we brought you shoulder-high.
Today, the road all runners come,
Shoulder-high, we bring you home,
And set you at your threshold down,
Townsman of a stiller town.

—To an Athlete Dying Young, A.E. Housman

Midcourt in a basketball game is a terrible place to die. So is the five-yard line of the Chicago Bears. So is the center ring at Madison Square Garden.

Age 23 is a terrible time to die. But, then, so is 63. Maybe no one is ever ready.

"Ventricular fibrillation" is something palsied old men get, not power forwards. Doctors might be tempted to disbelieve their instruments.

How could Hank Gathers, 6 feet 7, 210 pounds, a franchise basketball player, fast, strong, a stupendous physical specimen, be a walking invalid? How could Lou Gehrig, the most powerful baseball player I have ever seen, be a victim of a disease so terrible it would reduce him to a man without the strength to lift a cup of coffee? What kind of cosmic joke is at work here?

Death should stay away from young men's games. Death belongs in musty hospital rooms, sickbeds. It should not impinge its terrible presence on the celebrations of youth, reap its frightful harvest in fields where cheers ring and bands play and banners wave.

But it does. Sudden-Athletic-Death syndrome is all too common. Medical symposiums have been held on the subject.

Yet it is shocking when it comes. It is resented. Death should know its place. How dare it claim our youngest, our fittest, our future? The inexorable workings of God? Or the inevitable blundering of man?

Obviously, Hank Gathers should not have been playing basketball. The awful result makes that abundantly clear. He fainted at a free-throw line as recently as December. Dying men should not be at a free-throw line. A slam dunk is not recommended therapeutic care for an arrhythmic heart. The doctors are very clear on that.

As long ago as 1985, cardiologists met and addressed the problem with a finding of their society that no one with cardiomyopathic problems should be playing pressure competitive sports.

But how do you tell a kid whose whole life, whose every dream, has been built around a sport? How do you say, "Tough luck, Hank, but you're going back to the projects. It's all over. You've got all the tools, size, speed, reflexes, but there's this one tiny muscle that's out of sync—your heart." How do you tell a guy who led the nation in scoring and rebounding and led his little school into the gaudy NCAA tournament that he doesn't belong out there?

Mickey Mantle probably should not have been playing big league baseball. He had osteomyelitis. Players like Norm Larker and Rick Reichardt had only one kidney. Earnie Shavers fought with a detached retina. Sam Langford fought with two of them.

Russ Christopher pitched for seven years in the majors with what was described as "a hole in his heart." He pitched till 1949 and had 17 saves in his last full year. He died in 1954. He was 37 years old.

There is a young man playing basketball in South Carolina now, Joe Rhett, who began having fainting spells. His heart stopped altogether for five beats under testing. He has been fitted with a pacemaker to keep the heart jarred into activity.

Should he play? Doubtful. Will he play? Doubtless.

One of the greatest athletes the San Joaquin Valley, which was a hotbed of them, ever produced was a young man you never heard of. Leon Patterson put the shot more than 60 feet the first time he ever picked it up. He was the first high school athlete to throw that far. He threw the discus 167-10 the first time he tried it.

He ran the 100 in 10.1, pole-vaulted 12 feet in high school on a steel pole—when the Olympic record was 14 feet—threw the javelin almost 200 feet. He was a good-enough football player to have Notre Dame after him and he high-jumped 5-11 in high school, wearing a baseball uniform. The Olympic record was 6-8 that year.

Leon Patterson had his heart set on the 1956 Olympics at Melbourne. He was a threat in the shot and discus and a natural for the decathlon.

He went out to get a summer job in the oil fields near Coalinga and, when he took the physical, they found albumin in his urine. It could have been any one of a number of things. In Leon's case it was the worst—Bright's disease, a catastrophic disorder of the kidneys, incurable and, in that year, largely untreatable.

He could live 10 years, the doctors said, if he gave up sports and strenuous activity. Leon compromised. He gave up football. He clung to track and field.

He got married. Ten years can be long enough if you play it right, he and his bride told themselves. Besides, doctors can be wrong.

The doctors were wrong. Leon Patterson didn't have 10 years, he had two. He died screaming after a summer spent loading 40-pound crates of grapes onto boxcars in the broiling valley sun, sometimes working 17 hours a day.

Did Hank Gathers know the direness of his plight? If so, would a life as a might-have-been be acceptable to him? Should he have had a say in the matter? Could he have believed the doctors?

Marc Buoniconti, the son of pro football's Nick Buoniconti, suffered a severed spinal cord while making a tackle in a college game. He was quoted in the papers the other day as saying, "I've always said that a young player will always want to play, whatever the risk. It's up to the doctors and trainers to stand between him and the field."

But the poet has said, "I must have my dreams if I must live." The athletes are wrong to risk all for a career in the light, a life in the center ring. We, in crabbed age, know that. But did we know it at 23? Remember, young men march off, singing, to war.

And round that early-laureled head
Will flock to gaze the strengthless dead
And find unwithered on its curls
A garland briefer than a girl's.

• • • • • • • • • • • • • • • • • • • •

MARCH 18, 1990

Old 98: Something Special to the End

He used to call me "the boulevardier." It was our own wry joke because my socks didn't always match, my ties were sometimes an off-purple and my sports coats glowed in the dark.

I showed up at the Winter Olympics in Grenoble in 1968 in wing-tip shoes, alpaca sweater and a topcoat you could see through. He took one horrified look and hustled me over to Geneva ski stores where I got the apres-ski boots, fur-lined jacket with hood, ski poles—everything but the surgical cast autographed "Better Luck Next Run—Jean Claude." He might have saved my life. I had walking pneumonia by the time he took charge.

Taking charge was his stock in trade. The world knew him as Old 98 or Harmon of Michigan. I knew him as friend. I called him "The Fox" because he always ran through life as if something was chasing him. Tom was not a guy to sit still.

No one ever ran with a football any better, not the Galloping Ghost, The Gipper, O.J., Walter Payton, Gale Sayers—nobody. He was almost the last of what they used to call the "triple threat" players.

He lived a life right out of Frank Merriwell. Campus god, war hero, celebrity, he was a James Bond come to life. He married a gorgeous movie star and they had the most beautiful children this side of the "Sound of Music" cast.

Death caught Tom Harmon from behind the other day. Believe me, it never would have happened if he had had a football in his hands. It came so quickly he didn't have time to change gears or stiff-arm it.

He didn't die the way most people do—in a hospital bed or under round-the-clock care. He died, so to speak, under his own power. He died, in a manner of speaking, coming out of a locker room. He had just shot 18 holes of birdie-riddled golf, he had showered, he felt good, and he was off to a travel office to get airline tickets for a golf tournament, the Bogey Busters, in Dayton in June. Tommy had no idea the game was in the fourth quarter.

The phrase "All-American" was invented for guys such as Tom Harmon. He had the name, the game. He bought the whole ethic. He had the kind of football career no one will ever have again. For all his marvelous skills, Bo Jackson will never play defense. Harmon did. Skillfully.

He punted, passed, ran, kicked field goals and points-after-touchdown. He ran for 33 touchdowns at Michigan, passed for 16, scored 237 points. He won the 1940 Heisman trophy, the sixth collegian to do so.

He was a combat pilot in the war, shot down over China and crash-landing in South America. He was a survivor. He walked out of both crashes. They made a movie about his life. He joined the Rams after four years in the war and he still has the team's third-longest run from scrimmage (84 yards against the Bears) behind Kenny Washington (92) and Eric Dickerson (85). He holds the record for the second-longest punt return (88 yards vs. the Detroit Lions) in Ram history. If it had to do with football, Tom could do it. Harmon seldom went down from the first hit. It was said in college he led the conference in torn jerseys and broken noses. There were no facemasks in the Big Ten in the '40s.

I knew Harmon as a broadcaster and golf partner in late years. He was a man of great pride. Whatever Tom Harmon did, he wanted to do well. He never got more than a few pounds over his playing weight, his dress was impeccable, his habits beyond reproach. He radiated dignity and reserve, but he was a staunch friend.

I remember once our rotund friend, the columnist Bud Tucker, whose forte was Don Rickles' type of insult humor, was trying his routines on a glowering stranger at the hospitality suite in Baltimore during a World Series. Suddenly, the fellow lunged at Tucker with intent to do great bodily harm. Harmon shot out of his seat, collared the combatant, wrapped his arms around his neck and hissed, "You gonna sit down and be quiet or do I snap your head off?" The fellow sat down. Quietly.

Another time, we were playing golf at Augusta. The club permitted us media types to play the course the morning after the Masters, and Harmon had played a typically fastidious Harmon game when an interloper took up heckling. What was so great about Tom Harmon? he sneered. Why, he went on, he bet Tom couldn't even beat him running. Oh, said Tom, when and where? Here and now, the guy answered. As they lined up, the guy, a little unnerved, wanted to know: "You ever run on a track?"

"A little," Tom answered. (He was the Indiana state sprint and hurdle champion.) As they lined up for the start, the fellow looked nervously at Harmon. "Aren't you going to take your coat off?" "Why?" Harmon answered coolly. "We're only going to run, aren't we? We're not going to fight or anything?" Harmon won the 60-yard dash by 10 yards.

He called everybody "Pappy." He enjoyed celebrity but he had a sense of humor about it. He was twitted once at a testimonial as speaker after speaker extolled him for bravery in being shot down or crashing on two continents. "Hey, Harmon," the emcee told him. "Your plane went down in China and South America? I don't know how to tell you this, but we were at war with Japan and Germany. What were you, on your way to bomb Peru?!" Harmon laughed louder than anybody.

He used to tell the story himself of the time when he came to California and his colleagues on the Rams were Les Horvath and Glenn Davis, Heisman trophy winners, both. And, when his wife dusted off his trophy and announced proudly it was the Heisman, Ruth Hirsch was to blurt out "Oh, is that what that is?! I thought everybody had one!"

At the height of his career, in a celebrated case up at Strawberry Canyon in Berkeley, a fan came out of the stands to tackle him as he was on his way to a touchdown. I like to think Death had to come out of the stands or Harmon would have eluded it, too. He died as he had lived—a hero. You never went into a room with Harmon without someone coming up to you and recalling "the day you beat us at Minnesota," or "the day you ripped through the Buckeyes."

He takes an era with him. When Tom came on the field, it was still a game for raccoon coats, hip flasks, porkpie hats and the last of the flappers. He helped the game become the big time it did.

Some guys, when their career is over, get out of shape. It's hard to believe they ever were athletes. Not Harmon. Right to the end he looked like a guy who still could go all the way.

Wherever he is today, I hope they have a football. And a guy who can block. I know one thing: The number 98 won't be taken. There was only one.

• • • • • • • • • • • • • • • • • • •

APRIL 17, 1990

By George, This Book Beats All

I always thought I had this understanding with political pundit George Will. He would take care of the day-to-day stuff, such as what to do about Lithuania, how to handle Kadafi, who should be President. You know, the minutiae.

I, on the other hand, would handle the really important matters of our time, such as how to pitch to Tony Gwynn with men on, whom to start in the All-Star game, whether the designated hitter is good or bad for baseball.

I would leave the running of the world to him. I had more pressing responsibilities—running the American or National League.

I figured he was busy enough telling George Bush what to do next. I had the tougher assignment—telling George Steinbrenner.

So, you can imagine my chagrin the other day when I picked up a book by Will and found he had left the posh areas of journalism—the relative inconsequentialities of Mideast policy, the European Economic Community, what to do about Noriega—and ventured into the treacherous shoals of infield fly rules, bunt signs, pickoff plays, back-door sliders and double steals.

The title of the book was "Men At Work," so I knew right away it wasn't about Washington, D.C. What I didn't bargain for was that George would presume to instruct me in the nuances of a game that I've been covering, man and boy, since—well, since Brooklyn was still in the league, the Braves were in Boston, the Athletics in Philadelphia and the Orioles were the St. Louis Browns.

I think the only fair thing now is for me to write a book analyzing the State Department's policy in Latin America, which, come to think of it, is not too different from the St. Louis Browns' at that.

You would not expect George Will to be handling any subject sub-Arnold Toynbee and a book by him subtitled "The Craft of Baseball" would be a form of literary slumming.

Not to George Will. To George Will, baseball is an American institution as lofty as the Supreme Court, the State Department or Capitol Hill. Gibbon never put more devotion, concentration and attention to construction in "The Decline and Fall of the Roman Empire" than George puts into his examination of the grand old game.

"I feel as if my life will be downhill from here," he notes. "It was the hardest work I've ever done. There was always more to say. You know, W.H. Auden once said that no poem is ever finished. It is abandoned. That's the way I felt about this book. I had to yield it up to the publisher, but I made changes in it right through the first press run."

Will feels his lifelong love affair with baseball is requited. "I wrote the book as a kind of thank-you letter to baseball," he explains. "A thank-you for what it has meant to me and my family. To me, baseball is a gift. A legacy. I see baseball as a realm of excellence, a pool of craftsmanship in an ocean of shoddiness."

Adds Will: "If America made its automobiles with the same care and precision baseball brings to its craft, the streets of downtown Tokyo would be jammed with Fords and Chevys."

George's book is not for the casual fan. It delves into the clockwork of baseball. It is a surprising book to a fan used to a chronicle of the frivolities of our national pastime. It lingers lovingly on the inner game, the microchips, if you will. If you want to know what Bo Jackson is really like, or what Jose Canseco had for breakfast, or is driving these days, this book is not for you. If you want to know how to pitch to Bo or Jose or when to pitch to them, George brings you the answers of experts.

It is not an ivory-tower book. George crisscrossed America's locker rooms in search of baseball's secrets.

George Will has been known to come down hard on the striped-pants diplomats of Foggy Bottom, but the pinstripes of baseball draw his unbounded respect.

He defends the game as eloquently as any man who ever collected a bubble-gum card or caught a foul ball. So far as George is concerned, the national anthem should be "Take Me Out to the Ball Game." He doesn't care if he never gets back, either.

Will reserves his scorn for those who find the game dull: "Red Smith put it best. He said baseball is a dull game only to dull people."

Says Will: "People speak of the game as 'unhurried' or 'leisurely.' That's silly. There's something going on every minute. There's barely enough time between pitches for all the thinking that's going on. Baseball action involves blazing speeds and fractions of seconds. The pace of the action is relentless. Folks from the serious quarterlies like to say baseball 'has the pace of America's pastoral past.' This is nonsense on stilts. Any late 20th-Century academic who thinks a 19th-Century farmer's day was a leisurely and unhurried stroll from sunup to sundown needs a reality transplant."

A born-and-bred Cub fan, Will knows what makes a true baseball fan: suffering. The book was more than a labor of love. It was an effort to know the game better. "I don't write to tell what I know. I write to find out what I know."

What he has found out he knows about baseball is considerable. The book is replete with nuggets of facts more often overlooked in the grand scheme of things. For instance, did you know that Babe Ruth, no less, stole home 10 times in his career, Ty Cobb stole home 45 times, while the all-time base-stealing champion, Lou Brock, never stole home? Rickey Henderson has stolen home only four times and not once since 1982.

Why? Will provides the answer: With the renaissance of base-stealing, with the artificial surfaces, pitchers don't take a windup with a man on third anymore.

When Will wants to find out why there are no more .400 hitters, he goes to the record book to find out how many hits Cobb got on his fourth and fifth times at bat. (A lot.) Reason: Relief pitchers were not in vogue in those days. A reliever was just a mop-up sore-armed ex-starter or a junk-throwing kid without an "out" pitch, not the formidable specialist of today.

But the significant thing is that our important thinkers have finally come to the realization the important concern of our day is not the situation in Berlin or cabinet meetings in Vilnius, it's can the Cubs ever win the pennant with Don Zimmer?

If the master historians of our day are going to invade our territory, it's only fair play for us to move into the political arena and tackle comparative issues such as, can George Bush go to his left? Can Dan Quayle bat cleanup? Is James Baker a sucker for Reds' pitching? Frankly, from what I can see, George, America needs more power in the lineup. We've become a bunch of Punch-and-Judy hitters; we need the big inning.

• •

MAY 23, 1990

Smell of the Grease, Roar of the Engines Endures in Him

INDIANAPOLIS—When I first came to the Indianapolis Motor Speedway, the engines were in the front and canted to the left to keep the cars going in that direction. You turned right to go to the cemetery.

They were all built in garages in Torrance by guys with screwdrivers and rubber hammers and pinups of Marilyn Monroe in the buff on the wall. There wasn't a computer in sight. The cars used to go in the high 140s in speed. When they hit the wall, the driver got a fire in his lap and maybe in his hair.

They had 750-horsepower supercharged Novis that made an ear-splitting noise as long as they lasted, which, fortunately, was never long. The other engines were mostly Offenhausers and they were almost as homemade as the cars.

As a proving ground, Indy mainly proved that cars could burn. So could drivers. And, in some cases, so could spectators. The Hollywood Freeway had already amply proved all of that, but Indy was as American as apple-bobbing and the apotheosis of America's love affair with the automobile.

Nowadays, the engines are all in the rear and they're all made in a laboratory in England. Indy became about as American as the Duke of Kent some time in the early '60s, first when a stoic young Aussie named Jack Brabham came over with a funny little car that not only had the engine in the back but developed only 92 horsepower and went through the corners like a scared mouse in a burning building.

In the boxing game, they rate a fighter "pound for pound" the best in the world. Pound for pound, Brabham's car was the best in the race and, within a year or two, the front-engine car was doomed and the Speedway was never again given over to the do-it-yourself grease monkeys and speed freaks of old.

Indy has changed. The cars cost $240,000 now, not counting tires and shocks; the engines go for $100,000, and the day of the independent entrepreneur is long gone. You get $100,000 from PPG just for winning the pole now. You used to get a gold watch and a free lunch.

The race can be run—and won—from the pits now. The cars go so fast they are tracked by radar, like fighter planes, and racing "teams" are really corporations. The cars go faster than World War II fighter planes. They are not driven, they're flown.

It has been pointed out that the speed that barely put the driver in this year's race in the 33rd and last spot—211.076 m.p.h.—would have put him on the pole five years ago. And would have put him in the Cleveland air races 20 years ago.

One thing hasn't changed at Indy in all those years—the driver in Car No. 14, the honorable Anthony Joseph Foyt Jr., the terrible Texan.

A.J. Foyt is not your grand old man of racing. At an age when he should be the grand marshal or, at best, the driver of the pace car, A.J. is nobody's token old-timer. A.J. drives to win, not show. And he is solidly in the race in the middle of the third row with an average flying time of 220.425 m.p.h. A.J. doesn't intend to be in anybody's rearview mirror. After all, he's only 55.

Much is made of a ballplayer who is still solving curveballs at the age of 42. Nolan Ryan still whistling 90-m.p.h. fastballs at 43 boggles the imagination. An Archie Moore or a George Foreman contesting for the heavyweight title at 40 or 41 evokes admiration and awe.

Foyt is driving an automobile through traffic on the most dangerous racecourse in the world at speeds up to 240 m.p.h. and he's on his way to being a great-grandfather. He is, by all odds, the most remarkable athlete of his time.

When you consider that, when A.J. Foyt first teed it up in this race—in 1958—Rocky Marciano was only two years retired as heavyweight champion, Eisenhower was President, coffee was a dime and the Berlin Wall had not even been built.

Technology has improved a lot of things at the Speedway, but they haven't figured a way to improve on A.J. Foyt. He's still the same cantankerous, get-out-of-my-way, lead-footed guy he was 32 years ago.

What would an Indianapolis 500 be without A.J. Foyt? Just another traffic jam. A race, not an event. News, but not history.

There was an Unser in the first Indy I ever saw. But that was Bobby, a whole generation of Unsers ago. He hung it on the wall after one lap. The other people in the race are long since pictures on a wall. Parnelli Jones won it that year. The late Jimmy Clark in the little British-made Lotus-Ford was second and rookie of the year.

But A.J. Foyt was already a seasoned veteran and former winner. He was driving his sixth Indy 500. He was third, only a fraction of a mile an hour behind the top two.

Foyt could drive this Brickyard blindfolded. Which is a good thing because your eyesight at 55 is not apt to make you handy at squirrel hunting.

It was never advisable to suggest to A.J. Foyt that he was in the race to do anything but win, to imply that he was merely another Sunday driver. Foyt's temper always had a very short wick on it and could go up like Krakatoa.

This reporter can remember a time he approached the great Foyt on the pit wall during practice. It was not the best of times. When something went wrong with the car, plenty went wrong with Foyt. It was like approaching a lion with a sore paw.

"Can't you see we're working here?" he snarled at the reporter.

"What do you think I'm doing?" I shot back.

Foyt, thank God, laughed. Foyt, laughing with a sick car, should have made the Guinness Book of World Records.

In those days, Foyt was either in a car or under it. He never got his cars built by some guys who spoke English with a funny accent and called racers "motor cars." Foyt put his cars together on a lube rack in Houston. The only thing high-tech in them was Foyt.

That day is long gone. But Foyt isn't. He's a genuine American heirloom, like the Alamo, or Ford's theater. He hasn't won this thing since 1977. But he was fifth last year. He's running with the youngsters. If there's a Foyt in the race, it's the original, not a Roman numeral. There's only one.

When Jack Nicklaus won the Masters golf tournament at 46, the whole sports world gasped. But if A.J. Foyt were to win his fifth 500 at 55, it would be like George Burns winning a tap-dance contest with Gregory Hines. To everybody but Foyt. He thinks he should be favored.

August 26, 1990

His Touch Made Dodgers Special

Now that it's the 100th anniversary of the founding of the Dodgers, a few of the savants were sitting around trying to decide who was the most valuable Dodger in the history of the franchise.

That's easy.

The most artful Dodger of them all never hit a homer with the bases full, stole home in a pennant race, struck out the side with the tying run on third or got Willie Mays to pop up with the game or the championship on the line.

In fact, the most valuable individual never played an inning, made out a lineup, moved an infield in, picked up a ground ball, laid down a bunt or stole a base.

He never made an error, either.

He's left-handed, reads lips. You can count on him for 150-160 impeccable games a year. He always shows up ready for the game, never hits the disabled list. He's a manager's wish, an owner's dream.

I would say, off hand, the only one who comes close is Jackie Robinson. Robinson's contributions, too, were more than just on the ballfield.

But when you look down the all-time roster and see the glorious names of Dazzy Vance, Sandy Koufax, Robinson, Roy Campanella, Pee Wee Reese, Duke Snider, Don Drysdale, Maury Wills, Don Newcombe, Max Carey or Van Lingle Mungo, you figure some guy poring through the rubble of an archeological dig one day will not have even heard of my candidate. His lifetime average isn't in there—but he was a .400 hitter, all right, and hc had an awesome assortment of pitches.

Vincent Edward Scully meant as much or more to the Dodgers than any .300 hitter they ever signed, any 20-game winner they ever fielded.

True, he didn't limp to home plate and hit the home run that turned a season into a miracle—but he knew what to do with it so it would echo through the ages.

It's impossible to overestimate Scully's value to the Dodgers. His mellifluous tone, wafting over the evening air in a ballpark because every transistor in the stadium is tuned to it, has made baseball a field of dreams for three generations of fans. Once, an umpire named Beans Reardon barked at an impatient manager, chafing because the ump waffled over a decision: "It ain't nuthin' till I say what it is!" In a sense, 35 years of Dodger fans could say: It ain't nuthin' till Scully tells us.

Scully made an art out of baseball broadcasting. He also made journalism out of it. In a profession so full of "homers"—not the four-base kind, the kind where the guy in the booth root-root-roots for the home team—Scully distanced himself from partisanship. In 1959, in a surprised moment as the Dodgers won a pennant on a throwing error, Scully blurted, "We go to Chicago!" It became an L.A. catch-phrase but, so far as is known, it is the only time Scully used the pronoun "we" instead of the Dodgers on the air.

He leveled with the fans. They could trust Scully. "It's playable!" he would assure them of a long, high drive that some shriller denizens of the broadcast booth might want to milk for some suspense.

It was a masterful job of self-control because Scully was as closely identified with the fortunes of the Dodgers as any manager, player or owner they ever had. Scully really told it like it is—always.

It wasn't that he didn't love the Dodgers. It was just that he loved the game. "I remember when I first got the job," Scully says. "I was just a kid, a street kid. And here I was broadcasting the Brooklyn Dodgers!"

His awe never compromised his neutrality. "I think it was a New York thing," he says. "We were above cheerleading. I remember once we went to Philadelphia, and a Philadelphia writer showed up in the press box with a Phillies cap on. He was scorned. We felt in New York we were reporters, not pompon girls."

It's not possible to overstate what Scully meant to the franchise shift to L.A. Here was this team, in the mold of carpetbaggers, pulling into a strange town 3,000 miles from their home base and trying to blend in. Scully midwifed this delicate process. Some front-office colleagues took the typically New York attitude that they were slumming among the uninitiated, rubes who knew nothing of the game of baseball. Scully tactfully took to going to as many luncheons as they could schedule. He put the right smiling face on the community's new neighbors—and representatives. He took the "we" out of broadcasting but put the "our" in community relations.

"I knew they knew baseball out here," Scully says. "It was just some of the individual players they weren't familiar with. Oh sure, they knew the stars, the Reeses, the Drysdales, Sniders, Furillos. But I take no credit for the transistor tune-ins. You have to remember when we played in the Coliseum, some of those fans were 79 rows up, a half-mile from the action. It made sense to bring a radio."

It was Scully's finest year, 1958.

"We knew we had a bad team," he says. "A decision had to be reached whether to go with the established stars or try to run in a bunch of unknown kids. It was decided to go with the name players."

Scully sold Los Angeles on the Dodgers—with a team that finished next to last. Scully was the master at distracting attention from the inept, the boring. He didn't broadcast a game, he narrated it.

Scully could have left the Dodgers. Network contracts in the high millions were dangled. And sometimes accepted. The temptation not to have to get in a car and drive down the freeway to the ballpark every night must have been enticing.

But he found life without the Dodgers unthinkable. Scully without the Dodgers was Caruso without an opera, any troubadour without a song.

He kept his feet in the shoals of celebrity. "In New York, I was a guy who rode the subway to work and lived in a fifth-floor walk-up. To the neighborhood, I was just a guy who worked nights."

He still works nights. And the Dodgers are glad of it.

Scully was probably the least surprised guy in the ballpark when the Dodgers blew an eight-run lead in the ninth the other night. "The Dodgers never do anything easy," he says. "They don't win easy—and they don't lose easy. But I'll tell you something: They have seemed to be touched ever since they came to L.A. Call it magic or luck, but just when things get to their worst, somebody touches a wand and here comes a Koufax or a Larry Sherry or a Maury Wills or a Kirk Gibson."

The Dodgers are an outfit you'd want to get next to in a lifeboat.

But if there's one thing Scully decries today, it's what he calls "single-file baseball." He explains: "We used to do things together. So did the team. We went by train but even when we moved West, on the days off, the whole organization got together for a golf outing.

"Now, the players arrive in single file. They get dressed in single file. If they do get on the team bus, they get on one by one. They sit behind each other on airplanes. Sometimes you think it's a clubhouse of strangers."

The Dodgers are 100 years old. Scully has been with them almost 40. In that time, attendances of 2 million—thought impossible for a baseball franchise—became commonplace in Los Angeles. Then, 3-million attendances were achieved six times.

Scully was there for all of them. It may have been a coincidence, but I think not. Scully will never be MVP—most valuable player. But he has to be MVD—most valuable Dodger.

• •

October 26, 1990

All He Needed Was A Mask and Gun

LAS VEGAS—What do you want to say was the biggest heist in history?

The Brink's robbery?

John Dillinger's holdup sprees? Bonnie and Clyde's? The theft of a Van Gogh from a Paris art gallery? The looting of the art treasures of Europe by Nazis? The S&L swindles?

How about the Buster Douglas Caper?

James (Buster) Douglas pulled a heist here Thursday that, for its sheer audacity, pales all these others by comparison.

Buster walked off with almost $20 million by the mere expedient of showing up with a satchel (not to mention the one around his middle), scooping up the money and running.

Buster slickered the American sporting public and the promoters as surely as any embezzler who ever took a plane to Rio with the bank's receipts. W.C. Fields would be open-mouthed with admiration. So would anyone who ever absconded with a widows and orphans fund.

You'd have more respect for him if he did it with a gold brick—or a gun. He did it with a smile and a wink. He got almost $20 million for pulling off the most elaborate practical joke and swindle in the annals of the heavyweight fight division.

You see, Buster, for his millions, had made a compact with the public that he would show up in some kind of physical shape and make an honest effort to defend the heavyweight title he won so shockingly from Mike Tyson in February.

Buster Douglas entered the ring looking like something that should be floating over a Thanksgiving Day parade. He ran a crooked wheel, is what he did. He dealt from the bottom.

You know, when an actor agrees to play Hamlet, he doesn't show up and do baggy pants shtick. If a guy agrees to sing "Carmen" and shows up drunk singing Irving Berlin, they throw eggs at him. And refund the money.

It's very clear Buster Douglas had little or no intention of doing any real fighting Thursday night. He came into the ring as out of shape as King Farouk and went through the motions. Jack Johnson put up a better fight against Jess Willard—and that fight was in the bag.

You knew there was going to be no fight when Buster stood on the scales Wednesday afternoon in the hotel ballroom and they topped out at 246 pounds. Now, that's OK for sumo wrestlers or a major league umpire, but it doesn't work when you have to get into the ring with a fighter who looks like something they found in a Greek ruin.

Buster took us, ladies and gentlemen. He made suckers of us all. He just sat there and lapped up the calories and lived the good life and took the suckers for everything they had—or almost $20 million, which is close enough—and laughed all the way to the refrigerator.

He got annihilated by a guy he outweighed by 38 pounds.

Lots of guys drank their way out of the heavyweight championship. Buster ate his way out of it.

He had a compact with the public and he mocked it. In the old days, they would hold up the purse when things like this happened, when one guy showed up in no shape to fight.

Buster has a history of this kind of hanky-panky. You look on his ring record and there is a telltale "NC" on it for a fight in Columbus in 1984. "NC" stands for "No contest" and it indicates a bout where the referee threw both contestants out for not trying or otherwise making a travesty of the sport.

Buster had his second No Contest at the Mirage Hotel here Thursday night. Only this time, his opponent would have none of it. Evander Holyfield came to fight, all right. He cuffed Buster around at will from the opening bell. It was almost as if Buster hadn't shown up, just his shadow. In effect, that was correct. Evander wasn't even breathing hard when the fight came to its sudden but predictable end when Holyfield threw a short but explosive right hand in Buster's fat mouth.

In the shape he was in, Buster probably couldn't have gotten up at 10 if he tripped over his own shoelaces. But if he made any effort to get up, it didn't show. He appeared to find it very comfortable on the floor, like a hammock, and the suspicion lurks he'd spent plenty of his time prone since he won the championship.

Did he just run into a buzz-saw? Well, Evander Holyfield is not exactly The Brown Bomber or the Manassa Mauler himself. He has 20 knockouts in his pro career, but the likes of Tyrone Booze and Eric Winbush have gone the distance with him, to say nothing of Lionel Byarm. Dwight Qawi went 15.

Evander Holyfield liked the sensation of punching a fat old party around. He announced after the fight his next opponent would be George Foreman. It's too bad Elsa Maxwell or Orson Welles isn't with us anymore. They might get a shot.

Still, I guess it was a triumph for clean living, hard work and a lean cuisine. Horatio Alger would approve. So would Frank Merriwell. Buster could have set dieting back 100 years and bankrupted the country's fat farms if he prevailed.

He didn't prevail. The worst part of it was, he obviously knew he wouldn't. He was observed doing roadwork two days before the fight on a golf course and he looked like a guy chasing a slow bus. Buster had the look on his face of a guy dreaming of chicken and gravy.

The only way he could have beaten Evander Holyfield Thursday night was to eat him.

• • • • • • • • • • • • • • • • • • • •

DECEMBER 9, 1990

He Knows Easy Rides Are Rare

The fourth race at Hollywood Park that day wasn't much. The six plugs they loaded into the starting gate were a sorry lot, the riffraff of the track, plating horses. None of them had ever won a race and three of them were 4 years old. You knew right away you weren't dealing with any Secretariats or Man o' Wars here.

It was a $60 ride in a $29,000 race on a no-chance 4-year-old for jockey Chris McCarron, a man who has won the Kentucky Derby, the

Preakness and million-dollar purses in the Breeders' Cup. But he'll never forget it.

On the far turn of the seven-furlong dash, McCarron's mount, a shadow-jumper named Full Design, was tucked down along the rail, boxed in by those rank-running cheap horses when, suddenly, the horse in front of him snapped an ankle and went down in a heap. So did Full Design, followed shortly by Chris McCarron, who was cartwheeled out in the middle of the track in the path of oncoming traffic.

"At first, I thought I was all right," recalls Chris. "And then I felt these three blows to my legs and arm."

McCarron had just lived every rider's nightmare. He had been run over by the field. He looked down at his left leg. It seemed there were two of them. And they were pointing in opposite directions. His other leg and arm were a little better. They were broken, all right, but not in two. The medics wouldn't need a picture to put them back together.

Now, then, sports fans, what, would you have to say, would be the most uneven matchup in all the world of sport? Tyson vs. Spinks? Joe Louis vs. anybody? Notre Dame vs. Harvard? Man vs. a mountain? The 1940 Bears vs. the Redskins? The Christians vs. the lions?

None of them is more of a mismatch than a 100-pound jockey vs. an 1,100-pound stallion. A thoroughbred race horse would be a handful for Hulk Hogan. You look at a 5-foot jockey like McCarron, with these ringlets of red-gold hair and big Orphan Annie blue eyes, and you wonder how those tiny fingers can handle a wild animal going 40 m.p.h. in a panic.

He'd be almost as well off riding a shark. The last thing in the world a horse wants to do is run in a race. It's up to the jockey to make him.

The public has no difficulty in comprehending that a guy who climbs into a 200-m.p.h. race car is overmatching himself. They shake their heads when a guy perches on the ledge of a mountain and pushes off with only a hang glider to save him from becoming a pile of scattered bones.

But they take no thought that the undersized young (or not so young) fellow on a temperamental horse's back is taking his life in his hands every furlong. They marvel at girls in a circus who ride elephants at a slow walk, but they snarl at race riders who finish sixth well out from the rail, "Boy, you rode that horse like a taxi—what merry-go-round did you learn to ride on?"

What they don't know is, the insurance companies rate jockeys right along with auto race drivers, skydivers and guys who put out oil well fires for a living. Channel swimmers can get insured for only a couple of dollars a year. It costs Chris McCarron $18,000. Insurance companies don't trust horses, either.

McCarron might be as good a rider as there is on a racetrack today. Whoever is first, Chris is in the photo. No one ever called him "the Slasher," or "the Pumper," or "Geronimo," but he gets out of a horse whatever the horse has to give.

McCarron once set a record for victories in a year, 546, that held for 19 years, until Kent Desormeaux broke it. McCarron is currently the leading rider at Hollywood Park with 36 firsts, 24 seconds and 23 thirds and an astonishing winning percentage of 26.

But there was a certain poetic irony in McCarron being the one who found himself lying on the track last June 3 with an ambulance coming and a doctor poking a needle in his leg and asking, "Can you feel this?"

It all began three years ago when Don MacBeth, the terminally ill ex-rider who had been injured in a race spill, came out to Santa Anita to get the Georgie Woolf Jockey Award. McCarron and his wife Judy had lunch with the dying jockey and found out that racing had no funds for indigent or ill ex-riders.

"We found that in only five states do jockeys come under workmen's compensation," McCarron says. "Every other state considers us independent contractors, and disabled riders had nowhere to turn."

The McCarrons and comedian Tim Conway founded the Don MacBeth Fund and have since raised hundreds of thousands for downed riders.

For McCarron, every accident is not a disaster. In 1986, he was to ride the 2-year-old champion, Demons Begone, in the Breeders' Cup Juvenile when he broke his pelvis in a spill at Santa Anita. At that time, jockey Pat Day was the regular rider for Jack Van Berg's colt, Alysheba.

With the ride on Demons Begone open, Day took off Alysheba and elected to ride Demons Begone in the 1987 Kentucky Derby instead.

It's an old, familiar backstretch story. Only a month after getting off crutches, McCarron got the mount on Alysheba. He won the Kentucky Derby, the Preakness and the Breeders' Cup Classic. Demons Begone bled and finished last in the Derby and dropped out of racing.

But Chris McCarron knows you can't always count on a happy ending. That's why when he remembers the acclaim and thrills of Kentucky Derbies and Preaknesses and Breeders' Cups on national television, he can also recall a June 3 maiden race at Hollywood Park and rejoice that those hoofs hit only his arms and legs.

1991

• •

JANUARY 6, 1991

Now, Here Is a Golfer to Admire

CARLSBAD—I like to watch Lanny Wadkins play golf for the same reasons I liked to see Bob Gibson pitch, Rocky Marciano fight or Fred Astaire dance. I like guys who just do it. Like the others, Lanny does it quickly, aggressively, stylishly, with a minimum of posturing, capering, temporizing or delaying. Lanny gets it over with. He acts like a guy who is double-parked and on the lam.

You never see Lanny walking ahead of his ball or pulling out a notebook, calibrating distances, conferring with his caddie, waiting for a ruling or doing any of the things so favored by other players. Lanny gets on with it. Lanny simply squints down the fairway, pulls out a club and slashes at the ball and runs after the shot. He is in the great tradition of Doug Ford, another exponent of fugitive golf who always played as if the sheriff were after him. Like Arnold Palmer, Lanny doesn't play a golf course so much as he hunts it.

He goes for the jugular. Lanny never tries to jab a course to death. He goes for the knockout. He hurries after each shot like a guy chasing a bus. When he's on his game, it looks as if it's raining golf balls.

You're happy to see Lanny win golf tournaments because it gives the right message to every 20-handicapper in the country.

Look. Don't you hate to see the pitcher in a drawn-out game staring at the batter, or taking a stroll around the mound or conferring with the manager before finally releasing the ball? Like to see a fighter skipping around the ring, falling into a clinch, spinning and whirling and never throwing a punch? Get tired of seeing a team or a player stalling for time, stopping the action, boring the gallery?

Golf is not brain surgery, but golfers, as a class, act as if they are in a life-or-death operation where, if they wait, all conditions will improve, nerves will be calmed, the grass will grow to optimum length and Jupiter will be in Neptune's house and all putts will be short and lies playable. They are like a general who must wait for all the reserves to pull up before he can muster the attack. Some guys stand over the ball till they gather dust. Still others, such as Cary Middlecoff, used to fidget so much they looked like someone in the final stages of St. Vitus' dance.

Golfers hate to do anything in a rush. They are conservative, cautious, deliberate. They do not have an impetuous bone in their bodies. They spend their whole lives in slow motion. They walk slow, they talk slow. They even eat slow. It is said that if a golfer fell off the Empire State Building it would take him a week to hit the ground. He would be checking the yardage all the way down.

On a golf course, he acts as if the thing he dreads most in the world is hitting a golf shot. He will do almost anything to avoid it—wipe his club, hitch his trousers, confer with his caddie, throw grass into the air, stare at the sky, growl at photographers—then step up to the ball and waggle his club to death before launching a swing. If he had any mail, you're sure he'd take it out and read it.

He has hit probably 10 million golf shots in his career, but he acts as if this is the first one he's ever hit. He has hit this shot probably 50,000 to 100,000 times. There's nothing new about it. Even if he went into a trance, his muscles would probably remember exactly how to shoot it for him. Yet, a film will come over his eyes, his breath will get short, he will button and unbutton his glove. You would think he was going to the electric chair.

Not Lanny Wadkins. Lanny is a gimme-the-damn-club-and-stand-back player. Lanny disdains all the theatrics. Lanny walks up to the ball and swipes at it like a guy swatting a fly. Usually it sails unerringly up to a green and settles uncannily in one-putt range, and Lanny merely snaps his fingers and chalks up another birdie and steps quickly to the next tee.

That is why a lot of us were glad to see Lanny doing so well down here at the Infiniti Tournament of Champions this week. Golfers imitate success. If a guy made birdies standing on one leg because his ankle hurt, by the weekend, every golfer in the state would be playing on one leg.

If Lanny wins playing fast, you can bet every hacker in the country will start copying it. Which will be a good thing for golf.

If Lanny were merely the fastest player out here this week, it would hardly be the story. But he may also be the best.

If he wins here, he becomes the winningest active player on the tour save for Tom Watson and Raymond Floyd. Victory here would give Wadkins 20 victories on the tour. Only 28 players in history have won more.

It's not necessary to play slow to win on the tour. One of the players tied with Wadkins at 19 career wins is Doug Ford, who couldn't have played any faster if he were on fire. If Wadkins and Ford were in a twosome, they would be at best a blur and at worst a rumor.

Lanny couldn't move fast enough Saturday to keep the field at bay in the 39th Tournament of Champions, an event he has won twice. The cold round that attacks all players for one of the 18 holes came on Lanny. But Lanny didn't start studying his nails, studying putts from 17 or more angles, backing off approaches, stalling for time, throwing clubs, glaring at spectators. Lanny charges at 73s with the same skill and enthusiasm as he does 65s.

He lost his lead but not necessarily his momentum. Fred Couples caught him, Tom Kite passed him. But only on the scoreboard. If they paid off on speed as well as numbers, Lanny would make the world forget Ben Hogan. Or, at least, Doug Ford. Jack Nicklaus won 19 tournaments in a little more than four years. But Lanny Wadkins won 19 in an elapsed time of a little more than 60 hours. If the 24-second clock ever comes to golf, Lanny would be harder to beat than four aces.

•••••••••••••••••••

FEBRUARY 19, 1991

Even When Celtics Take a Fall, They Rise Again in the East

The Boston Celtics are to the NBA what the old New York Yankees were to baseball, what Calumet was to horse racing, Notre Dame to college football.

They represent the highest state of the art. They're not a team, they're a mystique. It used to be, when they walked onto the floor, they were carrying a 10-point lead with them just because they were the Celtics.

Sometimes, it looked as if they had two or three more players on the court than the poor guys they were playing. They moved quickly, they struck fiercely. They were always in fine, furious motion. The fast break may have originated with them.

A player automatically moved up in class when he played for the Celtics. For one thing, his surrounding cast had high standards. It was like acting in a movie with Tracy, Hepburn, James Stewart or Fred Astaire. You had to turn it up a notch or get run over.

It used to happen on the old Yankees. Players who were journeymen elsewhere became All-Stars when they put on the pinstripes and got to play alongside Ruth, Gehrig, DiMaggio, Mantle, Munson. Same with the Celtics. Players like Don Nelson, John Thompson, Larry Siegfried rose to the occasions when they had to share the ball with the likes of Cousy, Heinsohn, the Jones boys, Russell, Sharman and Havlicek.

Arnold (Red) Auerbach gave them their edge. Like Branch Rickey in baseball, Red Auerbach could spot a star player from the window of a moving train or in a crowd shot at St. Peter's Square. If Red tapped you, you could play. It's hard to believe five teams passed on Larry Bird in 1978. It's hard to believe St. Louis gave the Celtics Bill Russell for Ed Macauley. The rich got richer.

Basketball needs the Celtics. It's no fun beating the Charlotte Hornets or the Miami Heat. Beating the Celtics is climbing Mt. Everest, swimming the Channel, breaking the bank at Monte Carlo. Beat the Detroit Pistons and the country goes "Aargh!" Beat the Celts and it goes "All r-i-i-i-ght!"

The Celtics have fallen on lean times. They haven't won a championship since 1985-86. They haven't even been in the finals since '86-87.

Well, they're back. They beat the Lakers at the Forum Friday night for the first time in five years. It was the first time in two years the Celtics had beaten the Lakers anywhere. They're leading their division by—count 'em—12½ games.

The Celtics are like an old dowager. They never throw anything away. They keep trunkfuls of good players like old dance cards. They spot-play them as artfully as a riverboat gambler making good use of an ace showing.

Robert Parish is the oldest player in the NBA. A lot of teams would have talked him into retiring. The Celtics talked him out of it. He's like the proverbial old-timer. He's not as good as he once was, but he's as good once as he ever was. He threw in 21 points in the first quarter against the Lakers the other night. He played only 20 more minutes, but he had buried the Lakers. The rest of the game was just a function of shoveling the dirt back in with defense.

Kevin McHale played no minutes. He sat in the locker room with his injured ankle elevated. He is not the oldest player in the league, but he is no pink-cheeked rookie either.

Coming into the game Friday, McHale was the leading scorer on the '91 Celts. He has since been passed by Reggie Lewis, but should be back in the lineup momentarily.

The hard corps of the Celtics is still Parish, Bird and McHale. The team counts on them for 30-35 quality minutes a game and surrounds them with a chorus of net-picking young gunners like Lewis, Brian Shaw, Kevin Gamble and Dee Brown—16 to 18 points a night quick-draw artists.

"These guys have added to our careers," McHale acknowledged as he sat with ice around his sprained ankle Friday night. "They give us good ball movement. When you're playing on a team with six guys in double figures, as we are, the defense doesn't know where to go first. They can't double-up on you. You get more easy baskets. You don't get as worn out going to the hoop.

"These young guys give us back the Celtic game. The fast break, the smooth transition, the open man. The game is more guard-oriented today, and this plays into our hands."

What is good for the game might not be good for the league. The old Boston dynasty teams—nine championships in 10 years, 11 championships in 13 years—were such foregone winners, the season got to be just a formality. Did McHale find the old hostility returning? Had the Celtics become the league bad guys again? The despots of basketball?

"Not at all," McHale claims. "You find Celtics fans everywhere. Even the people that love to hate us, love us. You heard them tonight. Almost as many cheer when the Celtics scored as when the Lakers. Happens everywhere.

"You don't win championships in February. But being a Celtic means never having to settle for losing. It means never expecting to lose. This is a team that doesn't stay down. You lose a Cousy, and K.C. Jones takes up the slack. Then comes Nate Archibald and Dennis Johnson. You lose a Russell, and a (Dave) Cowens comes along. You lose Cowens, and Robert Parish is there. You play at home under all those championship banners and you don't want to let them down.

"What would the game be without the Celtics? I'll tell you—a whole lot less fun. You beat the Portland Trail Blazers and everybody says, 'Who?' You beat the Boston Celtics and everybody says 'Wow!'"

• •

MARCH 10, 1991

Read Between the Lines When Talkin' Baseball

It's March. Everybody wins the pennant. Every pitcher is Cy Young. Every batter is Ty Cobb. Buy me some peanuts and Cracker Jack, I don't care if I never get back.

Opening day is just around the corner. April is waiting for the fools. Baseball is a game of optical illusions anyway. The ball doesn't really curve. Stealing is legal and the spitball isn't as outlawed as the commissioner thinks it is.

You can't play any sport without being an optimist. But baseball is the only one that comes with the spring of the year when the ground thaws, the Yukon breaks up, the trees bud, the birds return and hope is reborn.

As noted, spring and baseball are perfect for each other. Forty-five-year-old pitchers who haven't thrown anything that curved for seven years suddenly think that age is an illusion, like the curveball. Ted Williams says that the hardest thing to do in the world of sport is to hit the curveball, but 100 rookies dream of solving the secret.

But spring goeth before the fall. Managers appear to be the worst of the lot. But that's only an illusion, too. Managers have been around too long not to know that a Willie Mays only comes along once in a generation, that everybody else is a journeyman trying to put together that one magical year that will enable him to coast to his pension.

Pay no attention to what the manager says in public. He's just trying to sell tickets. What he says and what he thinks are as different as—well, spring and fall.

Below, what the manager says. In parentheses, what he thinks:

"We can play with anybody in the game." ("We can play with them, we just can't beat them.")

"We're as good as any team in the league." ("The Carolina League. Is there still a Three-I League?")

"This team doesn't know the meaning of the word choke" ("This team doesn't know the meaning of a lot of words. The only thing lower than their batting average is their IQ. The only word they know right offhand is renegotiation. They learn that right after Momma.")

"These guys remind me of great combinations of the past." ("Laurel and Hardy. Curly, Shemp and Moe. Groucho, Harpo, Zeppo and Gummo. The Keystone Kops. Chaplin on a banana peel was never any funnier than these guys.")

"The trade with the Mets gives us the best balanced outfield we've ever had." ("One guy can't catch the ball, one guy can't hit the ball and the other guy can't throw the ball. How's that for balance?")

"This is a team with a lot of desire." ("Just ask any waitress in town. Or just add up the paternity suits and sexual harassment charges. These guys make Porfirio Rubirosa look like a monk.")

"We're going to emphasize fundamentals." ("What else can you do with a bunch of .218 hitters, wait for three-run homers?")

"This team isn't afraid to get its uniforms dirty." ("It's their fingernails they worry about.")

"I got a guy here who's a regular Ruth." ("Or Dora or Emily or Sarah. What I mean to say is, he runs and throws like a girl.")

"We're going to surprise a lot of people." ("Particularly the owner, who shelled out $30 million for this pile of crud—overpaid underachievers.")

"These guys don't sell themselves short." ("Particularly the left fielder. He was born on a dirt floor in a cane field where the nearest running water was the Mississippi River, his first pair of shoes had cleats in them and he now says he can't live on $2.3 million a year.")

"He's going to be my stopper!" ("He couldn't stop a nosebleed in a rabbit. The last time he got the side out, Eisenhower was President. The only thing he'll stop is a winning streak—in the unlikely event we ever have one.")

"My bullpen has the best firemen in the game." ("They should call it 'Gasoline Alley.' These guys should be arrested for arson. You've heard of pouring oil on troubled waters? These guys would pour oil on forest fires. Around the league they're known as 'The Towering Inferno.'")

"All this club needs is another bat in the center of the lineup." ("All this club needs is another lineup—the 1927 Yankees, say.")

"This is a hungry club." ("If you don't think so, just check room service. My infield set two records last year, one for throwing errors, the other for steak sandwiches at 2 in the morning. This is also a thirsty club. It has its own bartender and a beer truck follows the infield around on the road. I won't say these guys lead the league in hangovers but you don't dare light a match in the clubhouse before day games.")

"These guys could get in the World Series. All they need is a few breaks." ("Yeah, Roger Clemens needs to break his arm, Jose Canseco needs to break a leg and the Kansas City Royals have to hit a mountain.")

"This team just has to learn to relax." ("Relax? I can hardly keep them awake through the seventh inning. If this team relaxed any more, you could take their pulse with a calendar. It's not a team, it's a coma.")

"These are the finest bunch of young men I have ever managed." ("Fine young men don't win pennants; nasty, blue-bearded, redneck, tobacco-chewing, snarling loudmouths do. Home runs win pennants, not homebodies. Give me someone who wants to win ballgames, not friends. Don't give me someone who's good to his mother, give me someone who'd throw at her with men on base. I want to win a pennant, not a popularity contest.")

"I'm confident this team will play up to its potential." ("I'm not confident they will, I'm afraid they will. This team will play up to its potential, all right—sixth place.")

APRIL 14, 1991

When He Drives, It's Beautiful

The other drivers called him "Hollywood." They thought he was too pretty to be in a race car. The back seat of a limo, perhaps. His profile would get mussed, his hair out of place. This wasn't Warner Bros., they warned him. This was for real. Nobody would call "Cut!" if the car turned right. He couldn't hire a stunt man for the race scenes. You had to do your own stunts here. There were no happy endings guaranteed. The star could get killed off in the first reel in this melodrama.

The first time he saw A.J. Foyt in his rearview mirror, they predicted, he would go running back to makeup. Or the comparative safety of driving a cab in New York. They figured he was being a race driver just to have something to do till polo started up. Or he got tired of the yacht club. He would be out of there the first time he hit a wall or spun in traffic.

That was nine years ago. Danny Sullivan is still sitting in a race car every week strapping a helmet on, revving an engine and crossing himself. When A.J. Foyt—or any Unser, or any Andretti, or any Fittipaldi, for that matter—sees him in the rearview mirror, he knows he'd better turn up the boost.

You're supposed to get race drivers out of Torrance garages, not posh military schools or state universities. They're not supposed to have movie star good looks or rich fathers.

In Europe, royalty races—but boredom is the enemy of the titled classes. In America, the privileged get into the bond market, not the Indy 500. You don't get race drivers out of Yale—or, in the case of Danny Sullivan, the University of Kentucky. You get them out of lube racks, off drag strips.

It wasn't long before "Hollywood" became "Sully." "Danny Boy" became "that *&!%!! Sullivan!"

There have been race drivers who were perceived as dilettantes before. They weren't. Peter Revson and Mark Donohue both died in race cars. They were the real article. They rode to win. So does Danny Sullivan.

You're not a race driver till you run at Indy. You're not a star till you win. Danny Sullivan not only won the world's most prestigious race, he did it surviving a 360-degree spin in the north chute and through a shower of crashing cars and runaway tires. An Indy race always manages to look at some point as if a naval engagement were in progress, but Danny's year was a banner year for flying debris.

He and the wall at Indy are no strangers. Kissing cousins, you might say. He kissed it in his rookie year. He smacked it again in 1988 after leading the first 91 laps. And he hit it again in 1989. He drove with a broken arm that year. He twice set the single-lap record at Indy—both times it was broken by teammate Rick Mears. He has started in the front row twice but won from a start in the middle of the third row. If his cars are fast, he makes them faster.

He is the most famous Sullivan since John L. Race drivers tend to live in Indianapolis or Houston or Albuquerque, the gasoline alleys of America. Danny lives in Aspen. "I think so" is a long answer for most race drivers, followed sometimes by "Get outta here!" Danny hires a high-powered Hollywood firm, Rogers & Cowan, to handle his speaking engagements and public appearances. He has appeared on episodes of "Miami Vice." He is no Garbo, but he avoids on-track friendships since his best friend on the track, Gunnar Nielsen, died tragically. "You sort of dare not get close," he explains.

His life would be a nice part for Paul Newman, except Danny could probably handle it himself.

He didn't set out to be a racer. He was well on his way to being a chorus boy. "He went to New York for a weekend and stayed three years," recalled his mother, Peggy, at a prerace party for the Long Beach

Grand Prix the other day. He was a waiter, cabdriver, chicken farmer and playboy.

The family dispatched a family friend, Dr. Frank Falkner, to see if they could find him and rescue him from his young-man-about-Manhattan lifestyle before it became a way of life and he became a kind of complicated mannequin. "Check the tennis courts," they told him.

Falkner promised the young Sullivan he would get him into auto racing if he would promise to return to college. The doctor then sent Danny not to Lexington, but to his native England to driving school to learn how to take Formula Ones into the corners. "He's the best we have here, a born driver," the school informed Dr. Falkner. The good doctor was appalled. "How can I tell his family?" he groaned.

He needn't have worried. "Nothing Danny does surprises us," Peggy Sullivan told him cheerily. "He never does what you want him to anyway."

Danny Sullivan is at a crossroads in his career as the traveling Indy car circus arrives in Long Beach for the Toyota Grand Prix this weekend. Cutbacks in the highly competitive, highly expensive racing car market have seen him cut from the lordly Penske team, the Notre Dame of racing. He leaves the tried-and-true Penske Chevy for the newcomer Alfa Romeo.

A fourth-place finish in the opening competition of the PPG Indy Car series at Queensland, Australia, gives Sullivan 12 points (to winner John Andretti's 20) in the 17-race rodeo, which has stops at Indy, Elkhart, Monterey and the streets of Cleveland, Detroit, Denver and Vancouver before the season is out. It's a championship he won once, in 1988, and he was sixth last year.

He qualified 16th for today's race.

But even if he were to race in a stock pickup with a dog in the back, no one is putting Danny down anymore or suggesting he go back to Central Casting and get into a surfing movie. No one says, "What's the matter—skiing bad?"

The girls might not like the classic profile covered up in a bubble helmet and flameproof bandanna, but Danny Sullivan, movie-star good looks and tango dancer's figure and all, is tough competition on the streets or ovals. No one wants him in the rearview mirror, either, although if he's not there, it might be because he's half a lap in front.

• • • • • • • • • • • • • • • • • • •

APRIL 20, 1991

He Passes the Test of Time

ATLANTIC CITY, N.J.—One guy looked like a Greek god. The other looked like a Greek restaurant.

The heavyweight champion of all the world, old What's-His-Name, beat George Foreman in the Convention Center here Friday night.

He ought to be ashamed of himself.

If you ever have seen a train run over an elephant—and seem to get the worse of it from time to time—you have a picture of Friday night's fight.

One guy looked like a statue. The other fought like one.

Evander Holyfield, who was 10 when George Foreman won the heavyweight championship, hit the old man with every punch in his arsenal. But when you come right down to it, Holyfield seemed to annoy Foreman more than hurt him.

Holyfield is a fitness freak. He has his own ballet teacher, gym teacher, he has this high-tech menagerie of equipment, things to make his punches resistant, things to beef up his long muscles, the whole health religion.

George looks a little like a plate of hamburgers or a pizza with everything.

I would say the good news is, it's OK to pig out on junk food. Throw away that skim milk and get a double malt. Don't be afraid of ice cream.

Holyfield didn't even come close to putting that fat old party down. George came into the ring looking like something that should have a guy in a turban riding on his head. Holyfield was skipping and dancing around the ring like a kid with a puppy.

George stepped in from time to time to rap him upside the head and teach him some manners as if he were a kid skipping school or stealing pies.

You have never seen a more frustrated fighter than the heavyweight champ in the middle and late rounds. The punches that bounced Buster Douglas, Alex Stewart and all those kids all over the ring bounced off George Foreman like raindrops.

George didn't telegraph his punches. He sent them by fourth-class mail. Nevertheless, Evander Holyfield, the product of a dawn-to-dusk fitness regime, couldn't seem to get out of the way of any but the slowest.

They said George would get tired and fall like an old tree in the forest along about the seventh round. Hah!

Holyfield appeared to be counting on it. He stepped back periodically in case George didn't have room to fall. George didn't have reason to fall.

Usually, watching an old faded champion failing in a comeback against a young bull of an opponent is a sad sight. I'm sure people wanted to cover their eyes watching Jack Johnson at Havana, Dempsey in the 10th round against Tunney, Louis against Marciano and Ali against Holmes.

But the crowd was on its feet chanting "George! George! George!" this night. It was magnificent, really. The ringsiders kept waiting for the telltale "thud!" that never came. George didn't even sit down between rounds.

They thought they would have to carry George out of the ring along about the fifth round. I'll tell you something: George took a pounding to the face, but he can walk up to anybody today and say, "Yeah, but you should see the other guy!" By the ninth round, George was throwing punches from memory. But they hurt. Even when his trademark chopping right was more of a paw than a poke.

He almost dropped young Master Holyfield in the seventh at a time when much of press row still had the fight even.

The old man was glassy-eyed but still proud. His tormentor was leaping at him like a dog pack on a wounded bear, when suddenly George called upon remembered skills, skills he used to practice when Evander was in grade school, and he almost swatted the champion to one knee.

Right then and there, it seemed to this ringsider, Holyfield abandoned his grandiose schemes of a ringing knockout and settled for a nice safe decision. He was like a pitcher who stops challenging the hitter and resorts to junk and curves or a tennis player who settles for the baseline and returning serve.

"George earned a lot of respect from me," Holyfield said after the fight. "I learned very quickly I couldn't run him over and I had to change to a tactical fight. I knew then I had to fight the best fight of my life.

"At 42, who would think George would be able to go 12 rounds with me?!"

George Foreman, that's who. The magnificent old man taught young Holyfield—and anyone else who was watching—to respect his elders. He absorbed punishment without flinching. He carried the fight to the younger, faster opponent. He never once relied on clinching or hanging on. He fought three minutes of every round, as best he could. From time to time, it was the younger Holyfield who seemed to want the breather.

It reminded me, incongruously, of Hemingway's classic "The Old Man and the Sea." In that, you will remember the old fisherman tries to reel his marlin all the way back to shore, but little by little the sharks eat away at it until he only has the bones—and his pride—left.

Holyfield is still champion, but Foreman is of the folklore of pugilism. He has redeemed a star-crossed career. It will be recalled he was humiliated by Muhammad Ali in Africa all those years ago and, despite grandstand stunts like fighting five guys in one night and knocking out Joe Frazier for the second time, he couldn't coax Ali back into the ring, and finally had to retire in discouragement.

He has come out from under that cloud. He lost a fight is all. But the guess here is, in the annals of pugilism, he won a championship. He is almost America's Sweetheart.

• • • • • • • • • • • • • • • • • • •

JULY 11, 1991

The Shoe Says He Will Win This One, Too

I talked to the world's greatest race rider the other day.

I asked him how he thought he was going to do.

"Bet on me," Bill Shoemaker said. "I should be even money in here."

You never could get much of a price on Willie Shoemaker. It never was advisable to bet against him.

But he's not getting ready for a Gold Cup this time. This is not the fourth at Arlington. Even the Kentucky Derby pales beside this challenge. The Belmont distance of a mile and a half is a sprint compared to the distance of ground Shoe has ahead of him. The track is greasy, and you can't even see the homestretch.

The man who won four Kentucky Derbies, two Preaknesses and five Belmonts—to say nothing of 8,822 other races including 11 Santa Anita Handicaps—is in the ride of his life.

Anyone else would scratch.

Shoe is not getting the mount on Swaps for this Derby. He rides a wheelchair. He's paralyzed from the neck down. If he feels movement in even a finger, it's cause for a party. Happiness is a twinge in your elbow.

Shoemaker was the best there ever was at taking the mount they said couldn't be ridden and bringing him home by eight lengths.

Horses, like people, loved him.

As usual, he's got a rogue to bring home this time. If anyone can do it, he can. It's a longshot—the longest shot he ever rode. But as usual, with Shoemaker in the irons, the odds will drop.

The man who handled 40,343 mounts, shadow-jumpers, lug-ins, biters, kickers, 1,200 pounds of malevolence or laziness, couldn't handle a Ford Bronco. It jumped the track on him one chilly night last April. When they picked up the 95-pound, 4-foot-11 body, there was no sign it was alive. He could hardly breathe, talk, frost a glass, and his blood pressure had dropped, so they had to inject him to get any.

Of course, Shoemaker has been there before. Fifty-nine years ago, in the little town of Fabens, Texas, the doctors gave him less chance than they do now. He weighed in at a little over two pounds at birth, was barely a hand's length long and was as purplish-blue as a twilight. "That baby'll be dead by morning," the doctor told the mother.

Shoemaker beat the price, as always. Fed by an eyedropper like a bird till he was several weeks old, his whole life was spent, so to speak, on the rail.

He became one of the great figures in sport for his time and for all time because of his ask-no-favors personality and ability to take on adversity. Red Smith, an admirer, once wrote that if Shoemaker were 6 feet tall and weighed over 200 pounds, he could beat anybody at anything.

He asked little of life. And got it.

"Can you imagine?" he said ruefully the other day. "I rode 40,000 horses—and an auto got me."

The auto got him, all right. It toppled him off an off-ramp and piled him up on a freeway 45 feet below, and he fractured the fifth, sixth and seventh cervical vertebrae in the fall, with subsequent damage to the spinal cord and cessation of the ability to move muscles. Simple term: quadriplegia.

He was on his way home from a golf course at the time, but if friends he was drinking beer with blame themselves, Shoemaker doesn't. Not his style. When he stood up in the stirrups in a Derby in 1957, the ready-made excuse was that the finish pole was confusing in the longest homestretch in racing, but Shoe would have none of it. "I blew it!" he admitted.

He still doesn't sound like a man looking for something or someone else to blame. "I have great memories. I've had a great life. I'll have a great life again. It happens. You live with it."

As usual, he's confounding the doctors. Seven weeks ago, he could move only his eyes. Now, he can move a wheelchair. "I blow into it!" he tells you proudly. "I can drive the thing by myself! I drive it by mouth. By air power, you might say! It works with compression. It's amazing what you can do with your mouth!" The air pressure propels the vehicle. "I was down at the stables just this morning!" Shoe says excitedly. The stables are not at Santa Anita, they're at Craig Hospital in Englewood, Colo., where Shoemaker will be spending the next few months. "Did you see any Swapses or Ferdinands down there?" he is asked. "Naw! They're all jumping horses," he tells you.

A month ago, the only place he could see a horse was on a television screen. He could get off a respirator only a few minutes a day. His conversation was restricted to blinks. Now, he's off it all day. He's on the phone more often than George Bush.

He was getting ready to watch the All-Star game the day I called. But he uses his television screen and special satellite dish largely to check the progress of the horses he trains. His assistant, Paddy Gallagher, films the works and transmits them to the hospital room.

He lives in a metal halo, a modern orthopedic version of a medieval torture chamber the Borgias would have been proud of, but it will be removed when it has held the fractures in alignment and promoted growth.

Will Shoe make the winner's circle again? Will there be a hole on the rail he can get through to the roses as he did with Ferdinand in the '86 Derby? Will this trip, bad as it is leaving the gate, end up in winner's circle No. 8,834, the most important one he's ever made?

The whole world hopes so. Shoemaker knows so. "Bet on it," he advises us.

Horses have been trained from wheelchairs before. Shoemaker is sure he not only can do it, he will do it and be back on a track in time for the Oak Tree meeting at Santa Anita in October. He'll never go there on horseback again, but you can go to a winner's circle by chair, too.

Any horseplayer in the country can tell you it's the first place to look for Willie Shoemaker.

• • • • • • • • • • • • • • • • • • • •

AUGUST 4, 1991

Sampras' Good Game Is Good for the Game

Sports, like Hollywood, needs heroes. Stars. That's why they put numbers on the backs of players. It's all very well to talk of team exploits, but it's individuals who sell tickets.

Tennis needs them more than most. It especially needs American heroes. The game foundered periodically here with the flood of skilled but alien Australian players. Of late, the superior practitioners of the game seem to come from Europe.

Tennis has always needed the Big Bill Tildens, Jack Kramers, Arthur Ashes, Donald Budges. Jimmy Connors and John McEnroe filled the bill for a time, but they came into focus as something of anti-heroes, skilled players but a long way from the Frank Merriwell traditions of another generation. Kind of embarrassments, really.

McEnroe and Connors are all but gone, and the game has weathered the Scandinavian onslaught (Stefan Edberg appears to be the last of the great Svenskas).

The lists are filled with journeymen, quarterfinalists at best, players who might rise to an occasional challenge but who are inconsistent, incomplete, lacking true star status. That's why the game was really ready to throw its racket in the air, leap the net, and send up a volley of cheers when Pete Sampras became the first American in seven years to win our Open, in fact, the first American to reach the final in six years.

Pete Sampras is tall, dark, handsome, as American as a malt shop. A hero right out of Central Casting. He plays the American big game, serve and volley. A home run hitter. A bomb-thrower. Dempsey. Joe Louis. A take-no-prisoners game. He doesn't have to chip and dive for his points, hug the baseline and wait for the breaks. Sampras is a terminator.

American tennis is overjoyed. At last, a guy on a white horse. A guy whose idol was Rod Laver, not Charlie Manson. You can root for Pete Sampras. No ugly American here. You don't have to hold your breath for fear he will insult the Queen, make a gesture at the royal box, ask the Pope for a light.

Like all power hitters, he tends to over-rely on his big weapon. Baseball sluggers either hit a home run or strike out. They rarely bother with the small skills, hitting behind the runner, working the count, moving the man over, bunting. Power quarterbacks go for the long one, they don't work the ball downfield one first down at a time. Mike Tyson isn't looking to win the decision.

Sampras, too, is like a railroad gun. When he's on target, havoc. When he's not, oops!

He served 13 aces against a moderately skilled international player, Amos Mansdorf, at the Volvo/Los Angeles tournament at UCLA the other night, but had to rally from a 1-4 deficit in the second set to pull out the match. His games sometimes tend to look like Bugs Bunny cartoons with the wily rabbits turning his own big game back in on him.

He threw 100 aces at the field in the U.S. Open last September, 24 of them at Andre Agassi in the final. It was like arguing with King Kong.

But what happens when the ball comes back? What happens when the KO artist throws his Sunday punch and the other guy doesn't even blink? Or gets up at the count of two and charges?

"Fastball pitchers say there are some nights they don't have that fine line," Sampras is advised. "Are there some nights the serve is off? What happens then?"

"The ball comes back," Sampras admits. "You're startled. You go to Plan B."

Does he have a Plan B? Sampras thinks so. He doesn't plan to revert to baseline tennis. "I get a lot of easy points, but I play aggressive tennis. I keep the pressure on."

It's a risk game. It is an axiom of pugilism that great punchers have their biggest problems with jab-and-run artists, clinchers who neutralize onslaughts—boxing's version of baseline tennis. Home run hitters can't handle junk pitches as a rule and quarterbacks hate safeties who play zones.

Pete Sampras faces a foe in the Volvo final today whose game is hardly as nuclear as his. Brad Gilbert may think it's raining tennis balls by the second set, but if he can contain the fallout and get the ball back in play, Sampras may need to play his aces as usual.

Bill Tilden had more than a big serve. So did Don Budge, Rod Laver, Bjorn Borg. But none of them won the U.S. Open singles championship at the age of 19 years 28 days.

A cannonball serve is no more a guarantee of immortality than a 350-yard drive in golf or the 100-m.p.h. fastball in baseball. You have to be able to chip and putt. You have to have a curve, a change and control.

And you need passing shots, lobs, drop volleys and second serves in tennis. The game should take up a collection to ensure that Pete Sampras gets them. If he doesn't make it, the whole game goes back to the baseline. To say nothing of back to the Borises and Ivans and guys who speak English in the singsong smorgasbord of Stockholm.

• •

AUGUST 29, 1991

Sack Dance Sacked? Good!

I'm going to hate myself in the morning. I know this is not the popular stand, but I have to weigh in with the minority report on a major controversy confronting the Republic.

The question of the breakup of the Union of Soviet Socialist Republics? Saddam Hussein? New rounds of taxes?

No. Sack dances.

It seems those eminent killjoys, the competition committeemen of the National Football League, have banned end-zone celebrations, on-field gloats and other demonstrations of unseemly jubilation over fallen foes.

Well now, the media have descended on these old mossbacks, the owners and general managers of pro football, in full fury. My friend Curry Kirkpatrick, writing in the current issue of Sports Illustrated, dismisses them as "ancient, Geritol-guzzling, fuddy-duddy relics, rooted in the 1950s and '60s."

Well, leave out the Geritol and Curry could put me in there.

My problem is, I could never abide bullies or bullying behavior. Sack dances are anathema to me. I used to find it painful to watch Mark Gastineau prance with glee after he had just cold-cocked a quarterback who weighed a hundred pounds less than he did and never saw him coming. I was never so happy watching TV as the day the Rams' Jackie Slater came across the scrimmage line and gave Gastineau a dose of his own medicine in the middle of his sack dance.

Who says you have to crow and strut over a vanquished opponent? What kind of message is that to send out to kids? You wonder why we have street gangs emulating this unseemly behavior? These guys are role models, for crying out loud! No matter how you cut it, this is glorifying kicking a man when he's down.

We admire anti-heroes. I'll never forget the shock I felt at a movie in New York one night when the "hero," in a fit of temper, sweeps a table in a diner clear of ketchup bottles, sugar, glasses of beer, coffee cups and plates of hamburger, and smashes it at the feet of a tired, 60-year-old waitress to clean up—and the audience stood up and cheered!

Curry Kirkpatrick thinks there's a generation gap at work here, and maybe he's right. "We have players who were brought up on glitz and MTV," he writes. To say nothing of "Saturday Night Live" and movies in which we have good guys as well as bad guys kicking people in the face.

Well, we were brought up on John Wayne and Frank Merriwell and Joe Louis, guys who spotted the villain the first draw, guys who never taunted opponents, never gloated when they won or threatened when they lost. Joe Louis always made it a point to leave a fallen contender a modicum of pride. "Another lucky night," he would breathe into the microphone just after he had obliterated some contender. The only thing lucky about it was that Joe hadn't killed the guy.

I guess it was Muhammad Ali who brought the art of the braggadocio into the sport of boxing, but with Ali it was a prefight hype designed to sell tickets and borrowed from the on-camera arsenal of wrestling. In wrestling, it's pure hokum because the "bouts" are as prefabbed as a military barracks and as choreographed as a Busby Berkeley movie.

In "Sunset Boulevard," playing a fading silent movie star, Gloria Swanson, scorning the modern talking pictures, says: "We had faces in my day!" Well, we had heroes in mine.

Picture John Wayne doing a sack dance after he has killed Geronimo or saved the fort, can you? Expect Joe Louis would go on the air to say "I should have killed the sucker," would you? Figure Frank Merriwell would point a finger at an end he just slickered for a touchdown? No way.

Let me lay a bit of history on you. Hitler did a sack dance at Compiegne after the fall of France. Look it up. But General Grant returned

General Lee's sword to him. Then, there was the admiral in the Spanish-American War who said as the enemy ship went down: "Don't laugh, boys. The poor fellows are dying."

Whatever happened to our notions of sportsmanship and chivalry? Have we become a nation of toadies, glorifying taunting, gloating tantrums in tennis, mockers of valiant effort just because it loses? Has this attitude slopped over into the stands, where minority rooters get assaulted into a coma?

When did it become fashionable to be a loudmouth, a bully? The Bible tells us the meek shall inherit the earth. If so, they're having a terrible first half. Did Burt L. Standish have it all wrong? Are pluck, perseverance, diligence and graciousness in victory poor substitutes today for cockiness, arrogance, insolence and disrespect? Outlined against a blue-gray October sky today are the new Four Horsemen—Greed, Avarice, Cupidity, Malice.

But if you like sack dances, end-zone shuffles, finger-pointing, boasting, don't worry. The "punishment" voted by the league office is—are you ready?—a five-yard penalty.

Well, that should be a big deterrent. But it figures. We give ax murderers three-to-five these days.

NOVEMBER 10, 1991

Warning, HIV: No Hiding Now

Never see Magic coming down the floor with the basketball again? Never see this little lopsided grin as he chivies the defender around like a yo-yo, then suddenly bursts with a behind-the-back, no-look pass to an open teammate for a baseline jumper? Never see that again?!

Magic, the most unselfish great player I have ever seen in any sport?

Magic, the superstar who actually liked us ink-stained wretches of the press, who stayed in the locker room until the last notebook was filled, the last microphone talked into, the last hand shook?

Wait a minute, God. Please! You can't do that to us! Not Magic. Tell us it's not Magic. There has just been a terrible mistake made here. Magic doesn't deserve this. We don't deserve this.

You can't take away Showtime USA. Those happy nights at the Forum when Magic had the ball and everything was going to be all right and the audience was standing and cheering and laughing and it was good to be alive and at a Laker game and you went home and petted the dog and kissed the kids and reminded yourself to give at the office so the poor people could feel as good as you did.

Magic did that to the community. Shucks, he did that to the game. You mentioned Magic's name and you smiled. So did the one hearing it. He brought a smile to L.A.'s face. He shouldn't be breaking our hearts now. Not Magic's style. I tell you, it's a ghastly mistake. Somebody up there goofed.

What's Jack Nicholson going to do? What are the Lakers going to do? Go back to being the somber bunch they were before Magic came, a cast of characters who looked—and played—as if they were on their way to the electric chair or just got word the dam burst. Magic turned them into the happiest band of troupers this side of the Seven Dwarfs.

And how he could play basketball! The game was invented for people like Magic. It was like watching Nureyev doing "Swan Lake," Astaire dancing down stairs. I always said Magic Johnson with the basketball was Babe Ruth with a bat, Willie Mays with a glove, Rocky Marciano with his nose cut, Caruso with a high C, Nicklaus with a one-iron, John Wayne with a horse. It was one of the great sights and sounds of our age. The throaty roar built as he moved. Not moved, flowed.

He had this marvelous charisma on court. He is 6 feet 9, 225 pounds, and, if you were a defender, you wanted to call 911 when you saw him coming. To a backpedaling guard, he must have seemed like the iceberg bearing down on the Titanic, but he managed to look like Bambi out there. All innocence and grace.

The Lakers were Magic's team. He made the shots, he called the shots, he took over the game.

What's Larry Bird going to do without him? Isiah? Hell, what's basketball going to do without him?

I remember the first time I saw Earvin Johnson. It was in 1979, the Lakers had just signed him and owner Jack Kent Cooke had arranged an interview for me. I was having catastrophic eye problems at the time and could hardly see across the table. But you could see Magic's smile anywhere. It was gracious of him to consent to this awkward interview, but Magic was, above everything, gracious.

You perceive a lot when you can't see, and what I heard in the voice of this new young recruit was kindness. Compassion. I realized this was not just some cocky young jock, this was something special. Such a happy, upbeat person. Magic brought no baggage with him. Magic seemed to feel his mission in life was to make everybody feel good. Magic wanted to be liked.

He was the biggest star in L.A., but I would often chance upon him walking the shops of Century City by himself. No entourage. No flunkies clearing the way as if he were in a sedan chair. He parked his own car—a Jeep. I remember thinking many a time, someone did a nice job in bringing up this young man. To know him is to like him. I never saw a glower on his face.

We knew we had to lose him eventually—say about 2001. But not this way. Magic should have gone out with a farewell tour, with flowers at his feet, balloons over his head, outpourings of love and gratitude, gifts, plaques, streets named after him.

HIV may have picked on the wrong guy this time. There's a way to play HIV—go into seclusion, shut off your phone, cancel your mailing address, go into a cave of your own fears and hide.

But there's a way to play Larry Bird, too. And Michael Jordan. That's to take it to them. Pick them up in the backcourt. Draw the foul. Steal the ball. Make them work for it.

It should come as no surprise to anyone who knows him that's the way Magic is going to play this latest foe, too. If AIDS thinks it has a clear shot to the basket, it hasn't been paying attention. Magic is not about to put his hands up in the air and take this lying down. Magic is going out to meet this terrible foe, too. Take the ball away from it.

HIV may have blown its cover this time. A plague works best in darkness and silence. Embarrassment is its ally.

Magic is not going to let it get away with it. He served notice by appearing forthrightly in public, baring his soul, knocking the chip off the enemy's shoulder. He's going to block this shot, too. A champion does not quit in his corner. A hero does not cower in the dark.

Magic wants this ball, too. He got a rotten break. But the great ones do not foul out. HIV may have gotten a rotten break, too. Heretofore, it has had things all its own way.

Nobody has things all its own way against Magic Johnson. Ask Bird, Isiah, Dominique, Jordan. Magic may be winning something far more important than a Final Four, an NBA championship, player of the year. Magic may be winning for a whole generation. Let's pray he can slam-dunk this one. Let's hope he can find the open man at the top of the key at the buzzer in this one.

If he can, I want to see that smile!

1992

•••••••••••••••••••••

FEBRUARY 2, 1992

A Hit That Changes Your Life

The trouble is, there's no warning. It's not fair. It's not even human. It's nature at its most diabolical.

One minute, you're a vibrant, healthy, happy, eager young athlete. You're chasing a football over a grassy field on a glorious afternoon.

The next moment, you're unable to move. One minute, you can run the 40 in 4.4. Your future is all roses—or, at least, Rose Bowls. One minute you're following in your father's footsteps. You're going to leave your own footsteps in the sands of football glory. The next minute, you're a crumpled heap. You'll never leave a footprint anywhere, any time.

You're Mike Utley of the Detroit Lions. Or, you're Marc Buoniconti of The Citadel.

You usually get some warning when catastrophe surfaces. You're driving too fast, you're drinking too much. You're daring fate and you know it. Or you notice this lump under your arm. Your pulse is erratic or your breathing is labored. You're running a fever.

But, when you're a linebacker, and son of a linebacker who became one of the legends of the game, life is just a romp. Your blood pressure and temperature are perfect, you can see 20/20, hear perfectly, run fast, hit hard. Life is third and short yardage.

It was just a nothing game. East Tennessee State vs. The Citadel at that hub of college football, Johnson City, Tenn. ABC wasn't there, just a few under-excited reporters, a fair crowd, cheerleaders and the school band at halftime.

It was a game that will outlive many others in the region's history. For Marc Buoniconti it was more than a game, it was a life. One minute, he was sliding toward a sure tackle. The next minute, he was as inert as a fallen log, unable to right himself, hardly able to breathe.

Marc Buoniconti was doing what sons have been doing since time immemorial—trying to emulate his father. Father Nick had been a mainstay of the great Miami Dolphins teams of the '70s, including the only pro team in history to go 17-0 and win a Super Bowl. Nick was probably the last of the 218-pound linebackers but he was a sure, deadly tackler, a play-stopper, a pass rusher with an uncanny instinct for the football. He had played for 16 years without getting a bad nosebleed.

There was some controversy as to whether his young son should have been playing that afternoon in Johnson City. "He had on a contraption that fastened from his face mask to his shoulder pads," his father was to recall grimly. "He had been injured two weeks before. He hadn't practiced because of it, but played in spite of it."

The media likes to describe a hit as a "bonecrushing tackle." This was exactly what young Marc Buoniconti put on the ballcarrier. Except the bone was his. "His neck was turned to one side and dislocated. He had crushed his spinal cord at the C-3 level," explains his father. Prognosis: lifetime inside a body that was a prison, not a servant. Messages from the brain could no longer be carried out. They were short-circuited at the neck.

For Nick Buoniconti, the accident was devastating. "You get no warning, no way to prepare yourself for this."

The father remembers mostly the desperation of that first night, the most terrible of his life. The doctors at the facility at Johnson City were candid. "His lungs began to fill up with fluid. His condition worsened. They told me 'He'll die if you leave him here.' "

Nick Buoniconti recalls spiriting his dying boy out of the trauma center to air-vac him to Miami. "It was 3 o'clock in the morning. It was cold—30 degrees—and damp. A 15-mile ride to the airport took two hours. He was just clinging to life. I remember thinking 'If he makes it through this night, we'll have him.' "

That was 1985. Marc Buoniconti was 19 years old. No time is a good time to become a quadriplegic but 19 is obscene. He not only couldn't move, he couldn't breathe.

There are two things you can do when life deals you a hand like that: You can rail against the fates, scream "Why me?" sulk and hide. Or, you can say "I'll play these."

The father and son diagnosed the play. They were bucking a stacked deck. "I was shocked to discover there was almost no research into spinal cord injuries out there," said Nick. "There are over 600,000 people in wheelchairs or suffering from those injuries. There are 14,000 added every year. Average age: 19. Over 80% of them are male. Apart from the automobile, most of them are sports-related injuries. These people are the risk-takers, whether it was diving into a wave or diving into a line."

The cheering stops and faces are averted when the game is over and the victim can't run the 40 in 4.4 any more. The Buonicontis sued the college for medical negligence but they mostly turned their attention to determining what was to be done now that the goal posts have been torn down and the school fight song is over and "playing hurt" becomes not a heroic but a mockery.

For a 218-pound linebacker who thought nothing of hurling himself at 300-pound pulling guards, not even paralysis was too big a foe to be met head-on.

Nick and some new teammates formed a project which, because of its proximity to and association with the University of Miami, came to be known as The Miami Project to Cure Paralysis. "From almost no research labs and a skeletal crew working on spinal cord injuries, we've grown to 25 labs and over 70 researchers all over the world." he boasts proudly.

They've already begun to probe enemy weaknesses in this real life Super Bowl. "They said there was no way human nerve tissue could regenerate. They're finding out it can. In five years, we may be able to have a breakthrough and be able to restore some function to a paralyzed person."

The gains, warn the Miami Project scientists, are "in inches." To Nick, that's preferable to the ailment's former position—a regular 100-yard loss. "We're very optimistic," insists Nick. You don't always win every game to win a championship.

The program can be kept alive only by massive doses of money and frequent fund-raisers. One such will be held on February 11 at the Beverly Hilton here where The Paralysis Project, the West Coast affiliate of the Miami Project, will hold a Great Sports Legends West Dinner, an annual event supported and attended by the likes of the great Joe DiMaggio, the great John Unitas, the great Stan Musial and the great O.J. Simpson.

From his wheelchair, Marc Buoniconti speaks for a half-million of his fellow patients who have been immobilized by the tragedy of spinal cord damage. "I still look down and see my body motionless, feelingless. But I have to put all that behind me."

The success of the project is not for him. It's for that 19-year-old coming along who will be strapping on his helmet, putting on the pads and neck brace and going smiling out to that line of scrimmage from which he will never emerge erect. It comes without warning but it should not go without challenge.

• • • • • • • • • • • • • • • • • •

FEBRUARY 16, 1992

This Decision Isn't a Knockout

The first time I met Mike Tyson, we were riding in a white stretch limousine to be on Roy Firestone's show. Tyson was about 19 at the time. He was not yet heavyweight champion, but everybody knew he would be. There was nothing in his way but a lot of has-beens, never-will-be's and fat old parties with a history of drug abuse.

"Did you ever dream two years ago you'd be riding around Hollywood in a stretch limo to go on national television?" Tyson was asked. "Two years ago, if I was around this limousine, I'd be stealing it," the young Tyson said with a smile.

Tyson was a curious study. He would scare you to look at him. The eyes kind of glittered at times. The gold in the teeth glinted. His squat, massive body looked carved. You pictured him on the street with a knife in his teeth and you shuddered. You knew he could kill you with one blow.

But he had another, almost appealing side. He spoke with this almost sing-song voice with a little lisp. He didn't look vulnerable, but he managed to sound it. He had this sense of humor. He was not educated, but he was intelligent. He spoke in full sentences and not in the cadence of the streets.

You wondered if you had another Rocky Marciano here. Marciano was a frightening physical specimen, too. In the ring, he was a bull, wild, homicidal. Out of it, he was as gentle and self-effacing as a butler.

Tyson would climb into the ring like a mugger. He scorned the niceties of showmanship. He wore no socks; his shoulders were covered with a frayed towel.

Other fighters came into the ring in jeweled robes, high socks, shoes with tassels. Tyson came into the ring as stripped for action as a tiger.

But he remained almost deferential in his early career. When he threw in a lackluster fight against Bonecrusher Smith in Las Vegas, he came into the media room afterward to apologize, almost as if he had done something dishonorable or was ashamed of himself.

It's hard to pinpoint when he began to change. Sometime after the death of his mentor, Cus D'Amato, to be sure. He became contemptuous. He would put his head down and pretend to sleep at news conferences, rousing only to bait his opponent with sneering, schoolyard insults.

He became a walking 911 number. He got in 4 a.m. street brawls, he crashed cars into trees, he harassed women, he slapped parking lot attendants. He cut loose from Bill Cayton, the last voice of reason and responsibility in his camp, and threw in with Don King, a man who was in no position to moralize, a man who would be selling snake oil if this were another time, another place.

Not even getting knocked out could bring Tyson back to reality. History tells us that when the great Joe Louis got suddenly, shockingly knocked out by Max Schmeling, it might have been the best thing that ever happened to him. Tyson's knockout by Buster Douglas actually seems to have escaped his notice.

But could anyone have predicted he would be so out of touch with reality as to commit rape? Against an 18-year-old beauty queen with impeccable academic credentials? This was no bimbo from the pages of the supermarket tabloids, no groupie, this was a girl of such spotless record even the defense lawyers couldn't find witnesses to mar it.

It was a blowup of volcanic proportions. But, like the Douglas knockout, Tyson seems to have persuaded himself it never happened. The law had never scared him on the streets of Brooklyn, and it didn't now.

Date rape is a new concept in the annals of crime in this country. Thirty years ago, the chances of a successful prosecution would have been nonexistent. Rape, by its nature, usually is a crime without third-party witnesses and was almost never punished when the victim knew the criminal.

Should the young woman have been in Tyson's room at 1:30 in the morning? Of course not. Oh, Gloria Steinem would say she had a perfect right to be there if she wished, it is her constitutional right. I have a constitutional right to walk through Central Park at 1:30 in the morning, too. But I don't think I'll exercise it. Criminals seem to be the only ones able to exercise constitutional rights these days anyway.

Has Tyson even now faced the reality of his situation? The gravity? It's doubtful. He is, after all, a valuable property, a walking vault of money to so many people. They are all there, television networks, cable companies, hotels, tours, ticket brokers, advertisers. They are already coming out of the woodwork. Donald Trump has already come forth with the proposal that Tyson be allowed to fight again as long as he contributes parts of his purses to rape victims.

To accept Trump's deal would be a cynical reaffirmation that, if you have enough money, you can get away with any crime, no matter how heinous.

Will Tyson fight again? Very probably. After all, a conviction today is only a semi-conviction and Tyson has the money to go to the Supreme Court.

When the heavyweight champion Jack Johnson flouted the law (even a law that was aimed discriminatingly at him), he had to flee the country and, ultimately, defend his title in Cuba. But Tyson probably will be able to have his title fight right here in the good old U.S. of A.

Wouldn't the "public" boycott such a fight? Are you kidding? They'd break down the doors. The guess here is, Tyson will be able to have his title fight. There's too much money at stake. There will be a public outcry from certain quarters. But from the country at large? Not the way to bet. Many of us would go to his hotel room at 1:30 in the morning.

••••••••••••••••••••

FEBRUARY 23, 1992

For the Drifter, Another Town and Another Job

Larry Brown, America's Bedouin, the Vanishing American, the now-you-see-him-now-you-don't artful dodger, was in an unaccustomed pose—visible from the front and not disappearing through a closing door.

He was standing in a locker room under the Sports Arena, where his Los Angeles Clippers, whom he has stuck with through thick and thin for almost 17 days now, had just met the team they have to beat.

The Clippers had just beaten, no, humiliated, the once-proud Los Angeles Lakers, 125-94, but you had to wonder if Larry's car was parked outside the door with the engine running and the bags packed and the trunk locked.

Larry has gone through more towns in his career than the Mississippi River.

The only known photos of him are from the back. The last guy to skip this many towns this fast, the sheriff was after him.

No one knows what sends Larry off to the horizon so often. Maybe some day, his friends think, he will disappear altogether.

Usually, when a guy shakes the dust of a community from his boots, it's to get away from failure. He's fleeing bankruptcy, alimony, felony, bad debts or even a bad romance or broken marriage. Unrequited love.

Brown is always trying to get away from success. Most of the places, he has left with them crying for more, in fact, hanging onto his coat sleeves and begging him to stay.

It was no use. Brown was just a drifter. He is like that proverbial husband who goes out for a pack of cigarettes and never comes back. Basketball's tumbleweed. As rootless as sagebrush. Git along, little dogie.

It was probably to be expected. A boy born in Brooklyn, raised on Long Island, in military school in Virginia, in college in North Carolina, on teams, variously, from Akron, New Orleans, Oakland, Washington, Virginia and Denver in his playing days.

Then as a coach in the pros at Carolina, Denver, New Jersey and San Antonio and in college at UCLA and Kansas, Brown could be pardoned for thinking he was as stateless as Gen. Noriega. He was double-dribbled through life. Have ball, will travel.

You picture him calling downstairs in the morning to see where he is. And, wherever it is, wanting out.

Larry Brown is the last coach who put the UCLA Bruins in the Final Four, in 1980. And, a year later, he had headed off in the direction of Kansas, where he put the Jayhawks in the Final Four. And won it.

And headed off.

Kansas did everything but block the exits, but Larry was packed and moving by morning. He was in such demand, he promised both UCLA and the San Antonio Spurs he would show up there next.

San Antonio won temporary custody. Basketball's version of Damon Runyon's permanent, established, floating crap game threw out the anchor in San Antone for a time. He kept the Bruins standing on tiptoe. But never kissed them.

This time, Larry didn't go over the wall. This time, the town helped him pack. "Can't win the big one," they said, even though his last record for a full season there was 55-27.

So now, Larry Brown is coaching the Clippers, who make a practice of helping coaches pack.

They can't even win the small ones. This is not a team, it's a collection of underachievers. It has not had a winning season in 12 years.

When it drafts someone (see Danny Ferry), he runs clear to Italy and, when he returns a year later, he announces that, all things considered, he'd rather be in Cleveland.

You would expect Larry Brown would have his camel double-parked to get away from this one he's landed on, the Clippers.

Teams like this have put men on ledges, never mind out-of-town buses. Coaching the Clippers is a good job for someone just passing through, anyway. It's unclear if some of the past ones gave their right names. It's where old coaches go to die—professionally, that is.

On the other hand, maybe this is what Larry Brown has been looking for all along.

He went to the Final Four with UCLA. And got out the road maps.

He won the Final Four with Kansas. And hit the ground running.

He went 57-27, then 47-37 with Carolina in the old American Basketball Assn. And hit the road.

He was 65-19, then 60-24 with Denver. But got restless.

He went to New Jersey, where he was 44-38 and 47-29—and when last seen New Jersey was putting up 19-63 and 17-65 seasons. It didn't matter. Larry was outta there.

Larry gets claustrophobic. He'll pick any direction, including straight up. He doesn't even leave a note.

Maybe he can't stand success.

If so, Larry seemed to have come to the right place. The Clippers are a team every guy who ever turned over a trey as a hole card can relate to.

They were star-less, win-less and luckless. Larry Brown had trouble with his teams in playoffs. But he wouldn't have any trouble with the Clippers in the playoffs. They never got in them.

Only now, under Larry Brown, they've won five of seven. They made the hated Lakers look like a blacktop pickup team.

That's the bad news. Because if they start looking like contenders, they may find Larry Brown down looking at travel posters.

Clipper owner Donald Sterling is ecstatic. He thinks Brown is a new John Wooden.

"It was my dream to sign him," he burbles.

Maybe so. But a few years back, there used to be this popular song, "Did You Ever See a Dream Walking? (Well I Did)."

• •

MARCH 19, 1992

Let the Record Show That Bo Is a Legend

Whenever sports fans gather late at night and the conversation turns, as it will, to discussions of "the best I ever saw," you can always depend on someone throwing a name in the conversation you never heard.

For example, one may say smugly: "Oh, sure, Koufax was all right in his way, Ryan gets a vote if you throw out all those walks, Johnson could bring it, but you really have to put Steve Dalkowski in there, now, don't you?"

Steve Dalkowski?

Right. Steve Dalkowski was a cult figure to end all cult figures. He was a minor league pitcher of such legendary velocity there wasn't a hitter in the game who could stand in there against his fastball. It was not only invisible, it was inaudible, his fans would tell you. It gave off a high-pitched sound only a hound dog could hear. He could throw a ball through a brick wall—if he could hit the wall.

But don't look for Steve Dalkowski in any of baseball's voluminous record books. He isn't there. He never pitched a day in the big leagues. The legend of Dalkowski was word-of-mouth only.

What brings this to mind is the sudden thought that succeeding generations may think us quaint cult worshipers when we talk of a quite extraordinary athlete of our time—one some will hold was the best ever.

We will sing his praises so vociferously that our listeners will be impressed enough to sidle over to the baseball encyclopedia and look up this paragon. Under "Jackson, Vincent Edward," they will find his "exploits" listed and they will wonder what all the shouting is about.

For, under his birth date and the information "Nickname, Bo," they will read: "Games 567, at-bats 1,837, runs 278, hits 460, home runs 109, runs batted in 313, batting average .250."

In the fine print, they will be told that Jackson, Vincent E., held the league record for strikeouts in 1989 with 172, that he struck out nine times in a row once, and struck out twice in the same inning in a game in 1987.

Now, these are not the statistics of a superstar, these are the statistics of a journeyman. These figures wouldn't make much more than a good two seasons' work for a Cecil Fielder.

The ballad of Bo Jackson is a sad song, a threnody, a lament for what might have been.

Bo thought it was all going to be easy. He came out of Auburn University with a Heisman Trophy and such a set of school records—43 touchdowns in 38 games—that the sports world thought he was going to make them forget Red Grange, O.J. Simpson, Jim Brown. They were shocked when he chose baseball.

It was a complicated choice. It had more to do with Bo's annoyance with the Tampa Bay Buccaneers—Bo is easily annoyed—than with any desire to become the next Henry Aaron.

But Bo was a proven football commodity. The ability to hit a pitcher from Georgia Tech is no guarantee you will hit Nolan Ryan.

The late Fresco Thompson, when he was vice president of the Dodgers, had a stock question he would pose to young athletes whenever they came to him, wondering whether they should opt for a job in baseball or in football: "What do you want, son? A career—or a limp?"

Bo Jackson didn't exactly opt for the limp. It came looking for him.

He was safely locked in a baseball contract in the spring of '87. He was batting .344, the curveball had gotten less mysterious to him, his home runs were prodigious. He had passed up the football draft the year before. Very few football franchises knew he had an escape clause that permitted him to jump to football if he so chose.

Al Davis knew it. The pro football draft had gone through seven rounds and 182 players when, suddenly, the selection of Bo Jackson by the Raiders was announced.

Al Davis had taken a calculated gamble. After all, a 183rd draft pick is not much of a risk.

Bo Jackson should have run for the exits. Instead, he was intrigued. He renegotiated his baseball contract to permit the playing of both sports. He wrested from the Raiders the right to report to the NFL a month late. He was to get $1.5 million to play football.

It wasn't enough.

Did Bo think he was invincible? Indestructible? No. In his book, co-authored by Dick Schaap, "Bo Knows Bo," he compares the sports with uncanny prescience:

"Why did I pick baseball in the first place? Well, I liked batting practice. I hated football practice. I liked the idea of a long career. I hated the idea of a knee injury."

Excelling in both sports, Bo became instant legend. Part Paul Bunyan, part Superman. Faster than a speeding bullet, able to leap tall buildings at a bound. Madison Avenue couldn't believe its good luck. Bo became more than a celebrity, he became a myth. He sold more shoes than Michael Jordan. He was so much larger than life size, people were surprised to see him getting on a plane. They didn't think he needed one.

His exploits will grow in the retelling. It's the nature of myths. Hogan never missed a green. Ruth never took a called strike. Magic never missed a jumper.

And Bo Jackson ran 92 yards every time he got his hands on the ball. He hit three home runs a game, threw baserunners out by 20 feet, broke bats in half with his head.

And, then, some spoilsport will haul out the record—.250 average, 600 strikeouts, 5.3-yard rushing average and 13 touchdowns in three years in the NFL.

Cult hero? No. The records don't tell the tale. He was the real thing. When you talk of all-time greatest athletes, there's Jim Thorpe. And then there's Vincent Jackson.

• • • • • • • • • • • • • • • • • • • •

MAY 19, 1992

Indy Speed Rarely Kills as in Past

In 75 years of 500-mile racing, 52 men have died—or suffered fatal injuries—in a race car at the Indianapolis Motor Speedway.

That's not that bad when you consider there have been more than 2,500 drivers and several hundred mechanics in the 500-mile race.

That doesn't even put it neck and neck with the Hollywood Freeway.

But you have to bear in mind these were the finest drivers in the world. None of them were drunk, all could see perfectly. None of them were lost and consulting a lap map for directions. Their cars had to pass the most rigid inspection, the tires were always brand new, the brake linings not worn. There wasn't any traffic coming the other way. The radio wasn't on, the weather was always perfect or you weren't out there, you didn't have to watch out for cops, pedestrians, road construction, streetcars or railroad crossings. If the road got so much as a gum wrapper on it, they stopped and vacuumed it.

You could go as fast as you'd want. And therein lies the rub. Cars might be built to go 240 m.p.h. People aren't.

But it seemed the faster men and cars went, the safer it got.

It used to be in this country that one out of every three men who climbed in a race car died in a race car. And that was when 100 m.p.h. was considered scorching.

The last fatality on the Speedway before this year was 10 years ago. You will find no comparable span of time between fatal accidents. The Speedway served up an annual fatality. Some years—1933, for instance—there were as many as five.

Many of these accidents took place when the average race speed was 104 m.p.h. In the years no fatalities occurred, it ranged from 185 m.p.h. to 162. Qualifying speeds in the multiple-accident years were 116 m.p.h. This year, they reached 230 m.p.h.

Death seemed finally to be taking this holiday. It defied logic. It was eerie. The Indy track was still only 50 feet wide. They still had those unforgiving concrete walls. Even if the cars had changed, drivers hadn't.

There were something like 14 crashes at the Speedway this year. Some of them lit the sky. Car parts flew through the air, wheels soared skyward. Rick Mears slid along the wall upside down with a disintegrating front end and a car churning like a washing machine. But, incredibly, he walked away. And got into another race car. Driver after driver walked away all month.

Until Friday. Edward Jovy Marcelo, a 27-year-old rookie from the Philippines, joined the ghostly parade of those who didn't.

Death is capricious. Marcelo lost his life driving 173 m.p.h. Drivers going 230 climbed safely out of their crashes. Death doesn't care if you are going fast or slow, racing, practicing or qualifying.

It is uncanny how many times—19 to be exact—the words "in practice" appear in the roll call of the fatally injured. Eight of the last 11 killed at the Speedway died in practice. To die at 172 m.p.h. is the ultimate irony. Indy drivers come into the pits faster than that. It is like that soldier killed in the war reaching for a butterfly.

Any death is too many. But the death of an obscure rookie driver from Manila does not command the media attention the death of an icon of the sport would.

The icons of the sport have been spared in large part. The last marquee name to get killed at Indy was Eddie Sachs in 1964. Foyt, the Unsers (one brother did die in a race car— in practice), the Andrettis, Mears, Fittipaldi, Sullivan, Rahal elude the ultimate black flag whether through superior driving skill, experience or simple intelligence. Indianapolis is lucky. If A.J. Foyt were to die in a race car, the hue and cry of those who would have the sport abolished would be deafening.

Fourteen crashes in two weeks would seem to be trying to tell the track something. The old saying goes: To finish first, first you have to finish. The tubs, or cockpits, surrounding the driver might be all but impregnable, cars might be constructed to break away like sets for movie fights—but people can't break away. It's nice to try to go fast enough to arrive at Victory Lane. But you don't want to say, "I'll give it my all" or "I'll die trying." Because you might.

•••••••••••••••••••

JULY 26, 1992

Reveling in Spotlight Of World

BARCELONA—All right, Miss K., take a memo to Baron de Coubertin, wherever he is today:

"Dear Baron:

"About your Olympic Games? Those celebrations of youth and fitness you put into effect a century ago to produce a race of happy people who would never again have to go to war? Which would draw the whole world into a pageant of health and happiness and combat in sport, not in warships?

"Well, it's gotten a little out of hand, Baron. It's become a celebration of power and money. Instead of athletes, we're getting power brokers, ad hucksters, bickering boardroom types. They're using the Olympic Games to sell shoes, soft drinks, even postal services.

"There are more sponsors than there are players on the U.S. basketball team. The Olympic flag should be a pair of shoes rampant on a field of dollar signs. Instead of 'Citius, Altius, Fortius,' the Olympic motto should be 'Sell, Pay and Bank.'

"But there's one corner of your Olympic ideal that I have to think is what you had in mind and it is alive and well and, this year, living in Barcelona.

"This is the parade of the nations that opens your Games. This is the lump-in-the-throat ceremony that sets the mood and tone of the event and is the hardest ticket in the Games because it's not about money or winning or records, it's about joy.

"This is where the infighting stops, the commercialism plays out. This is where the Games begin and end. This is what they should be all about.

"It's not just a parade, it's really a moment in history. Always a highlight. It's the only thing in the Games that hasn't been commercialized or politicized.

"Not everyone recognizes a decathlon or a pentathlon or the Harvard Four With Cox, but everyone loves a parade. I love a parade, you love a parade, the whole world loves a parade—and the whole world is in this one.

"It's fireworks and card tricks and it's a chance for the host country to show off its creative capacities and stage an extravaganza that C.B. DeMille would envy. It's overdone, over-staged, over-produced—but it's marvelous.

"It's a three-handkerchief production. As Marc Antony said, 'If you have tears, prepare to shed them now.' It's as wholesome as hot apple pie and as sentimental as a valentine.

"But what makes it is the march of the athletes. I didn't count them, but I'm told there were 12,000. Most of them seemed to want to get their picture taken with Magic Johnson, but they represented 183 countries, the largest number in Olympic history.

"They didn't really march. They straggled. They chewed gum. They waved to the crowd. They got out of step. They got out of line. They carried cameras. Some of them carried each other. They put their arms around each other. They chattered. They took pictures. They exchanged pins. They had a ball. You looked at them and you figured things are going to be all right, after all.

"You see, Baron, your Games are indestructible. Neither wars, nor boycotts, nor terrorists, nor Depressions, nor economic hardships can kill your Games.

"All of the above tried to and couldn't. That's because they're a spirit, not a thing. They transcend a track meet, a basketball game, a fencing match. They transcend sport.

"An opening ceremony can sum up more than any philosopher's dogma, any political speech how people are the same. They come in different colors, they wear different clothes, they speak different languages, but underneath, they're the same. People are people. Athletes are athletes.

"You could chart world history by Olympic opening parades. You look and you don't see America, or you look and you don't see Russia and you know the sabers are rattling.

"You look this year and what was once the lordly and populous Soviet delegation is now a strange raggle-taggle crew known as the Unified Team of the Commonwealth of Independent States with places such as Azerbaijan and Kirghiz listed.

"You look and you know Communism is gone. We may not miss the philosophy or the regime—but we miss the team.

"The Games were opened by a real live king, a Bourbon, at that, but he's not a throwback to the crowned heads of Europe.

"He doesn't wear a spiked helmet with a plume on it or a jeweled sword or golden epaulets: He has a two-piece suit. He looks like a King from Wall Street.

"The only uniform worn in the Games was on Fidel Castro. He drew boos.

"The Germans came as one team and General Ludendorff would be ashamed of them. They didn't goose-step, they didn't look like parade-ground troops. They straggled, too. They bumped into each other, stopped to photograph American basketball players and, in general, acted like teenagers everywhere.

"You looked and you didn't see Yugoslavia, and you knew that politics still could rear its ugly head.

"The United Nations, no less, requested that the Yugoslav teams be disinvited, barred from the party for their belligerence and persistence in perpetuating civil war in their homeland.

"The president of the Barcelona Olympic committee acknowledged that his compliance had been sought—and agreed upon—by the secretary general of the United Nations.

"The Olympic parade gave ample evidence of the dissolution of Woodrow Wilson's great dream of unified ethnic groups: Splintered delegations of Bosnians and Slovenes and Croats marched instead of Yugoslavia and the Czech and Slovak Federative Republic marched instead of Czechoslovakia.

"Nothing's perfect, Baron. But, look at an Olympics this way: suppose you gave a party and everybody came? That's what happened this year.

"The head of the host committee, de Pasqual Maragall, spoke of 'the common language of sport.' And it's true.

"Sport, like music, is a language all its own. Love of sport knows no borders.

"In a century marked by regress and war, arrogant words and unfulfilled ideals, to meet from time to time to participate in sport, engage in a nonviolent struggle, may it be a celebration of the whole world. Long live the Olympic Games!

"Juan Antonio Samaranch, the Olympic head, called it 'the greatest festival of contemporary society.' He told the athletes and the hosts, 'Baron Pierre de Coubertin would have been proud of you!'

"So, rest easy, Baron. There's lots wrong with the world. But nothing guns and fire and killing can heal.

"I like your idea a lot better. I like Dream Teams and world's fastest humans, and world's greatest athletes, and canoes flying through the water and arrows flying through the air.

"In fact, they ignited the Olympic torch by an archer firing an arrow into the saucer of gas. It's not exactly splitting an apple on your son's head, but it was an impressive piece of symbolism using an ancient weapon for a flame for peace.

"The Olympic Games do the same thing. They march for peace and brotherhood. And to get Magic Johnson's autograph."

• •

August 7, 1992

Lewis Is Again Good As Gold in Long Jump

BARCELONA—Do you have a clue what three centimeters amount to? A little more than the width of your thumbnail. Ten or 20 grains of sand in a row.

But for Mike Powell, three centimeters might as well be a mile. The hole he made coming down in the sand at the Olympic high jump pit was three centimeters short of the one Carl Lewis had made two hours earlier.

It was a melodramatic evening. Lewis had started the competition with a jump of 28 feet 5½ inches.

People thought that was going to be an appetizer. Turned out it was the main course.

For two hours, the best jumpers in the world couldn't come close. Powell, who jumped 29-4½ last year, was having trouble.

It came down to the last jump of the night. Powell had served notice by jumping 28 feet on his fifth jump—on a night when only three jumps were better than 28 feet.

He stood at the runway. He shook his hands, stared in concentration, then went into that funny, characteristic cakewalk, broke into a run. He hit the mark, leaped...

...and came down past the 28-foot mark. The crowd roared. Powell leaped from the pit, waved and bowed. Clearly, he thought he had won. Later, he said he "felt" it had been short. But how do you "feel" three centimeters? How do you even detect them?

In a way, Powell almost spoiled a great moment of history.

I guess a lot of people missed Sarah Bernhardt's farewell tours. Not many people were in the stands for Babe Ruth's last home run or Ted

Williams' last at-bat. Plenty of people who saw it wished they had missed Joe Louis' last fight.

We never got to see Jesse Owens make a farewell Olympic appearance. War intervened. He never got to defend his four gold medals.

But, we got to see Carl Lewis make what surely is his farewell Olympic long jump appearance—and go out on a high note.

Carl was never the beloved figure Jesse Owens was. Aloof, austere, difficult, even condescending, he inspired more awe than affection. You didn't know whether to curtsy or genuflect in his presence.

But for sheer brilliance, we may not see his like again.

Jesse Owens got shortchanged. In a way, Lewis has, too.

You measure excellence by historic comparisons, usually athletic. If a man is a great cook, you say he is the Babe Ruth of cooks. A man drives fast, the cop stops him, pulls out the ticket book and says, "OK, Andretti, you've just won the pole."

If you run fast or jump far, you are "a regular Carl Lewis."

Lewis has been the most consistent and versatile performer in track history for almost a dozen years now. Save for a boycott, he would doubtless be appearing in his fourth Games. It is not likely you will see athletes doubling and tripling in events as Lewis has done.

But, for all its incandescence, Lewis' career has, in a very real sense, been marked by frustrations. It is as if Ruth hadn't hit those 60 home runs or Ted Williams never batted .400.

As great as it was, it could have been greater. When he won four gold medals in Los Angeles in 1984, the public carped because he left the long jump pit after leaping only the obligatory 28 ¼ and passed up trying to improve it to save himself for the 200 meters.

He was the world's greatest long jumper for 11 years. He broke meet records, piled up gold medals. But, he was really chasing a ghost.

One fantastic afternoon back in October of 1968, a jumper of no particular distinction before that, Bob Beamon, electrified the track world by breaking the world record by almost two feet. No one had ever gone 28 feet before. Beamon went over 29. By 2½ inches. It was so eerie, they blamed the altitude.

The record became the longest-lasting in track history. When Carl Lewis came along, he went 11 years without losing a long jump, and he set out after the record like a Scotland Yard detective on the trail of Jack the Ripper.

He stalked it. He sought it. He dreamed about it. Track aficionados said he actually broke it in the 1982 Sports Festival, but an official thought he detected a foul. He didn't. There wasn't one. But the jump was never measured.

One trouble was, Lewis was more than a jumper. He was also the world's best sprinter. He was the first since Owens to make that difficult double in the Olympics.

Then, in Tokyo last year, he finally jumped 29 feet. Three times. He eclipsed Beamon's record.

But so did Powell. Only Mike did it by two inches. Lewis did it by a quarter of an inch—and the wind was too high to make it an acceptable jump.

Carl Lewis has seven gold medals and one silver. But, for a moment Thursday night, it seemed his curtain call was going to be on a sad note. A couple of grains of sand the other way and he ends his career shaking hands to congratulate someone else.

It was fitting it didn't turn out that way, that he went out a winner. I mean, would you want Ted Williams to go out with the bat on his shoulder and the bases loaded? Did you enjoy Louis lying on the canvas, Ali on the ropes unable to fight back in his last title bout?

If it was going to be three centimeters, it is altogether proper that they were on Carl Lewis' side. He'll never get his world record now. He'll never get in another Olympics. He thinks he will but he won't. He was the only man in history to win the gold medal in the long jump in two Olympics. Now, he has won it in three.

Even the man he beat, Mike Powell, was glad for him.

"Listen, I had to break a 23-year-old record just to beat this guy!" Powell said after the medal ceremony. "I have great respect for Carl

Lewis. He's been my motivator for a long while, ever since I was a high school kid. He's the best there ever was. Seeing Carl Lewis beat me, I can't get too upset."

If the guy he beat by only three centimeters can feel that way, the rest of the world should be throwing its hat in the air. It was poetic justice. Prose, too.

• • • • • • • • • • • • • • • • • • •

SEPTEMBER 17, 1992

The 'Tying Irish' Just Doesn't Make It

I don't think it occurred to Lou Holtz till he was running off the field and was stopped by a TV interviewer who wanted to get some light on a strange series of plays Notre Dame called with one minute to play. "My God!" Holtz probably thought to himself, "I've tied one for the Gipper!"

For the second time in 26 years, a Notre Dame coach was guilty of running up the white flag, seeking terms, hiding the football, saying, in effect, "I'll quit if you will."

Notre Dame is not supposed to do that. The typical last-minute desperation pass to win a football game is called the "Hail Mary" even by heathens. That's because its chance of success is dependent on divine intervention. Who better to call on that than the University of Our Lady of the Lake?

When Ara Parseghian put away his gun in the great shootout with Michigan State in 1966 and said "Can't we talk this over?" the derision was incredible. Notre Dame men hung their heads. Anti-Notre Damers had a field day.

It is the notion in some quarters that Coach Parseghian never fully recovered from that perceived stigma. And the perception was clear: Notre Dame ran and hid. "Fighting" Irish, indeed! "Fainting" Irish, jeered the rivals. Even the Michigan State team leaned across the line of scrimmage in the final minutes and mocked their opponents.

The next week, Notre Dame took out its humiliation on USC. It beat the Trojans, mercilessly, 51-0. That may have been a bigger mistake than playing for a tie. Parseghian did not beat USC again for seven years, and, in his last year, USC, behind 24-0 till a minute before the half ended, drubbed him, 55-24.

Playing to a tie, Bear Bryant once said, "is like kissing your sister." For Notre Dame, it was to prove a lot more exciting, more like killing your sister. Serial killers get better press than Notre Dame coaches who hide in the closet.

Coaches play for a tie all the time. That's all right at Princeton, Cornell or Iowa State, but Notre Dame is supposed to go out like John Paul Jones ("I have not yet begun to fight!").

It's the tradition of "One-Play O'Brien," "The Gipper." I mean, would the Four Horsemen start falling on the ball? What would Grantland Rice write? "Outlined against a blue-gray September sky, The Four Horsemen fell on the football"?

Would Rockne send in orders to pack it in and try to hide the football and sue for peace? An Irishman ducking a fight?! Say five Our Fathers at once!

It's a tradition nurtured by Hollywood—after all, a future President of the United States, no less, played the legendary Gipp in the all-time hit football film "Knute Rockne—All-American." Notre Dame never went for a tie on a sound stage.

So, outlined against a black and white sports page or color TV, Notre Dame comes across as a guy hiding under the bed. Notre Dame died (or tied) with its boots off, handing over its guns and putting its hands in the air. The subway alumni feel as if John Wayne gave up the fort.

Actually, the last-minute, desperation pass is more for image than hope of success. It gives the illusion of brave effort without the substance. What earned Coach Lou Holtz his scorn—and there were catcalls from the supposedly super-loyal home crowd—was his unconvincing, truculent attempt to head off criticism in his postgame TV byte.

Here was the situation: Notre Dame had just had its prayers answered when it blunted a Michigan victory drive on its 12 with an interception of an Elvis Grbac pass. There were 65 seconds left in the tie game.

First, the coach called for a line buck up the middle. The bad news is, it gained seven yards. The worse news is, it used up 30 seconds.

Holtz later explained resentfully he "was trying to see what kind of defense Michigan was in."

He apparently decided they were in a defense that was a sucker for another line buck. This one took the clock down to 12 seconds. Holtz decided to call time out.

This looked to the crowd—and the rest of the country looking on—like folding your hand. With aces in there.

In the Rose Bowl game after his mortifying 51-0 defeat at the hands of Notre Dame, USC Coach John McKay's Trojans went in for a touchdown in the waning minutes of the game against Purdue to bring the score to 14-13 in favor of Purdue. His dilemma: go for the sure tie with a kick—or go for the victory with a two-point pass play.

McKay never hesitated. He tried for the victory. The play got knocked down.

The record books show he lost, right? Uh-uh. No, he didn't. He went out with his guns out and his boots on. He didn't want the tie.

Holtz did. The record books show he got his tie. So he won? Uh-uh. The headline should probably read: "Notre Dame Loses, 17-17."

• • • • • • • • • • • • • • • • • • • •

SEPTEMBER 22, 1992

It's a Day Off, but No One's Off This Hook

There used to be a sportswriter, Jimmy Cannon, who was a pal and an idol of mine, who had this feature column he reeled off now and again when he was otherwise out of material. It was called "Nobody Asked Me But..." and it was good fun. It was also a day off.

Accordingly, I am going to resurrect this gimmick in honor of my late colleague. It's too good a vehicle to let lapse. I lack Jimmy's capacity for all-out indignation, but Jimmy was a Third Avenue guy till the day he died, never mind how many Presidents he dined with.

So, Nobody Asked Me, Either, But...

1. When I see a guy with his hat on backward, I figure his brains are on the same way.

2. I trust anybody who smokes a cigar—because my Uncle Frank smoked one.

3. I think Lee Harvey Oswald killed John Kennedy—period.

4. I can't stand Roseanne Barr.

5. I wish just once I'd sit on an airplane where the guy next to me was paying the full fare.

6. Any team that throws the football more than 50 times loses. Look it up.

7. I wish the top 10 teams in the Associated Press poll had more students on them than scofflaws—in other words, Rhodes scholars instead of rogue scholars.

8. I think that football coach who castrated a bull for the entertainment/incitement of his players should resign—from the human race.

9. I can't remember a time when the designated hitter won a ballgame. I think being a designated hitter ruins a ballplayer—baseball is

not a platoon sport.

10. I wish women would stop wearing ugly men's shoes, particularly boxing shoes. Not even Mike Tyson looks good in them. And the only thing that looks good in a leopard coat is a leopard.

11. I hope Magic Johnson plays for the Lakers this season, but if he plays for the Knicks, they'll win it all.

12. If you're ever in Spain, don't send out laundry. I had a $400 bill at a suburban Barcelona hotel for a laundering a few shirts and socks that weren't worth a tenth of that new.

13. Drinking coffee out of a plastic cup is going to ruin the coffee industry one day.

14. Guys over 50 shouldn't wear ponytails. Guys under 50 look bad enough. The only people who look good in ponytails are granddaughters.

15. I hate computers.

16. I wish they'd move the Atlanta Olympics to October. That's when they had the Mexico City and Tokyo Olympics and the world didn't come to an end.

17. When I was a kid, a film like "Basic Instinct" would have been a stag movie and the actors would have worn masks.

18. Movies described in the ads as "steamy" usually leave me cold.

19. I think Phil Simms is the most underrated quarterback in football. I put Jay Schroeder in there someplace, too.

20. I do, too, like tennis. It's the people who play it who sometimes get on my nerves.

21. I never knew a golfer who didn't think he was 10 shots better than he was.

22. I like Woody Allen movies, but I don't think I'd like Woody Allen. And I'm sure he wouldn't like me.

23. Guys who think I have it in for Notre Dame make me laugh. Hey! My name is James Patrick Murray!

24. Guys who get on an airplane carrying everything but the family Volkswagen make me see red. Hey! I don't like to wait for my bag-

gage either.

25. I think Julio Cesar Chavez is a great fighter, but he couldn't sell tickets if he fought Saddam Hussein.

26. I wish golf would get a star. The tour without a star is like home movies.

27. I think Jackie Robinson was the greatest athlete I have ever seen—but baseball might have been his third-best sport.

28. I wish we'd get a heavyweight champion named Joe or Jack again.

29. I don't find PeeWee Herman funny. But Bill Murray can make me laugh out loud.

30. I miss Johnny Carson.

31. I wish Toronto would get in the World Series—but I'm not sure why.

32. Every time I start to feel sorry for myself, I look at Jim Abbott.

33. If you'd told me 20 years ago that men would be wearing earrings and necklaces, I'd have thought you were talking about Borneo, not America.

34. All women look pretty in big, floppy hats.

35. I better get out of here before I make everybody mad.

• •

NOVEMBER 3, 1992

It's Mailman's Biggest Delivery

Karl Malone is a very formidable basketball player. He has size and strength—he is 6 feet 9 and 260 pounds—and speed. He is a 30-point-a-night scorer.

But he might have done something off the floor this week that neither he nor any other forward in the league could ever do on it—stop

Magic Johnson in his tracks. Take him right out of his game.

The story was in a corner of the New York Times sports sheet Sunday, not flamboyantly featured but right alongside the automotive column. It was easy to miss. But, as I read it, I realized that sportswriter Harvey Araton was bringing a ball up-court that was going to break the game wide open.

The headline was innocent enough: "Johnson, the N.B.A. and the Fear of AIDS."

But the story went right to the hoop, and began by quoting Malone, of the Utah Jazz, in compelling terms. Malone, the story said, was "challenging the accepted belief that Magic Johnson has been universally welcomed back to the (NBA) even though he has the virus that causes AIDS."

"Look at this," Malone was quoted. "Scabs and cuts all over me. I get these every night, every game. They can't tell you that you're not at risk (against a player with HIV), and you can't tell me there's one guy in the NBA who hasn't thought about it."

Now, this was not coming from some bigoted redneck, this was coming from the league's Mailman, a superstar in his own right, a man who had been a teammate, no less, of Magic on the Dream Team, which went to Barcelona for the Olympics last summer and won the gold medal.

Those quotes had to hurt Magic.

They had to play a part—maybe a big one—in Magic's abrupt decision to abort his comeback this week, to re-retire, hang up No. 32 once and for all.

His explanation was cloaked enough, but it contained the telltale phrase, "It has become obvious to me that the various controversies surrounding my return are taking away both from basketball as a sport and the larger issue of living with HIV...."

English translation: Magic feels his continued insistence on playing will do more harm than good for the fight against HIV and AIDS. Score a three-pointer for Karl Malone.

Araton's story also quotes Gerald Wilkins, a guard with the Cleveland Cavaliers, as saying: "Everybody's talking about it. Some people are scared. This could be dangerous to us all but you're dealing with Magic Johnson, so people are handling it with white gloves. They're not going to say how they really feel."

Several unnamed players and general managers were quoted as joining the anvil chorus.

The story additionally noted that, since Magic's announcement that he has HIV, players who get cut must now leave the floor immediately to get treatment to stop the bleeding. These precautions can hardly be reassuring to the playing personnel.

Magic on court has always inspired fear on the part of the foe, like Geronimo on horseback or Rommel in a tank—but Magic wants to inspire that kind of fear, not the fear of infection.

When I wrote a column some time ago suggesting the possibility of Magic's return, I received letters from doctors who held that a return to the stressful life of pro basketball was the worst possible treatment for his disease. Other doctors were not so sure.

Magic seemed to gravitate toward stress anyway. Shooting a three-pointer at the buzzer can be stressful—but so can criticizing the President of the United States. Magic was never one to go off to a mountain cabin and commune with nature and eat fruits and nuts and await his fate. Magic was a people person. Playing basketball might have been the least stressful thing he did.

The guess here is that the statements of ex-teammates, rivals and fellow players have done what the doctors, lawyers, his own manager and even Arsenio Hall could not do—persuade Magic to turn to the rocking chair.

Magic does not want to be anybody's Typhoid Mary.

How real are the fears? Very real to the players involved. Almost nonexistent scientifically. The possibility of transmittal is said to be in the zero to infinitesimal range.

That's not enough for some athletes. An unnamed guard in the

New York Times' story talks of "backing off" rather than guarding Magic aggressively. Fear of collision may dictate timidity.

The only segment of the population that could decisively influence Magic has done so. As Phoenix owner Jerry Colangelo predicted, "The only people who might have impact on Magic are the players."

Magic Johnson might have been the greatest player who ever lived. Certainly, he was the most unselfish. His 9,921 assists attest to that. His 17,239 points could have been infinitely higher—in the 30,000 range—if he had gone more for the basket than the open man.

A man who would go through a career thinking of others would not want to end it by causing pain or apprehension or fear or loathing in his fellow players. Magic would always give himself up for the team. Now, he's giving himself up for the game.

The Mailman always rings twice. Magic got the message.

1993

• • • • • • • • • • • • • • • • • • • •

JANUARY 2, 1993

The Whole Thing Seemed Offensive

Let's face it. It was the So-What Bowl. No Heisman controversy was at stake, no national championship.

Fittingly, it was a sandlot game. It was like a fight in a bar at 2 a.m. All offense.

If you're into trivia, the score was 38-31, Michigan. But it will never make anyone's highlight film.

You ever see a major college football game where neither team can break serve? That's what happened here. Whoever got the ball won at love. The last time you saw tackling this sloppy, one of the parties was greased. And the other was drunk.

I knew we were in trouble when I sat in the regular seats in the first quarter and someone said, "Which one is Washington?" This was solidified when another asked, "What's a Wolverine?" The answer came back, "It's a female wolf."

About 9,000 people managed to miss this Rose Bowl game. I think the last time this many eschewed this Tournament of Roses party, it was still a chariot race.

Nobody ran the wrong way, no substitute quarterback named Doyle Nave came off the bench to pull out a game against an unscored-upon opponent in the gloaming.

Still, it was exciting. Correction: It would have been exciting—except that "exciting" requires that you care who wins, that something be at stake. Nobody south of Puget Sound or west of Ann Arbor saw this as having any more significance than, say, Yale-Harvard.

Any time you have two presumably quality teams in a postseason game and the total scoring tops out over 68, there is a hole in one or both teams. The defense looked most of the day like Oliver Hardy chasing a chicken. While trying to look dignified.

It may have been Washington Coach Don James who could say, "Nice mess you got us in here, Stanley!" We may have seen the last of the storied James Gangs. Those Washington gangs of James wouldn't give up 38 points a season, never mind in one Rose Bowl game. And if you can believe the reports, it turns out Don has been getting his gangs the same way Jesse did. From wanted posters in post offices.

The reality of the Big Ten-Pac-10 pact is, it works best when a California school is lined up. Cal and Stanford are allowed in—on a restrictive basis. Kind of like the guy who can play nine holes at the exclusive club. An occasional trek south by a Pacific Northwest school is tolerated.

But not when they overdo it. Don James didn't seem to get the point. He kept sending down these superbly conditioned, smart teams to elbow aside the California teams and cause the ticket-brokers to gnash their teeth. This was the third time in a row Washington came to Pasadena.

It looks as if Don won't be able to continue throwing overalls into the Rose Bowl's chowder. Don't look now, but Don's team seems finally to have been demoralized by the scandals. When a Don James team gives up 38 points, it needs a shrink. It has something else on its mind.

James' teams have given up 80 points in their last two games, both losses. That is major league leading with your chin. A Don James team is not normally that susceptible to roundhouse rights. But on Friday, they got floored more than Ernie (The Rock) Durando.

If the game is at all historic, it will be for the 88-yard run from scrimmage peeled off by Michigan tailback Tyrone Wheatley. It was, as it happens, the longest run from scrimmage in Rose Bowl history. It put Michigan ahead, 24-21, a lead the Wolverines lost but regained. It came on the first play of the second half and seemed to put Washington into the posture of a guy trying to look over both shoulders at once the rest of the game. The Huskies were to score again but never regained their poise.

It is customary for a losing coach to rely in the postgame interview on the hoary, well-worn explanation, "We didn't execute." Coach James offered instead, "We didn't wrap up." English translation: His tacklers let their quarry slip through their grasp. Wheatley was one who escaped the packaging. He ran for 235 yards, an average of 15.7, and two other touchdowns.

What Don didn't wrap up were his overzealous boosters. They did more to break up his team's concentration than Tyrone Wheatley. Wheatley ruined a game. Those other guys ruined a career.

• • • • • • • • • • • • • • • • • •

FEBRUARY 2, 1993

Image Problem Is Everything

The night before the game, the powers that be were panicky. They were afraid it might rain on their Super Bowl.

Hah!

Why didn't they come to me? Never mind the weather bureau, isobars, occluded fronts and all that malarkey.

I don't have to know meteorology. I know L.A.

I could have told them that old trollop would never let the rest of the world see her in hair curlers, no makeup, a ratty robe tied in the middle, shuffling around smoking and drinking reheated coffee.

No way!

When L.A. knows the world is going to be looking in on her, she gets out the eye shadow, lipstick, puts on her net stockings, her highest heels and shortest skirt, piles her hair up in a beehive, bats her eyes and adopts her most seductive pose. She looks like the first runner-up in a pageant.

What I'm trying to say is, like an old-time movie star, she always looks her most glamorous in public.

It sometimes rains here. But you would never know it from the telecasts of major sporting events.

Do you know how long it's been since it rained on a Rose Bowl game? Since 1955. Thirty-eight years. Now, the law of averages would dictate that it would rain on Jan. 1 more than once every 38 years. I mean, it does rain here. But never on New Year's.

We do have smog, fog, fires, wind. But never on Channel 4—or 2 or 7 or whatever network is televising the latest international event. We have had seven Super Bowls here. But we didn't even have dew on those days.

I remember when we had the Olympics in '84. A crew from British television came to my home. They began the interview with negatives. L.A. would be too hot, too smoggy, the traffic would be horrendous. And so on.

I sighed.

"Let me tell you something," I said to them. "L.A. will be gorgeous. Sunshine, palm trees, card tricks. The traffic will be nothing. We get 100,000 people at the Coliseum lots of times. We get a million and a half in Pasadena every New Year's. We handle it. There won't even be any smog. That old strumpet L.A. will be at her chamber-of-commerce best."

She was. I think it was the only time in history, or since the invention of the motor car, there wasn't even a rush hour.

The problem is, this kind of false advertising brings new hordes. People in the rust belt look up and see these people in January sitting in the sun, bare to the waist, eating ice cream cones and drinking beer, and they wonder what they're doing there with that snow shovel. When I came to this state, its population was around 8½ million. Now, it is more than 30 million and climbing. I blame television.

It can rain right up to the morning of the game. Then, as they used to say in the old Ralph Henry Barbour novels, "The day of the big game dawned bright and clear."

San Francisco doesn't have this problem. They got in two World Series. The first one, it rained five straight days. The second one, they had an earthquake. Some cities have all the luck. Well, no, there's nothing lucky about an earthquake. Let's say some cities tell it like it is.

I have addressed this crucial situation before. Basically, it's one of image. We somehow have to counteract the notion that we live in La-La or Lotus Land, that this is really the Good Ship Lollipop out here.

It's not easily gotten around, given the coquettish instincts of our lady. We have to convince the world that this isn't a Shirley Temple set out here. We have to stanch the immigrant flow or face getting pushed into the Pacific ourselves.

Accordingly, the demon real estater from Pasadena, Mr. David Bryant, and myself got our heads together a few years ago for a set of rules regulating sporting event telecasts from our too-fair city.

And I would like to reprise at this time, as this latest Super Bowl shows that L.A. has no intention of mending her ways and presenting an honest image to the world. You saw how it rained right up until midnight before the game and then beamed cloudless sunshine at kickoff.

We will get no help from the old bawd. We have to be resourceful to counteract her wiles. With this in mind, here are the rules:

1. For attendance at the Rose Bowl, it should be mandatory for all ticket holders to wear ski masks, mittens and earmuffs, to sneeze a lot on camera. The front rows will be restricted to those with runny noses, head colds, migraines or watery eyes.

2. Tickets will not be sold to anybody with a tan.

3. Sunglasses are to be confiscated on the spot.

4. Tank tops will be barred and anyone taking a shirt off will be summarily ejected, even if it's Cheryl Tiegs.

5. NBC will be forbidden to photograph the magnificent backdrop of the San Gabriel Mountains—unless they are on fire.

6. No one is allowed to broadcast that the windchill factor is 85,

under pain of getting the plug pulled.

7. The network will be barred from televising the Rose Parade, since we don't want to leave viewers with the impression we live in a place where you can grow roses in January. To discourage even attendance at the Rose Parade, we will lobby to have Saddam Hussein named grand marshal.

8. We will truck in mud and rain machines from the back lot at Fox.

9. No one wearing shorts will be allowed within 500 yards of the stadium. Anyone seen sweating will be required to take a cold shower before admittance.

10. We can publicize tornado warnings. Even though they are for Olathe, Kan., we can give the impression they are for Orange County.

11. Under no circumstances can we show orange or grapefruit trees blossoming. We can show the traffic jams instead, zeroing in on vehicles with vapor lock, or station wagons that haven't moved more than two inches in the last hour. Emphasize that this is not game related, but normal traffic going home from work on the 210.

12. See to it that the Buffalo Bills get in every time. That way, nobody west of Tonawanda will watch and all we'll have to worry about is a few stragglers from Olean.

These would help. So would real rain. But when L.A. knows the cameras are on, you can't even seed the clouds. There aren't any.

• •

FEBRUARY 23, 1993

Bolt Gave Golf Its Deserts

He was golf's Vesuvius. The rumbling would begin when the putts wouldn't drop, the galleries would move, the lies would be unplayable. By the 18th hole, you could sense the lava rising, the ash spewing, the top about to come off. Volcanologists would run to their instruments in alarm. Mt. Bolt was about to erupt.

Whenever word filtered down to the press tent that Tommy Bolt had double-bogeyed the 18th hole, every reporter worth his salt would head for the locker room on the double.

A shoe would come flying through the air, crash into a locker. The sky would turn blue. Bolt would be in fine, furious eruption. It made "The Last Days of Pompeii" look like a Sunday school picnic, Mt. St. Helens, a smog alert.

No one ever hit a golf ball any better than Thomas Henry Bolt, a.k.a. Thunder, Terrible, Tempestuous. He was one of the best strikers of the ball who ever showed up on a first tee. He could fade it, hook it, slice it, feather it, punch it, fluff it. Mostly, he could hit it straight.

But it used to seem that he never met a golf shot he liked. He never trusted a golf ball or a golf course in his life. He acted as if he were going through Indian country and could hear drums. It was not a game, it was a conspiracy. The game had it in for him. The world had it in for him.

The world didn't have it in for him. The world loved Tommy Bolt. He was every man who ever missed a two-foot putt, who wouldn't take a double-bogey lying down. Like hackers everywhere, Tommy knew what a two-timing tart golf can be. He let the world know what a trollop she was.

He was a perfectionist. He never let golf get away with it when it trifled with his shots. Every time a shot moved an inch off line, Tommy was furious. Other guys threw clubs. Tommy threw bags.

The stories about him are legend. How he came up to a 200-yard approach to a green and asked the caddie what the right club was.

"A seven-iron, Mr. Bolt," the boy answered.

"A seven-iron!" screamed Tom. "What makes you think I can get there with a seven-iron!"

"Because it's the only club you have left in the bag," the caddie said.

Or he is playing the Crosby. The wind is howling, the rain is falling, deer graze on the fairways.

"Listen!" screams Bolt as he passes Bing Crosby's home on the 14th green. "Get me a .45 and I'll put it to that crooner's head and see how he'd like to come out here and par 8, 9 and 10 and keep his sanity."

That was old Thunder. No compromise.

Golf is the most maddening game people play. That's because the failure is your own. In baseball, the pitcher strikes you out or the outfielder makes a leaping catch. In tennis, your opponent aces you. In football, someone else intercepts the pass.

In golf, you do it to yourself. Your rage is inner directed. You can't scream at the linesman, the guy in the chair, the ballboy, the umpire, field judge, referee or teammate.

No golfer finds this easy to deal with. But most mask their feelings.

Tommy Bolt never did. Tommy shook his fist at the heavens, kicked rakes, criticized courses. Tommy did not suffer failure gracefully.

Oddly enough, though, Tommy did not use the excuses a lot of more genteel golfers did. Tommy never suddenly noticed he got flu after shooting a few double-bogeys. Tommy took his lumps. Tommy stayed and slugged it out with the course. He hit back.

He didn't think so, but the public adored him. He didn't walk a golf course, he sauntered. And he always attacked it. Tommy took no prisoners.

The only golfer he truly respected was Ben Hogan. Everybody else was an opponent to Tommy. He glared his way around 18 holes—unless he was shooting a 63. Then, everybody was Tommy Bolt's friend.

Off the golf course, he was the soul of congeniality. On it, he acted as if he were on the deck of the Titanic and the lifeboats were full.

But what a player he was when the putts were dropping, the fairways were splitting and the water was merely scenery! There was no finer sound and sight in the game than Tommy Bolt winning a U.S. Open by four shots over Gary Player in Oklahoma in 1958.

Those who were there recall it as one of the purest victories in an

Open ever—or since Hogan's first. They are sure Bolt never had more than an eight-foot putt, there were no chip-ins, no-brainers or balls that hit cart paths and bounced into the hole. He hit 54 greens that week.

Bolt won 15 tournaments. The magic of that is, he won them in only 16 years on the tour. And he never teed it up on the tour until he was 34. He was a carpenter in Shreveport, La., when some tour players came through and Bolt took the afternoon off and found out he was two shots better than any of them.

He became one of the biggest tour attractions. People loved it when his ears got red and his face purple, but Lee Trevino, no less, rated him one of the five best players he ever played against.

The second tournament he won was the 1952 Los Angeles Open, where he beat Dutch Harrison and Jackie Burke in an 18-hole playoff. Bolt, who played in a felt hat and with a velvet swing, became an instant celebrity, playing the game with such a look of pure disdain that the galleries were fascinated. It was such a landmark event that the L.A. Open has made Tommy Bolt this year's honoree from the past for the tournament that opens Thursday at Riviera.

It has been a long, brilliant career for Bolt. Some years ago, in Arkansas, a man came up to him and reminded him he had caddied for him as a young boy. Fellow by the name of Bill Clinton.

Tommy sat in a restaurant near the golf course the other day. A companion pointed out a golfer sitting nearby. Payne Stewart. Bolt looked up at the young man sitting at breakfast in sweat togs and baseball cap.

"Are you Payne Stewart's caddie?" Bolt demanded.

"I am Payne Stewart," responded the other.

"Damn!" said Bolt. "I believe I must have played with your daddy! Ain't you from Springfield, Mo.?"

The two shook hands. Two U.S. Open winners. Bolt, in 1958, got $8,000 for winning his Open. Stewart, in 1991, got $235,000.

"It was a real pleasure to see you, Mr. Bolt," Stewart acknowledged. Bolt was entranced.

"You see how respectful that young man is?" he said. "Shows real respect."

Why shouldn't he? It was the tempestuous, terrible-tempered thunderers who made his game what it is.

Has the game gotten easier—is that why no one seems to lose his temper on the fairways anymore? Bolt is asked.

He sniffs. "They all have public relations experts telling them what to say. Jackie Burke looked like an altar boy, but he once told someone that if he said what he felt like on a golf course, he would make me look like Billy Graham."

So, do they shoot lower scores because they keep their composure?

Bolt looks scornful. "The equipment is better," he says.

Won't go as far when you throw it?

Bolt smiles. "I never threw a club that didn't deserve it."

APRIL 6, 1993

Golf's Most Revered Course Can Be Downright Devilish

AUGUSTA, Ga.—All right, all you tour two-putts, take the A game out of the bag. Put the eight-iron in a vise and see if you can get grooves that will make a ball stop on glass.

This is the Masters, Sonny. This isn't some amusement park four-ball. This isn't a romp through the cactus and tumbleweed in Arizona; they have trees here. This isn't a telephone company pro-am. If there are any "ams" here, they won the U.S. Amateur or the medal on the Walker Cup team. It's not the Kmart Greater Tuscaloosa Classic or the chocolate company invitational. It's golf, not pool.

You don't get any automobiles for holes-in-one here, you get in the history books. You are playing for the ages here, not a paycheck.

Bring the two-iron. Sleep with your putter. Get some old films of Hogan and Snead. Check your throat because the pressure will get to be about what it is 50 fathoms down in the Mariana Trench. You'll get the bends just driving into this place.

This is the Vatican of golf. The most magnificent 250 acres in the game. The azaleas, the towering pines, the ponds would move a poet to rhapsody—but if the ball goes in them, don't expect hymns. Just curses. You can't one-putt these greens. But you could ski them.

It's hallowed ground. Hogan won here. So did Snead, Nelson, Sarazen, Palmer. Nicklaus won six times.

The foreigners have all but taken it over with six victories in the last decade.

But don't expect an upset. "Unknown Wins Open" is a familiar headline. But "Unknown Wins Masters" is as far out as "Republican Captures Massachusetts." Hackers don't make it in this field. God wears a green coat. And carries a one-iron. Winning the Masters is a almost a religious experience. The winner is the Pope of golf.

A lot of people consider the Masters stuffy. It simply has a reverence for the past. What's wrong with that? Golf never was meant to be stick-ball in the street. You wipe your feet and take off your hat when you come to the Masters. You whisper here. No "You the man!" countenanced at the Masters. After all, this was founded by the honorable Bobby Jones, Esq., himself. It's a cathedral of golf courses. Enemy bombers would spare it in a war.

Outside its lordly magnolias, the surrounding countryside is Tobacco Road. But inside, you can almost smell the incense. It's not a course, it's a shrine.

They name the holes after flowers here. No. 1 is the "Tea Olive," for example. No. 2 is "Pink Dogwood," No. 3 "Flowering Peach." And so on.

But if you play it, you may have a different view. It may look more like 7,000 yards of hay fever to you. Walter Hagen told his partners to be sure to smell the flowers along the way. But the Haig made birdies. It's harder to smell them through the bogeys. They're just weeds to the guy who hits into them. He doesn't want to smell them, he wants to pull them.

So, romantic as they sound, I have to think the holes are misnamed. I have to think no golfer cards a 6 and walks off thinking, "Aren't the azaleas pretty?" I think the holes should be identified with the sounds you hear on these 18 public enemies masquerading as flower girls. For instance,

No. 1—This is not the "Tea Olive." This is "Oh, God, not over there!"

No. 2—"Pink Dogwood?" Uh-uh. This is "Anybody see where that went?"

No. 3—"Oh, hit another one. I was breathing on your backswing."

No. 4—"I think that's out. Got another ball?"

No. 5—"What'd I do wrong?"

No. 6—"Fore on the right!"

No. 7—"I don't understand. I got there with a four-iron yesterday."

No. 8—"What in the world did they put a sand trap there for? I hit that good!"

No. 9—"How could anybody putt this green? It's not a golf green, it's a hockey rink! Next time, hand me a puck. Or let Gretzky make it for me."

No. 10—"What do you think the cut's going to be? Do you think 11 over will make it?"

No. 11—"What have they got water over there for? What is this, a golf course or a hatchery?"

No. 12—"Where's that going? Come down! Bite! Bite!"

No. 13—"Sarazen made a double-eagle here? Well, let me tell you something: That's the only way the ball would go in the hole on that green. With a four-wood. You can't do it with a putter. As he would have found out. If it doesn't go in, he makes 6."

No. 14—"Where are the 'breather' holes around here? Even Notre Dame has a patsy now and then. And the 1927 Yankees had a couple of .200 hitters. This is the real Murderers' Row. Every hole is Babe Ruth."

No. 15—"Who designed this hole—Dracula? They should call this hole 'Silent Screaming.' What'd they do with the wolves?"

No. 16—"What is that out there—Lake Erie? Never mind the golf clubs, Get me a canoe and a ukulele. It looks like a U-boat pen. You don't know whether to swim it or play it. Maybe they thought this was a regatta."

No. 17—"They should call this hole 'Help!' 'The Nandina?' Don't make me laugh! Hah! 'The KGB' would be more like it. It's ruined more careers than Stalin. At night, you can hear the ghosts of guys moaning, 'I was sure it broke left.' Johnny Miller had its number. 'You hit three perfect shots—and you still have a 25-foot putt left.' "

No. 18—"The only good thing about this hole is, it's the last. You can go home and cut your wrists. You play it with a driver, an eight-iron—and a priest. You get a green straitjacket if you get above the hole. Which you will."

And when someone comes up and burbles, "the Masters is beautiful this time of year!" the golfer can look him (or her) straight in the eye and say "Yeah? So is Devil's Island."

• • • • • • • • • • • • • • • • • • •

APRIL 25, 1993

He Was the Key to the City

San Francisco is not so much a city as a myth. It is in the United States but not of it. It is so civilized, it would starve to death if it didn't get a salad fork or the right wine. It fancies itself Camelot but comes off more like Cleveland. Its legacy to the world is the quiche. People speak in whole sentences, and polysyllabically. It suffers from a superiority complex.

Which is why a lot of people were startled to see its reaction to the departure of Joe Montana. San Francisco didn't make that much fuss when they thought the Giants were leaving.

You would have thought they were losing the Golden Gate Bridge, Nob Hill, Coit Tower, cable cars, Fisherman's Wharf, the Embarcadero. It was "Say it ain't so, Joe!" all over again.

People were surprised because they didn't think San Francisco cared that much. About anything. They were losing a quarterback, not a landmark. The fog is still there. Joe Montana might have left his heart in San Francisco. But he took his arm to Kansas City.

He was the most visible symbol of the City by the Bay since Dirty Harry or Emperor Norton I.

You see, the city that had once been saluted as "the Paris of the West," that had once been the capital, the Parthenon of the Golden West, has been on a losing streak of sorts in recent years. Los Angeles, which it always regarded as a complicated hobo jungle to the south, has long since passed it as a center of commerce, finance, even—if Herb Caen will forgive me—culture. San Francisco has nothing but its frayed elegance left.

It can't seem to get it right. It gets in one World Series—and it rains for five days in a row. It gets in another—and gets upstaged by an earthquake.

It builds a ballpark—and it becomes a haunted house, a cold, dank, windblown hall of horrors with everything but wolf howls at midnight.

The old San Francisco Call-Bulletin once wrote a line—with a perfectly straight face—"Yesterday was the coldest day in San Francisco since last July 6." July 6! It's hard to take seriously a place that is fur-coat weather on July 6—and shorts weather on December 25.

Enter Joe Montana. He came in with no flags flying, no bands playing. He was, like, 82nd on the draft list. Third round. He had a great career at Notre Dame. But that was Notre Dame. What did they know about passing? Not even the fact that Joe Montana in his last collegiate game, the Cotton Bowl in 1979, took over an Irish team trailing Houston by 34-12, and, with only 7 minutes remaining, engineered a last-second 35-34 victory, could impress the pros.

Joe Montana brought a new element to the city—winning. He was the perfect operator for the complex pass patterns of the new coach, the patrician Bill Walsh, and he put the 49ers in four Super Bowls—and won them all.

San Francisco appeared stunned by this turn of unaccustomed good fortune, even embarrassed by it. They didn't quite know what to make of Joe Montana.

Even for San Francisco, Joe Montana was a departure. Pale, skinny, long arms, long pianist's fingers, he didn't look like an athlete, he looked like a cellist. He was as low key as a librarian, as unflappable as a British butler. He gave new meaning to the word cool. In fact, he had been held out of games in his college career because his temperature was below normal. He had the blood pressure of a coelacanth, the pulse rate of a turtle.

But he gave San Francisco super-respectability. The 49ers had never won anything like a championship in their 33 years previous to Montana-Walsh, but within two years they were not only champions, they were a dynasty. They brought dramas like "The Catch" and "The Drive" into the language of "The City" and made 49er games something other than a place to go before the cocktail party at the Mark.

In San Francisco where Joe used to mean DiMaggio, it came to mean Montana. Joe took his fame in stride. He didn't appear vain, cocky, conceited. His private life was private. He credited his coaches, his blocking, his receivers. He wasn't modest, merely gracious. He never starred in nightclub brawls, clubhouse controversies. He simply licked his lips and went out and threw touchdown passes. He was, like San Francisco itself, courteous, civilized, dignified. He didn't court the press but he accommodated it. Courteously.

No one I knew ever felt close to Joe Montana. With a football in his hand, he was an artist. With a microphone, he was bland. Uninteresting, almost. If you didn't follow football, you would have figured him for a stockbroker or real estate agent. He married a high-profile actress-model but they were nobody's Ken and Barbie. Under hobbies, you would have expected him to put "first downs."

He's going to be 37 before kickoff this fall. He has played two quarters of football in two years. That could be a plus. The minus is, Joe Montana will be going to a new team with new personnel, new expectations.

It is considered axiomatic in the NFL that it takes even the cagiest of veteran players a season to adjust to new surroundings, new personnel, new personalities, new coaches, new customs, new city, new state.

At 37, does Joe Montana have a year? It is a point of fact that the infusion of once-star quarterbacks into a new environment has not panned out. When John Unitas went to the Chargers after greatness at Baltimore, he was only going through the motions. Joe Namath, after being all-world in New York, was not even all-city in L.A.

Is there any reason to believe Montana will be an exception? Even though the Chiefs are planning to put in a system similar to Walsh's, it won't be exactly the same.

Should Montana have stayed with the guys who, so to say, brung him? Probably. He knew the system, he was comfortable in it. He helped invent it, perfect it. He would know he could look out there at any given play and know there would be that one receiver who always seemed to be open under the Walshian scheme of things.

Should the 49ers have kept him? Assuredly. He would be useful, perhaps even critical to them. He had put them in four Super Bowls. Although it's unlikely he can put Kansas City in one, it's in the realm of possibility that he could have put the 49ers into their fifth. Still, it isn't as if San Francisco was putting him adrift in a long boat on the open sea with a jug of water and an oar. Joe said all the right things—as usual—in his departure, but it was clear he hadn't relished playing behind Steve Young. That had to be humiliating to a guy who struck gold for the 49ers.

In a political debate some years ago, Lloyd Bentsen turned to Dan Quayle and said, "You're no Jack Kennedy." Presumably, someone could turn to Steve Young and say, "You're no Joe Montana."

But, at 37, in a new setting with new plays and no Jerry Rice out there to make them work, it may be that Joe Montana is no Joe Montana. In San Francisco, a tourist attraction. In Kansas city, a tourist.

• • • • • • • • • • • • • • • • • • • •

MAY 23, 1993

Palmer Had the Open; Andretti Has This Place

If, as has been said, it's never a good idea to bring up the subject of rope in the house of the hanged, perhaps it's not too advisable to bring up the subject of the Indianapolis 500 in the house of the Andrettis.

For too long, it has been a sore spot. The purists wince, the dedicated fans groan, and well-wishers shriek "Not again!" as the tragic words come drifting over the loudspeaker in the late stages of the race, "Andretti is slowing down!" Pit crews kick the fuel tanks, owners curse, wives weep.

It's a bit of historic injustice that happens every year. It doesn't seem to matter which Andretti—father Mario, or sons Michael and Jeff. Maybe, one of these years, it will be nephew John.

The Andrettis should enter this haunted house with dread. Trepidation. It's Little Red Riding Hood going to grandmother's house, Hansel and Gretel strolling through the forest, Snow White and her stepmother.

It's galling. It's particularly discouraging when it keeps happening to Mario. Mario Andretti is unquestionably now that A.J. Foyt is retired—the greatest race driver of our times still in a car.

The Indianapolis Motor Speedway was supposed to be to Mario Andretti what the stage of the Old Vic was to Olivier, the Met to Caruso, the Bolshoi to Nureyev, a ring to Muhammad Ali. A showcase for his great talents.

The first time he drove the 500, he dazzled the natives with the confident competence with which he handled it. He was a 4F driver—fast, fearless, feisty and (usually) first. He was rookie of the year. He finished third, only ticks behind winner Jim Clark.

When he won in 1969, it was freely predicted he might win a dozen of these before he was through.

He has won one.

Anyone who ever watched an auto race knows what a colossal bit of unfairness this is. Mario Andretti winning only one Indy is like Arnold Palmer winning one U.S. Open. Mario is the Arnold Palmer of auto racing. The gods of sport have it in for them.

You will remember that Palmer, too, in winning only one Open, was second in four of them and in playoffs in three of those.

Mario has won only once at Indy. But he has been second twice, third once and fourth once.

You might say he was in a playoff in 1981. That was the year Bobby Unser, driving one of Roger Penske's cars, arrived in Victory Lane, only to be told the next morning that he had been penalized a lap for passing cars under a yellow light. His "victory" was taken away from him and awarded to Mario Andretti, who had come from 32nd—next to last—on the grid to second. And then, apparently, to first.

Andretti got the traditional pace car at the victory banquet the following Monday—but without the keys in it. He got an envelope with the winner's check in it—but the check wasn't signed.

The race was turned over to the courts. The litigation dragged on until October, when a three-judge panel returned the victory to Unser—but by a vote of 2-1. Bobby got two-thirds of a triumph.

It was the longest, costliest Indy race in history, 4 months from start to checkered flag. It computed out at an average of about 6 m.p.h. Covered wagons might not take that long to make 500 miles.

So, Mario—like Palmer with golf—became synonymous with racing, a popular victim of what Aristotle called undeserved misfortune.

Arnold won 60 golf tournaments on the PGA Tour, fourth all time. Mario has won 52 Indy car races, second all time.

By rights, each should be multiple winners in his sport's showcase tournament.

The Open eluded Palmer once when he had a seven-shot lead with only nine holes to play.

Indy has eluded Mario when he was in sight of the checkered flag, had a clear track in front of him and plenty of fuel. In 1987, he had led the race for 170 laps when, on Lap 195 of 200, his car suddenly slowed and stopped.

In 1985, Mario not only saved Danny Sullivan's race, he saved his life. Andretti dived down beneath Sullivan's spinning car on Lap 120. Mario led that race for 107 laps, but finished second.

Shouldn't Mario stay in bed on race day? Or take the family to the beach? Get an insurance policy against even hearing the race?

Not Mario. He couldn't wait to get out on that track this year, as usual. He was first off the blocks on qualification day. He rolled out there and put himself solidly on the pole—for six hours—on a day the track was so hot it made pizza out of the tires and slowed the cars into delivery trucks.

But, Mario knows those corners like Palmer knows the greens at Augusta, and he put up numbers—223-plus—that stood until late in the day and the cool of evening, when Arie Luyendyk went out and took the pole away from him by a tick of the second hand.

Mario has won the pole three times at the Speedway. This will be the third time he has started from the No. 2 position. The first time he did, he won.

Does he feel snakebit at this citadel of motorsport? Is the Brickyard the graveyard for Andretti hopes?

"Well, when you consider I've led this race more laps than anyone in it—and more times than a guy who was a four-time winner (Rick Mears), you have to think something is at work here," Mario concedes. "Yes, I would have thought I'd be working on my fifth win by now."

Instead, he's working on his second.

It's the hardest race in the world to win. You don't even win it when you do.

Of the 1981 debacle, Mario says: "The rules say you can't pass (cars) under the yellow (caution flag). (Bobby Unser) passed 13 cars under one yellow. He put 13 cars behind him and the pace car. The pictures showed that.

"The rules are there. When Jerry Grant finished second (in 1972), they found he had pitted in Bobby Unser's pit and took on fuel there. They penalized him 12 laps. Moved him back to 12th and cost him a lot of money ($72,000). They penalized Johnny Rutherford for passing under the yellow one year (1985) when he was running third."

So, who won the '81 race?

"Penske's lawyers," Mario says.

Mario makes his 28th assault on the Speedway next Sunday. At 53, is he Don Quixote tilting at his personal windmill once again? Age 48 is the oldest anyone has won this race—Al Unser Sr.

Mario Andretti is not interested in trivia. The Indianapolis 500 owes him one. Auto racing owes him plenty. The hope in the infield is that this year the exciting news that comes spewing over the loudspeakers on Lap 198 is, "Andretti is speeding up!"

Even Arnold Palmer would applaud that. It would be fitting and just. But, if racing had any decency, Andretti would be on the pole. If it had a conscience, he would win. And we would all be 25 years younger.

• • • • • • • • • • • • • • • • • • • •

JUNE 6, 1993

Great Expectations Nearing Fulfillment

When Bruce McNall traded for Wayne Gretzky in 1988, we all knew he wasn't merely buying a hockey player, he was buying the Stanley Cup. It came attached to Gretzky. After all, he had won it four times for the Edmonton Oilers.

And, when he didn't win it, he was in it. The finals, that is.

No one in L.A. even knew what the Stanley Cup looked like. Or Gretzky, for that matter. All we ever saw of him was this guy skating around in a plastic helmet, waving a stick in the air after he had whipped in another goal against the Kings.

He got 56 of them and 170 points in only 63 games against the Kings. He found them barely harder to get through than Kleenex.

So, we hurried to the news conference when he was traded to get a fix on this new L.A. mega-star. I remember how startled we were at our first close-up look at him. I don't know what we pictured—your basic Canadian roughneck dripping tobacco juice, toothless, face stitched like a wall motto, parts of his ear missing, I guess. Something called "Boom Boom," or "the Rocket," or "the Golden Gorilla."

Heck, this guy didn't even look like Cowboy Flett. He had all his teeth, for cryin' out loud! Didn't have a stitch on him. He wasn't big. He looked too frail to be a hockey player. Not a tattoo anywhere.

He had this almost baby face, a nice smile, long blond hair. You would have figured him for a surfer if you'd run into him on the sand at Santa Monica. He could play the angel in a Christmas play.

This was a guy who had scored the most goals, 92, in a single season? Who scored the most single-season points, 215? Who scored the most points in the history of the game?

Our first thought was, those smart-alecks up in Canada had pulled a fast one. This couldn't be the great Gretzky, this—this altar boy. This was a fax.

But L.A. fans were patient. They told him to take all the time he'd need. Take a year, if necessary. We'd wait.

Then, they sat back to see how he would do it. Unfortunately, his teammates did, too. Some of them should have paid to get in. They didn't think Gretzky needed any help. All of them would have qualified for the Lady Byng Trophy, which they give in this league to the player who tries to kill the fewest opponents during the season.

Everybody figured this was Wayne's world. They stood around waiting for him to do it all. All they wanted to do was take the bows.

The public kept waiting, too. Each day it kept expecting to pick up the paper and see where Gretzky had exploded for eight or 10 goals, had performed a double hat trick—after all, 49 times in his career he has had three or more goals in a game.

But first you need the puck. The Kings could never seem to find it, get it to him.

Gretzky handled it well, tried his best. No one brought it up specifically, but as year piled onto year, you could feel the unspoken parts of the postgame interview as Gretzky would patiently account for another disappointment.

"Er, ah, Wayne. It's about the Cup. Er, ah, the—ahem—Stanley Cup? Er, when can we expect that?"

When it looked as if it would be never, along came 1993. It had not been a good season for Gretzky. All those years of getting hammered into the boards had paid off in a herniated disk. He never even got on the ice till the season was half over.

But that was the bad news. The good news was that the Gretzky who came back was the old whirlwind, the center iceman with the uncanny knack for being where the puck was, who could find the open man in the crowd at Times Square on New Year's Eve and get the puck to him at the precise moment the goalie was looking the other way.

There was also the likelihood the team had learned to fend for itself in Gretzky's absence. It had matured. The chemistry was there. Gretzky only ignited it.

The Cup playoffs were like old times. There was Gretzky making a playoff game look like an ice show, skating around and through the opposition, pulling hat tricks, slapping in winning goals.

Suddenly, the Holy Grail of hockey was right there for grabbing. The upstart Kings rolled through the Montreal Canadiens in the first game like the German army through Belgium. The only score the Canadiens had was kicked in by Gretzky.

The Canadian coach, a sly fellow, found a way out with one minute to play to win a game with a rule book instead of a puck when he invoked a hockey version of the corked bat to remove from the lineup a key player at the critical time. Hockey is one of the few games that do not play on a level field personnel-wise, and the hole in the lineup was fatal.

But if anyone doubted Gretzky's importance to his hockey team, Game 5 of the test matches would have overcome them. As these ice follies came to Los Angeles for the first time in history Saturday night, with the whole town waiting to form up for a ticker-tape parade, the Kings suddenly developed a case of what is known in the theater as flop sweat. They kept, so to speak, blowing their lines, falling into the scenery.

They fell behind, 3-0, and seemed to be looking around to see where to go to surrender.

Gretzky wouldn't let them. Suddenly, there he was behind the net with the puck. He spotted the open Luc Robitaille, flicked the puck to him for the score. The Kings were back in the game, calling for cards.

Nine ninutes later, after Tony Granato made it 3-2, there was Gretzky weaving down center ice with the puck on his stick, a sight no goaltender wants to see. Aaron with a hanging curve. Gretzky slapped it in from 30 feet or so. The score was tied.

It wasn't enough. For the second game in a row, the Kings lost quickly (34 seconds) in overtime.

But it couldn't obscure a central fact for the Kings. When Gretzky is on the ice, they are a Stanley Cup team. When he isn't, they are—well, maybe not a buttercup team but at least a hiccup.

He put them in the Stanley Cup finals. Will they come back?

Even if they don't, the fact that they're there means the community has now found out something the rest of hockey already knew. Wayne Gretzky is half a hockey team all by himself. Behind that choirboy exterior beats the heart of a train robber. The halo slips when he gets the puck.

He has finally done what he came to do. When you think of the athletes who came to this town with flags waving and bands playing but who crept out whining and complaining, Gretzky stands up and stands out. He starred for his sport and spoke for his sport. He put hockey on Page One and Prime Time. That's a hat trick all its own.

•••••••••••••••••••

JULY 6, 1993

He Makes the Most of His Run

It's not like Big D to leave us in the middle innings. Don usually went the route. Of his 209 lifetime victories, 167 of them were complete games.

He never needed much in the way of support. One or two runs were enough. And, with the Dodgers of his era, that was a good thing. That was all he got. It got to be a joke around the clubhouse. Captain Maury Wills would bunt for a single, steal second, go to third on a ground ball to the right side and slide home on a fly ball to short center, dust himself off and say to Don Drysdale, "There's your run, now don't squander it."

No one would laugh harder than Big D. Once, when he was in Washington for a presentation at the White House or some such, a messenger came in with the breathless news that his fellow Dodger Sandy Koufax had pitched a no-hitter in Philadelphia. "Oh, yeah?" shot back Drysdale. "Who won?"

He was a Hall of Fame pitcher and a Hall of Fame human being. Don's nickname at the time was the "Happy Warrior." He had the best sense of humor about himself of any megastar I have known. When the 1965 World Series began in Minnesota, Koufax couldn't pitch because it was Yom Kippur, a Jewish holiday. Instead, Drysdale started on short rest. Don loved to tell the story at banquets. How he got racked up for seven hits—including two home runs—and seven runs in a little over two innings, and how he said to Manager Walt Alston as he came out to relieve him, "I bet you wish I was the one who was Jewish."

Big D was like a big collie dog. You could almost picture him going through life with his tail wagging, an ongoing Lassie movie. He could always laugh at himself and the team.

He was mean on the mound, genial off it. He took the position that home plate was his office and you intruded at your peril. He often said he split the plate with the batters. They could have the outside part, but the inside and the middle belonged to him. I don't know how many times he hit Frank Robinson when Frank was with the Reds, but Robbie used to lean over the plate looking for the outside curve and Drysdale let him know he didn't belong there. "Let's see if he could hit it lying down," Drysdale used to laugh.

He holds the modern league record for hitting 154 batters. No telling how many hundreds got out of the way just in time. "If you're going to let them dig in, you might as well hand them your paycheck right now," he used to say. Fresco Thompson used to say of him: "He didn't care whether he knocked the bat off you or you off the bat."

Willie McCovey used to hit him like he owed him. One time, in San Francisco, McCovey touched him for a home run, knocking him out of the box. I went down in the locker room, where I was not supposed to be (and the Dodger clubhouse caretaker, Nobe Kawano, had a fit), but Big D was strolling around with his shirt off, his face black with rage. I looked. He had painful shingles all around his midriff. "What the hell did McCovey hit?" I asked. Drysdale glared. Then, his face softened. "Ball four," he said. And he roared with laughter.

That was Big D. He pitched in pain. He played hurt. He loved the game. He probably had better luck against right-handed batters. That sidearm fastball of his came in there like a hand grenade to righties. He threw a heavy ball. It was like hitting a shotput. He probably had better luck against Willie Mays than any pitcher in the league. ("Oh, yeah, I held him to triples," Don used to scoff.) And of Henry Aaron, he said: "Trying to get a fastball past Henry Aaron was like trying to smuggle a sunrise past a rooster."

He pitched probably the most gorgeous game I ever saw anyone pitch in the World Series. It was 1963 and he threw a three-hit, nine-strikeout shutout at the Yankees. His own team only got four hits—and one run. And those, bear in mind, were the Mantle-Maris Yankees who went whole seasons without being shut out.

One hot day in Cincinnati, Big D, his face and uniform black with sweat, was systematically cutting the Reds down when, suddenly in the ninth inning, he picked up a weak ground ball and tried to throw to first. But the ball went into right field, and the winning run scored. I wrote a lead that the only ball the Cincinnati Reds got out of the infield all afternoon against Drysdale, he threw out. The next day, I approached Double D's locker with trepidation. He glared, then broke into a grin. "You might have mentioned it was the best curve I threw all day," he chuckled. That was D.

It was a little-known fact that he always hankered to be a play-by-play announcer. It was his dream, even when he was a big star. You could often find him around the dugout or the bullpen talking into a spoon or a broom, broadcasting an imaginary game.

The batters got wind of this. I think it was Rusty Staub who said: "I hear Big D wants to be a broadcaster—I wish he'd hurry up and do it."

The batter's box with a 3-and-2 count would be a lot safer place.

Don never got lifted for a pinch-hitter. He was often the best the Dodgers had at that, too. But God took him out in the top of the seventh the other night. As usual, the game is a lot less fun without him. I guess God knew what he was doing. Maybe the batters up there need a little brushing back. Or they have to have someone who knows what to do with one whole run.

• • • • • • • • • • • • • • • • • • •

AUGUST 1, 1993

He Should Be Right At Home With Best

It was about 10 years ago. I was lying in a hospital room at Valley Presbyterian. I had been operated on that afternoon and I had bandages over both eyes. I was depressed. I had left strict orders there were to be no phone calls put through.

The phone rang. I groped for it, banged it against the bed, managed to get it up to my ear. I was annoyed.

It was Reggie Jackson. Reggie doesn't deal with the word no. He had charmed, bullied, cajoled his way through the switchboard. "He'll want to talk to me. I'll buck him up," he had promised the nurse.

He did. He didn't promise to hit a home run for me or bake a cake, but I remember he made me smile. That wasn't easy that night.

That was Reggie. Rules are not made for Reggie. They're for other guys.

When I first knew Reggie Jackson, he was on the Oakland A's and he had hit 45 home runs by the middle of August.

He had star written all over him. He had the most exciting at-bats in the history of baseball. He didn't swing at a pitch, he pounced on it like a leopard coming out of a tree.

He finished his swing like a pretzel. His left leg was in a kneeling position on the ground, his right leg looked like a corkscrew. He went around like a window shade going up.

You half expected to hear him flapping.

He looked better striking out than most guys do hitting a triple.

You have never seen relieved looks like those that pitchers got when they got the ball past him. They looked as if they had escaped a haunted house. Or won a lottery.

When he hit the ball over the fence—which he did more than 550 times in his career—he went into this leaning chug around the bases, the top half of his body stuck out beyond the lower half. He had a home run trot the ages could envy. Of course, he had a lot of practice at it.

Reggie was all show business. He had the flair for self-dramatization all the great ones have—part Babe, part Barnum. He was a dominant presence wherever he went.

I remember once after an Oakland World Series in which he had bopped the Dodgers, he sent down a crushed beer can to me in the press room. A colleague looked at it. "What'd he do—sit on it?" he asked. The messenger shook his head. "I think he crushed it between his thumb and forefinger," he said.

I still have that can. I loved Reggie for another reason: He wore glasses. But, it was a funny thing. On Reggie, you never really noticed. Energy just poured out of him. He was rarely still. I think he played cards standing up.

His finest hour, to be sure, was the World Series of 1977. He put on a home run display that would have popped the eyes of Babe Ruth himself. I remember he had hit two home runs in Game 6 and I had gone down in the bowels of Yankee Stadium to write my story when a shadow appeared in the doorway.

It was a colleague, Rick Talley: "The son of a blank just hit another one!" he said, laughing.

We scoured the record books. "That's four in a row!" I exclaimed.

"He hit a home run the last time up Sunday!"

It was inevitable that Reggie had to take the act to New York, of course. There was no way Reggie would round out his career in the relative obscurity of Oakland. Reggie was as right for Broadway as Lunt and Fontanne.

"They'll name a candy bar after me," he predicted when he signed. Reggie had no false modesty. Or any other kind.

The fur flew wherever Reggie went. But so did the pennants.

A lot of people were upset that Reggie carried a .262 batting average into the Hall of Fame. But of the last half dozen or more hitters inducted, only Rod Carew carried a batting average higher than .300. Rabbit Maranville got in with a .258 average. Luis Aparicio had .262.

You didn't measure Reggie Jackson by number of hits—although there were 2,584 of them—but by length. Almost half of them, 1,075, were for extra bases. He drove in 1,702 runs.

But you measured him by the soundest yardstick of all—championships. Teams Reggie Jackson played for got in an incredible 11 league championship playoffs, five with the Oakland A's, four with the Yankees, and two of the three the Angels have been in. Reggie made pitchers sweat—and pulled his team along with him. He got into five World Series.

He richly deserved his sobriquet, "Mr. October." Reggie hit 10 World Series home runs and drove in 24 runs and batted .357. Only Mickey Mantle, Babe Ruth, Yogi Berra and Duke Snider had more Series homers.

Even when he failed, it was high drama. One of the most dramatic confrontations I have ever seen in a World Series was Game 2 of the 1978 classic when, with his team down, 4-3, two out, and men on first and second, Jackson faced rookie fastballer Bob Welch in the ninth inning.

It was David and Goliath stuff. The Boy of Summer vs. Mr. October. The count went to 3-and-2. Reggie fouled off two pitches with a swing you could have tested airplanes in. Then, he struck out.

As the cliche goes, it was what the grand old game is all about.

Casey at the Bat revisited. Historians were ecstatic.

Reggie never did anything quietly in his life anyway. You always knew when Reggie came into a room. It was either Reggie or the circus.

He goes into the Hall of Fame at Cooperstown today. They build institutions like that for guys like Reggie. It'll be a livelier place with Reggie around. Trust me.

• •

OCTOBER 21, 1993

For Our Fall Classic, This Was a Real Classic

PHILADELPHIA—I saw it, but I still don't believe it.

This was one for the ages. But was it baseball? Lord! I hope you didn't let the kids stay up to watch it!

It wasn't a game, it was baggy pants comedy. What was that I was saying about this World Series being a fight between two drunks in a bar—all offense.

Well?

Baseball doesn't know whether to be embarrassed or proud. Two teams without pitchers are as defenseless as minnows in a shark tank.

But this one goes into legend. It was the highest-scoring game in World Series history. Never before have two teams scored in double figures.

They finally managed to take pitching out of the game. It was 4½ hours of batting practice.

But, Lord, it was exciting! This goes on the cassettes. This one goes directly to Cooperstown. A study in glorious ineptitude.

I still find it hard to believe Toronto won it. So, I have to think, does Toronto. The Phillies got four runs on one hit in the first inning, lost the lead, 7-6, in the third, then began to bombard the fences. They led, 12-7, 14-9, and appeared to be coasting to the hangar when their Wild Thing, Mitch Williams, came in to put a lid on the coffin in the eighth. The good news is, he wasn't wild. Or, rather, that's the bad news. He threw these nice straight strikes—and Toronto hit them all over the place for six runs and the victory.

When you score 14 runs, you expect to win a World Series game. To come up a buck short is enough to send you to psychiatry.

It set the art of pitching back to the Stone Age. It was sandlot baseball, but who needs classic baseball when you can get to see 31 hits, three home runs, two triples, seven doubles, 14 walks, two hit batsmen and two runs walked in?

It proved the adage, when you shoot at a king, make sure you kill him. The Blue Jays were like the corpse in those mystery movies where the hero leaves him for dead only to find him suddenly coming back with a drawn gun.

The Toronto batting order is like that—a killer on the loose who won't die.

Paul Molitor might be as good a hitter as this World Series has seen and maybe any since Pete Rose stopped appearing in them.

How good is he? Well, his manager sat the league's leading hitter down to make room for him in the lineup Tuesday night. That he could do that says a lot about two ballplayers—Molitor and the man he replaced, John Olerud. Not too many would take a demotion like that smiling. "Play me or trade me!" is the snarl most frequently heard in a major league dugout.

You get benched in a World Series and you feel like a fourth-runner-up in a Miss America contest.

How many clubs could bench a league-leading .363 hitter, a guy who batted over .400 most of the season?

It says a lot about Toronto that they could do that. It says a lot that John Olerud would let them.

John Olerud mouths all the proper platitudes. For the Good of the

Team. Manager-Cito-Gaston-Has-to-Play-the-Cards-He-Has. All that jazz. In a way, it's no disgrace to be lifted for a Paul Molitor. But the World Series is not just any old game. This is the Palace, La Scala, the Old Vic. Do it here, you belong to the ages. Get benched, the whole country wonders what's wrong with you.

Nothing's wrong with John Olerud. What he must want to say is "Bench me!? Are you kidding!? I was batting over .400! That's Ted Williams stuff! You gonna bench Ted Williams?!"

The good news was, he was benched for Molitor, probably one of the best strikers of the ball ever to pick up a bat. He hits the ball hard every time. Even the outs. He almost never pops it up, dribbles a handle hit weakly. He backs you up when he hits.

You would think, with his numbers—lifetime over .300, and .332 with 111 runs batted in and 22 home runs this year, he would be a statue in the park some place. A candy bar. He'd be nicknamed "the Man" or "Saint Paul" or such. If he played in New York, he'd be "Old Reliable."

But in spite of the honor, it's just possible John Olerud would rather have played. Lincoln used to tell the story of the man who was tarred and feathered and carried out of town on a slab by a mob and was asked how he liked that. And he answered, "If it weren't for the honor of the thing, I would rather walk."

Olerud knows how he feels.

When Molitor hit a triple and homer in Game 2, the manager's semi-promise to return the favor and bench Molitor for Olerud the next night went a-glimmering. He decided to put Paul on third base and keep Olerud on first.

So, why hadn't they done that the first night?

Manager Gaston had said that he didn't want to risk Molitor playing third base. That was arrant nonsense. Molitor has always been a third baseman by trade. He played far more games at third than first.

The controversy dimmed in the shot and shell of Wednesday's 15-14 game, baseball's version of Dempsey-Firpo, or even the battle of Gettysburg.

Eleven pitchers took the hill in the cannonading. Until, at one point, the Toronto brain trust had trouble contacting its relief corps in the bullpen when the score mounted in favor of the homer-hitting Phillie lineup.

The official explanation was, the bullpen phone wasn't working.

More likely, it was the pitchers who didn't want to be working.

It called to mind the story when another Philadelphia lineup was on the field, the heavy-hitting old Athletics. One day in Yankee Stadium, the Yankee manager contacted his relievers by phone. One of them, Henry Johnson, had just purchased a hot dog when the phone rang. "Johnson, get in there!" said the manager. "Who's coming up?" Johnson wanted to know. "Cochrane, Simmons and Foxx," came the answer, naming the most fearsome sluggers in the league. Johnson turned to his fellow relievers. "Don't touch that hot dog, I'll be right back!" he growled.

Relief pitchers were right back all night long. Eleven flingers tried to stem the tide while earned-run averages soared into the stratosphere.

It's no wonder they didn't want to answer the phone. They should have pitched under assumed names. It was great theater—but hardly pitching's finest hour. But let's hope there's more of it.

1994

• • • • • • • • • • • • • • • • • • •

January 28, 1994

The Coach and The Diplomat

ATLANTA—Nobody has been able to figure out why Marv Levy is a football coach except he's good at it. Jimmy Johnson couldn't be anything else but.

Marv Levy reads Dickens and Shakespeare. Jimmy Johnson never read anything in his life that didn't have X's and O's in it, and dotted lines.

Marv Levy is a very modest man, grateful to be coach of the Bills. Jimmy Johnson thinks the Cowboys are lucky to have him. They probably are.

Marv Levy is a good coach. Jimmy Johnson may be a great one.

Marv Levy runs a football team the way Plato might. Jimmy Johnson runs one the way Jesse James might.

You know how football coaches as a class are. The season opens, they say, "We may not make a first down." They have 90 of the finest athletes on the planet under their command, but they tell the world they have their work cut out for them.

Not Johnson. He goes into the most important football game of the season and announces his team is going to kick the San Francisco 49ers' butts. Calls up a radio station personally to make sure they get the message.

"It won't even be close," he vows.

It is such a shocking breach of the coaches' oath that the world figures Jimmy Johnson has become suicidal. Not at all. He just wants his players to know he has confidence in them.

"I'm a little different from your clone coach," Johnson boasts. "If you want a clone coach who gets up here and says the same thing every day, just get yourself a cutout and a tape recording. But I'd rather hear good questions. I'd rather have something to say."

Levy's game plan might be likened to a symphony, Johnson's to gangsta rap.

Levy tends to respect experience. Johnson prefers speed, which comes in the young. His teams are a blur. Two times, they ran down San Francisco's Steve Young from behind. Once, they even ran down Ricky Watters from behind. Now, that is speed. And sometimes they were defensive linemen, troglodytic in appearance but trackable only by radar when the ball is snapped.

Levy wants to stay at Buffalo forever.

"Amos Alonzo Stagg coached till he was 90," he reminds you. "You can stay young and coach forever."

Johnson never heard of Amos Alonzo Stagg. But he admits, "I get a little antsy, I get a little bored. I want a new challenge. I felt if I stayed at (the University of) Miami, I could have won a couple more national championships. But I wanted to take another challenge."

He may be looking for yet another. He allowed as how he might like the challenge of an expansion team at Jacksonville. But owner Jerry Jones reminded him he had a 10-year contract with five years left.

Levy's relationship with his owner, Ralph Wilson, is comfortable, non-obtrusive. Johnson and Jerry Jones were perceived by the public as joined at the hip, ex-college buddies who played on the same Arkansas team. Jones bought the team for Johnson, or so the story went.

The notion peeves Johnson.

"Just like I'm a little different from your clone coach, he's different from your clone owner," he says of Jones. "But people have this misconception we spend all our time together, an hour or two a day together. But, I'm a 5-o'clock-in-the-morning guy. I'm also a 10 o'clock in the night guy. That leaves about two hours a day we even could get together!" (Laughter.)

Not even the owner escapes the Johnson rag.

Levy takes the position his scouting staff brings him outstanding football players. Johnson figures he can evaluate football talent on the hoof as well as anyone in the game.

"We got guys on an hourly wage to look at film," he says. "We don't give 'em names, we just give 'em numbers—so they won't be influenced by preconceived notions or reputations. They watch performance, not stars. We don't tell them whether it's Charlie Ward or some backup."

Johnson wants you to know he was undone once by reputation.

"We (Miami) lost the Fiesta Bowl (to Penn State). We ran up 450 yards to their 150 or 200, but we had a quarterback who had been injured and he didn't have enough preparation and he threw three interceptions. But I wouldn't pull him because he was a Heisman Trophy winner. We lost."

So much for Heisman Trophy winners and other underachievers.

"You make a mistake when you let your heart make the picks," he warns. "I got Alonzo Highsmith with my heart."

There are those who think Johnson's heart is easy to overlook, that he does it all the time. But Johnson bristles at the notion that the Herschel Walker trade to Minnesota for a passel of draft picks "made" the Cowboys.

"It's what you do with the picks that counts," he says. "The Rams got a whole mess of them in the (Eric) Dickerson trade. If you pick up a bunch of schmoes, it doesn't do you much good."

Johnson hints that he picked up a bunch of all-pros, not all-schmoes.

"Besides, we made probably 40 or 50 (other) trades to build the team," he says defensively.

The Dallas Cowboys have had two coaches in their history—the legendary Tom Landry and Johnson. Under Landry, they became "America's team." There is some question Johnson wants to share the billing. They are Jimmy Johnson's team. Does Johnson want to be a legend?

"Naw, I'm not into that," says the non-legend. "I'm not trying to make a mark on history. I'm not into longevity. But I'm a very miserable person if I don't achieve what I set out to do."

Levy probably doesn't want to become a legend, either. He coached at Cal, about as far from being a football factory as you can get, west of Harvard. Johnson coached at Miami, about as close to being a football factory as you can get, football's version of the Dirty Dozen. Levy won eight games in three years at Cal. Johnson won 52 games in five years at Miami.

Levy has lost three Super Bowls. Johnson has never lost any.

Levy is gracious in defeat. Johnson is not particularly gracious even in victory. He has no patience with small talk, which he takes to mean any talk not including football.

"I don't want to go to some dinner party and have some lady in a bouffant hairdo lean over and ask me what a quarterback is," he grumbles. Talk football or shut up.

Johnson is not predicting victory Sunday. He probably thinks it's unnecessary. When asked if his team might suffer from overconfidence, given the outcome of last year's game, he frowned.

"Overconfidence is not a bad thing in football," he said. "As long as it doesn't boil over into complacency, where you think you're so good you don't need preparation. Underconfidence is worse."

Levy, of course, doesn't have to worry about overconfidence.

••••••••••••••••••••

FEBRUARY 22, 1994

Is L.A. Too Wimpy to Build New Stadium?

I'm worried about L.A.

Oh, no, it's not the earthquakes, the floods, the droughts, the fires, the riots. It's its soul I'm concerned about. It has lost it.

You know what kind of town this used to be? It was a shoot-the-moon town. Bet the ace. Call for cards. You're faded, buddy. Who says it can't be done? Get him outta here!

That's the way it was. You know, this is the town that built the Coliseum, the Rose Bowl, the first freeways, the movie business. This was the town that brought the Olympics to America in an era of worldwide Depression, when the whole world was broke.

This is a place that got things done. This is the place that, so to speak, made pro football, saved major league baseball, put pro golf on the map when it comes to that.

It had its naysayers, but L.A. laughed at them. Told them to shut up and deal. If they didn't want to sit in, drop out. Fold. We're busy here, don't interrupt.

In 1984, when the rest of the world found the Olympics too expensive and the Games were in danger of extinction, L.A. picked them up, dusted them off and took them again.

City Hall shook in its boots. So did all the wimpy politicians. They got hysterical and passed legislation that banned the expenditure of even one dollar to accommodate the Games. So, Peter Ueberroth said OK and rolled up his sleeves—and made $200 million on the Games and turned a lot of it over to the city.

We got the Rams here over the combined opposition of the colleges, the community penny-pinchers and, in some cases, pro football itself. They still thought this was Fort Apache out here. Only Charlie Chaplin and a few palm trees.

We went after the Dodgers over opposition just as furious—so furious they put a referendum on the ballot forbidding it.

We had guts, we had drive, we had vision. L.A. always just did it. They brought the water here in the early part of the century or L.A. wouldn't even be here. But nowadays some guy reviles the man who brought it here in print and film—as he sits by his swimming pool and turns his sprinklers on.

We're in an era of headlong wimpdom today—sometimes referred to as "political correctness" but more like political ineptness. Good Lord, even Christopher Columbus gets dumped on—by people who would be stomping grapes or picking tarantulas off banana bunches if he didn't have the guts to sail off to the end of the world in the first place.

We're scared to death of our lawyers and witless activists who know how to manipulate the system to promote their own agenda, which is frequently such a paranoid suspicion of the Establishment that it's a wonder they don't put a straitjacket on government altogether. We are afflicted with what I think of as a kind of "soup kitchen mentality."

Look, we need a stadium. That rotting pile of urine-stenched old stones out in Exposition Park has gotten hardening of the arteries. It's a municipal disgrace.

Don't take my word for it. The teams we lured to L.A. in the first place are now packing to leave. The best guess is, either the Rams or the Raiders will decamp shortly. Take their football and move to a place where the ballpark is new and state of the art and the revenue is a guaranteed sellout for 15 years no matter what kind of team you put on the field. The prospects are unlimited. L.A. is now in danger of becoming that municipal horror, a nice place to be from.

Now, I'm not advocating putting the taxpayers into hopeless hock to put up a place to play. On the other hand, how did they manage to build two stadiums (Coliseum and Rose Bowl) in the '20s? And what have they meant to L.A.? Two Olympics, World Series, Super Bowls, World Cup. Visit from the Pope. Title fights. USC-Notre Dame games.

You think the politicians who pushed those edifices through have to apologize to anybody? The only thing they did wrong was leave the running of them to bureaucrats and politicians.

I am sure there are entrepreneurs out there who are willing and able to do what their predecessors did 70-odd years ago—get a community center. Get a heart to Los Angeles.

But in an age full of people who might have gotten a restraining order against Columbus leaving Genoa, who's going to stick his neck out?

He would need civic cooperation. Remember, the city deeded over some hundreds of acres of Chavez Ravine to the Dodgers' Walter O'Malley in an admittedly one-sided exchange for Wrigley Field. But the cynics prophesied he would soon convert the land instead to more-profitable uses, condos and hotels. Well, Dodger Stadium is still there and the guess here is that if the stadium deal had been blocked, there would be gambling casinos there today.

I remember, in a hotel in Moscow in 1980, I was with John Argue, one of the moving forces in getting the '84 Olympics here, and John asked me what I thought the outlook was. I remember saying, "John, if L.A. can't put on a track meet, we are in a whole bunch of trouble."

We're getting so we can't put on a track meet. If pro football reverses the trend of past decades and goes out of L.A., it's not because pro football has changed, it's because L.A. has. We don't have any fun anymore. We're in thrall to a lot of guys who, if they were around to prevail in the '20s, the Dodgers would still be in Brooklyn, the Rams in Cleveland and the Olympic Games in bankruptcy.

The common plea in these parts used to be, "O give us men to match our mountains!" Now, we got men to match our geraniums.

• • • • • • • • • • • • • • • • • • •

MARCH 3, 1994

Agassi, Tennis Need Each Other

INDIAN WELLS—Every time I used to look at Andre Agassi, I would think of Eddie Stanky. You remember. The ballplayer of whom Leo Durocher once said, "He can't run, he can't hit, he can't throw. All he does is beat you."

Then Agassi won Wimbledon, and I realized I had misjudged him.

This was no good-field, no-hit banjo artist. This was a tenacious, dangerous, superbly skilled player who would take a lot of beating.

His on-court demeanor was intimidating. On court, his eyes were cruel, merciless, the eyes of a dictator. They had no interest in you whatsoever. You were a statistic, not an opponent.

From a distance, he appeared dislikable. He let his hair grow, his beard grow. He refused to tuck his shirt in, to wear white or do any of the things tennis used to make you do. He'd wear a tank top if he felt like it.

He was a rebel, but that had become kind of boring. Today, who isn't? He didn't appear to care whether you liked him or not so long as you gave him the line calls.

Oddly enough, he didn't seem to particularly care for his line of work. He dispatched opponents with the ruthless efficiency of a contract killer. When he got ahead of you, you were usually done for. He never really displayed a lot of emotion. It was unfortunate, but you were in his way. He was passionate, but not compassionate.

The public was fascinated by him. The groupies, of course, adored him. He managed to look cute in his kind of hyperactive way. But about the only concession he would make to the fans was, he would throw his sweaty shirt into a crowd of shrieking young girls at the end of a (winning) match.

Madison Avenue cottoned to him. He was not your monotonous serve-and-volley player. Two-shots-and-the-point's-over. His matches were brawls, not recitals. Cockfights. Not your basic, "Nice shot, Grizzy!" type of politesse.

He almost never lost his composure. Not for him the McEnroe or Nastase tantrums. He got even with a backhand down the line, not a stream of curses.

He hurried everywhere. No one ever saw him saunter, stroll or even sit still very long. He always looked like a guy running for a bus. He came on court like a whirling gust of woodpeckers. He never stood still a moment. His eyes darted around. He was in a hurry. He seemed to want to get it over with one way or the other. He had more important things to do.

Tennis had to respect him. He lost with a shrug. Sometimes, he won with a shrug too. He never seemed to change expressions much either way.

If he wasn't quite the image they wanted, he was a magnificent athlete. Charlie Pasarell, no less, thinks Agassi's hand-eye coordination was such that he almost never hit the ball anywhere but in the middle of the racket. He hit the ball exactly where he wanted to, most of the time. Usually, it was some place you had just left.

It was a funny thing, but he always appeared smaller than he was. He wasn't small. He was just a shade under six feet. But his legs were not long, nor his arms. He scurried around the court like a chipmunk; he didn't have the reach of those long-legged Tildens of yesteryear. But when the ball came down, he was, like DiMaggio, usually there waiting for it.

After winning Wimbledon—in 1992—his interest in the game seemed to begin to wane. He appeared overweight, listless. At times, not even competitive.

He had not come up through the traditional knotted-white-sweater, tea-between-sets atmosphere of tennis. Dad was a casino executive in Las Vegas, and young Andre was on the court very early and with much expected.

He was explaining the other night during the Newsweek Champions Cup at the Grand Champions resort here that he didn't have much of a choice in the matter. Someone put a tennis racket in his hands almost in his infancy. "I was packed off to a tennis camp when I was 13," he said. "I didn't have too many other options."

But last year, a sobering thing happened to Andre Agassi. His right wrist gave in to tendinitis. There was an operation. He suddenly couldn't play tennis at all.

And he found, somewhat to his surprise, that he missed it. That he was right where he belonged all the while. He fell in the rankings. At 23, he was yesterday's roses. Not bad news, no news. He wasn't a burnout, he was a flameout.

It wasn't St. Paul falling off a horse, but it was a revelation. "I realized tennis is part of who I am," he said. "I realized tennis was me. That tennis was something I did, something I wanted to do, something I needed. My profession is very important to me now."

He bought a gym, lost weight, skipped fast foods, trained like a prizefighter. A sleek, new, streamlined Agassi hustled onto the court here this week and it seemed like old times. Vintage Agassi. Although his own serve rarely exceeded 99 m.p.h., he easily returned 110-m.p.h. serves of his opponent. He easily dispatched Richey Reneberg, and visions of the Wimbledon championship began to dance in the heads.

He went before the press and termed his hiatus a "blessing in disguise," a turning point in his career. He added: "I am focused now."

Tennis was ready to circle the wagons. Agassi was back and better than ever.

Or was he?

Alas! Tennis being tennis, Agassi went out the next afternoon to play a journeyman—99th in the world—named Fabrice Santoro, a guy with no Wimbledon in his past—nor probably in his future.

He beat Agassi in straight sets, 6-4, 7-6. This is bad news to the tournament—and the game. It's nice to know Agassi now knows he needs tennis—because the game sure needs him.

• •

MARCH 13, 1994

Football Once Was a Sport

A fable, not by Aesop:

Once upon a time there used to be a sport in this country called football and it was played between competing elevens of students from the institutions of higher learning.

Sometimes they came out to the practice field direct from the chem lab or the library. They not only played for nothing, their parents paid for them just to go to school.

They really played for just a sweater with a block H or Y on it. The letterman was the real big man on campus, frequently the student body president and sometimes a straight-A student.

They played for the old blue and gold, alma mater dear. They had school songs like "Boola Boola" and cheers from a Greek chorus and classmates came in raccoon coats and beanies and waved pompons and the Yale-Harvard game sold out and so did the Army-Navy game, even though it was played with real undergraduates.

Coaches were really part of the faculty—Knute Rockne taught chemistry—who treated football as just another P.E. class.

It's hard to say when it changed. But the media got in the act. Intercollegiate athletics sold papers and the poets of the press box pulled out all the stops. Football players became mythic. They became Galloping Ghosts, Four Horsemen, Dream Backfields, Fighting Irish.

The coaches caught on. Somewhere along the line, one coach figured if he could find a way to get just one player out of a coal mine and smuggle him into school, he would have an edge. Then, some other coach figured he would top that by getting two players out of a coal mine, or a roundhouse, and he would go to a bowl game. They entered the mix. They told the story of the coach on a trip through Minnesota who stopped to get directions from a plowboy, and when the young man raised the plow with one hand to point the way, the coach knew he had his fullback—also his conference championship.

They called guys like this ringers. Pretty soon, the whole first team was composed of ringers, then the whole squad. The coach became a staff and you had more people teaching football on campus than physics. Students became walk-ons. They could pick up the towels.

Then, they began to figure ways to eliminate the middleman entirely—the college. Coaches housed their players in "athletic dormitories," segregated from the university as a whole. They found ways to eliminate annoying entrance requirements. The football team had as little to do with the university as the sanitation crew. Literacy was no longer an issue. You had guys who not only could not read or write when they entered college but, 4½ years later, they still couldn't. In the old days, someone with a weak mind and a strong back was given a shovel. Here they were given scholarships.

If their scholarship wasn't at issue, neither was their citizenship. They stopped looking for Eagle Scouts. Vultures were better. Football is not for the genteel, the role models. Football was for the kind of guys who might go join the Foreign Legion. They didn't need their pictures in Sports Illustrated, they needed them in the post office. You not only looked on the farms for prospects, you looked in the courts. You not only needed people who weren't afraid to hit people, you needed people who didn't mind it at all. You didn't need permission of the parents, you needed the permission of the parole officer.

Pro football entered the equation. When the bards of press row invented the Galloping Ghost and the Four Horsemen, the professional game was invented. Red Grange and the four Notre Damers against a blue-gray October sky sold more tickets than Dempsey-Tunney. In a sense, they invented the Green Bay Packers, Chicago Bears and, ultimately, the Los Angeles Rams and San Francisco 49ers. Football hit Wall Street.

Coaches were overjoyed. They had a new selling point. You were no longer playing for God, country and Yale. You were playing for the Dallas Cowboys, Washington Redskins, Miami Dolphins.

It came a long way from "Boola, Boola," Walter Camp, Hold-that-line! or "Far Above Cayuga's Waters." It is such a big business, you expect the Japanese to buy it any day now. The players today want to be paid to remove the last hypocrisy. It is claimed they bring money for the school, business for the community and sponsors for the telecasts. It can't be argued. Game day in, say, South Bend, is a fiscal bonanza.

But they are getting an education free of charge that is worth $100,000 over four or five years, to say nothing of future benefits.

That used to be enough. A football player named Eisenhower became a five-star general and President of the United States. A football player named White became Supreme Court Justice. A football player named Ford became President.

Football went from being a sport to being a business. It is a college dropout. But you knew it had to come to this the first time you heard a coach say, "Winning is the only thing." The rest was foregone. The game had left the halls of ivy and become just another mercantile or entertainment conglomerate.

• • • • • • • • • • • • • • • • • • • •

APRIL 3, 1994

Political Barkley Is Too Incorrect

I hate to say this—he's going to hate me for saying it—but I have to tell you Charles Barkley is a fake, a fraud.

How do I know this? Well, I've made a kind of study of the man. I read his biography, watched him play, sat in on his interviews, even urgently recommended him to Clipper owner Donald Sterling once when he came on the open market.

Look, Charles Barkley would have you believe he's the baddest dude in basketball, gives no quarter, takes no prisoners, defies convention. He's at pains to portray this image. He slugs barflies, spits at members of the audience, feuds with coaches, bad-mouths owners, snarls at media, takes pride in being his own man. A don't-mess-with-me attitude.

Fine. He's done all of those things. He's an intimidator. On and off the court. He's outspoken. Controversial, even. It's not advisable to come up and slap him on the back.

But, having said that, let's take a look at the man. He's not really Big Bad Barkley. He's not a pussycat, but neither is he a mountain lion. He's a sheep in wolf's clothing.

Watch him on the floor. He smiles a lot. He has a nice smile. He laughs easily. He shakes hands with the court-side customers he knows. Says hello to opponents before tipoffs.

He's a politician, for crying out loud! He's going to—get this!—run for governor of Alabama. Next stop, who knows? The White House?

Does that sound like the antisocial dude you've been reading about? The Charles Barkley who mugs the opposition, his own team or the paying customers with the same degree of skill and enthusiasm? The man you love to hate?

Barkley's big problem is he has trouble with the diplomatic lie. He might be governor, but he could never be secretary of state. World War III would ensue. Barkley would tell Yeltsin to sober up, tell the queen mother she was fat.

Barkley has great difficulty with the truth. Which is to say, he tells it. Which creates difficulty. The truth always does.

The other night at the Sports Arena, his team beat up a docile, uninterested bunch of L.A. Clippers so easily Barkley didn't have to play but 27 minutes.

The Phoenix Suns played him so little because they didn't need him to beat so inconsequential a bunch as the Clippers, Barkley told the reporters.

"You don't use your Mercedes-Benz to go to the grocery store. You save it for long, important trips," he said, dismissing the Clippers. "Their team doesn't try hard enough. Someone should tell them winning takes effort."

Vintage Barkley. In your face. Don't sugarcoat it. If the Clippers don't like it—well, it's a matter of complete indifference to Barkley.

Is Derrick Coleman a great player?

"Not as great as he should be," Barkley has evaluated.

Aren't the Knicks great on defense?

"They have to be," says Barkley. "They have no offense."

Barkley could spot the warts on the Mona Lisa. He never temporizes, says "No comment" or even claims he was misquoted. He was named to the all-interview team five years in a row by the beat writers. A dull game? Go find Barkley; he will liven it up for you. An open microphone and Barkley were like the iceberg and the Titanic. Once when he was criticized by an adversary, Byron Scott, Barkley said Scott was "last seen on the side of a milk carton." He once led an on-court brawl that set a league record for fines—$162,500, of which Barkley's share was $57,000 in fines and lost salary for suspension.

Reputation meant little to Barkley. He took over for Julius Erving in Philadelphia, where Dr. J was second only to Ben Franklin in community esteem, but it wasn't long before Erving was turning over the team leadership to the brash young Barkley—at Barkley's insistence. And Barkley once held Larry Bird with his arms pinned to his side while Dr. J belabored him with blows. Bird wore the wrong color uniform.

Sometimes, even the uniform didn't matter. When Barkley got traded to Phoenix, he chose the first practice to bounce teammate Cedric Ceballos on the floor as the team screamed at him.

In the Olympics, it was the Dream Team teammates who screamed at him when he elbowed a player from Angola in the ribs and stomped on his foot.

But for a guy who can dish it out, Barkley can also take it. When Bobby Knight cut him from the Olympic team in 1984, many thought it was because Barkley twitted the coach. The Barkley of those days was widely perceived to be a talented kid who was going to eat his way out of the game despite his undeniable genius for it. The "Round Mound of Rebound" was his nom-de-court in the better press releases. Knight wanted him to lose weight, but all Barkley did was lose interest.

But when Knight cut him, Barkley, astonishingly, defended him.

"I wasn't even close to the player I had been at the (Olympic) trials," he was to write. "I was just hanging out, having fun."

He actually thought Knight agonized over the decision to cut him.

"It's when I finally gained respect for Knight—realized we were very much alike—he couldn't take less than the best from anyone."

Barkley is also delighted when anyone stands up to him, which is not part of the image, either.

Now that I've blown his cover, shouldn't he rob a train, drown a canary or bad-mouth Mother Teresa to get his film-villain image back? First thing you know, he will be getting the basketball equivalent of hockey's Lady Byng Award, annually awarded to the player who passes out the fewest subdural hemorrhages, who uses his stick on a puck, not an ear.

But Barkley is the nearest thing to a megastar in the game, now that Michael Jordan has left. He put 16,005 fans in the seats at the Sports Arena the other night, and there was no doubt they were there to see him. Sir Charles. They booed him, of course. That's part of the pact.

If his team prevails and wins the championship this year, will he try out for the Chicago White Sox next year?

Barkley laughs. "No. I'm going to be trying for governor."

Will he make it?

"No doubt! By acclamation," he predicts.

"There's a sickness in our society today. Our idiots have given a message to our children that your life has no meaning unless you have a big house, a big car, expensive clothes and a lot of money. We've taught them that being a cop, an honest workman, a trash man or a carpenter, any of the useful things in life, are not meaningful. That needs to be addressed. The system isn't working. We need to root it out, remake it."

But can he kiss babies, eat the rubber chicken, make the promises and evade the pressing questions it will take to get to the state house? Can he get there by being Charles Barkley? Won't a couple of Charles Barkley answers torpedo the whole campaign?

Maybe so. But the fact of the matter is that despite his mouth,

Barkley is—come closer, I wouldn't want him to know I'm spreading this around—a nice guy!

• • • • • • • • • • • • • • • • • • •

MAY 15, 1994

Bulldog Lost Ace, Won Battle

Anyone can win a poker pot with four aces. Anyone can win an English spelling bee in Rangoon.

And anyone can win a Cy Young Award and set a shutout record when you have a sinking fastball that comes in at 95 m.p.h. and a curveball that tends to disappear on its way to the plate.

Orel Hershiser won 23 games when he had all those things in place. In 1988, he was not only the best pitcher in the game, but one of the best ever. He pitched the Dodgers to the World Series championship that year. You couldn't get a run against him the last month of the season. A hit was a moral victory.

But Hershiser was holding aces at the time. He was shooting with his own dice. It's easy to be the best speller when you have the dictionary. And when it came to pitching, he was the dictionary.

It was a lock for him to have won 99 big-league games in a bit more than six seasons.

It's for what happened after that point that Hershiser should get the Cy Young Award.

You see, Hershiser is not the Big O anymore.

He doesn't win games with his arm anymore. He wins them with his head. He's like a guy crawling through barbed wire with only a screwdriver, or a swimmer crossing shark-infested waters with a nosebleed. He must feel as if he's got a deck chair on the Titanic.

In 1988, Hershiser was this kind of pitcher: He threw five consecutive shutouts in September—really six because he threw 10 scoreless innings in a game the Dodgers were later to lose in the 16th. He was the Cy Young Award winner (unanimously), sportsman of the year in Sports Illustrated and male athlete of the year in the Associated Press. Among the 23 victories were eight shutouts.

He set the all-time scoreless-inning record of 59—but it was really 67 because he threw 8 1/3 scoreless innings in the first game of the playoffs that year. His earned-run average was only faintly visible—2.26.

There wasn't much you could do with a pitched ball he didn't do. He shut out the New York Mets in the seventh game of the playoffs. Then he shut out the Oakland Athletics in Game 2 of the World Series and pitched the Dodgers to the championship in Game 5.

It was one of the great solo performances in baseball history. In sports history.

But he was only four games into the 1990 season when the calliope suddenly stopped, the balloons popped.

At first, it seemed like only a springtime sore arm, one of those nagging pains. But a couple of X-rays and MRIs later, it was clear this was not a few adhesions or a winter lockup of the muscles to be pitched through. This had to do with the deterioration of a shoulder. This was more than serious, this was catastrophic. This had to do with ending a career.

Dr. Frank Jobe was blunt. No one had ever survived an injury of this kind and returned to pitching. You were lucky to return to combing your hair, never mind curving a baseball.

His manager, Tom Lasorda, has always called Hershiser "Bulldog," which was a mystery to press row. With his stuff, his image ran more to timber wolf.

But the rest of the league now found out what Lasorda was talking about. Hershiser refused to let go. He had the tenacity of an animal that would hang on to a rag even if you threw him out a window with it.

"Dr. Jobe said I had the wrong injury but I was the right patient,"

Hershiser was recalling the other night at Dodger Stadium. "I did what I was told. I did what was necessary.

"At first, I was scared. I thought 'It's over.' Then I thought 'Why?' It's only the first inning. They never knock me out of the box in the first inning."

No one in baseball expected to see Hershiser on a mound again. Except Hershiser.

For 13 months, he kept after his stubborn dream. He got a new battery mate. God was calling the pitches. "I couldn't have made it without faith," Hershiser insists.

The discouragements were relentless. The game humored him, but to a man they thought Hershiser should take his Cy Young Award and go on home and take up another line of work.

When he finally started to pitch tentatively, he found how little he had to work with. The fastball had lost 8 to 10 m.p.h., the sinker didn't sink and the curveball hung like washing on a line—or a ball on a tee.

"There is a whole range of formulas to pitching," Hershiser recalls. "One of the formulas was how to replace the lost skills. You lost velocity on your fastball? How do you keep that from the batter? What do you replace it with?

"There was a whole lot of bluffing going on. But it was stimulating. I found I relished the challenge. The whole upper end of the spectrum of pitching was erased, but I was not without weapons. I took it as a challenge. I reasoned that I had spent all those years pitching, I must have learned something besides how to rare back and say 'Hey! Hit this!' I think I became a professional pitcher. In other years, when all else failed, I always knew I could just muscle up and throw it past somebody. Now, I had to trick it past them. They would dig in now, which they didn't do before. But you had to find a way to use that."

There was also the pain. "You couldn't throw without wincing. But I got a series of programs I went through after and before my turn—three hours a day."

No one ever worked harder than Hershiser to stay on a roster. The pain subsided but didn't go away every day whether he was pitching or not.

He even consented to go back to the bush leagues. He tested his arm in Bakersfield, San Antonio and Phoenix. It was like asking Pavarotti to sing barbershop, but Hershiser wasn't worried about billing. He was relearning a profession. "I looked at all the pitchers in this game who have succeeded without the great velocity or sharp-breaking stuff and I thought, 'If they can do it, I can do it.'"

He has. The pitcher everyone thought was through on April 27, 1990, has won 31 games since then. He has pitched in 95 games, 591 2/3 innings and struck out 379.

The guy with the pair of treys can bluff the ribbon clerks. The guy who puts an "e" on"potato" can get to be Vice President.

And now that even the arm might be coming around and 3 to 5 m.p.h. might be returning to his fastball, Hershiser might come to feel that's nice—but he really doesn't need it.

MAY 24, 1994

Indy Mixes Old, New With Style

INDIANAPOLIS—The Indianapolis 500 is as American as, well, as American as an auto race.

Or apple pie, or hot fudge sundaes or harvest moons.

It's as modern as fuel injection but as old-fashioned as the bustle. It's nostalgic as moonlight on the Wabash, as Midwestern as a quilting bee. It is as much a part of Americana as soap operas, barbershop quartets, the Lincoln log cabin or the scent of new-mown hay. It is part picnic, part county fair and part band concert, although the music is made by 33 of the most highly tuned combustion engines in the world howling like banshees in the humid May air.

It's a sporting event that makes a Super Bowl seem like an intruder because it goes back to a kinder time four wars ago, when the cars—and the society—were not proceeding at near-sonic speeds.

There are certain things that will happen in an Indy 500 now:

1. It will be won by a foreigner. Foreign drivers have won three of the last five.

2. If the winner is not a foreigner, it will be an Unser. The race has been won eight times by two generations of Unsers.

3. If there is a fatal accident, it will probably be caused by a rookie driver. Rookies have racked up the field in about a dozen fatalities or near-fatalities, the most noted, the deaths of Pat O'Connor in 1958 and Eddie Sachs in 1964.

4. Don't consider the parade lap a formality. In 1992, Roberto Guerrero, who was on the pole as fastest qualifier, no less, crashed in the prerace turn around the track, hit the wall and was out of the tournament. Which was kind of like drowning in your own bathtub.

Jim Malloy hit the wall on the pace lap in 1970, making it the first time the race started without 33 entries.

The pace car crashed into a photographers' stand in 1971, injuring a dozen, one near-fatally. They used to let auto dealers and auto execs pace this thing but now they pick guys who could be in it—like Parnelli Jones this year.

5. Expect a close finish. The old days when drivers had to maintain their positions under caution conditions are no longer and cars can now close up and bunch behind the leader, who loses what might have been a half-lap lead. So, Al Unser won a race by 43 thousandths of a second in 1992. And Gordon Johncock won by 16 hundredths of a second in 1982.

6. Don't look for a rookie to win it. Six rookies have won it but one of them was Ray Harroun in 1911, when technically every driver was a rookie because it was the first Indy race. The last rookie to win was

> **"My, my, he was one hell of a writer, but he was even a better person, seemingly without ego, without pretension."**
>
> —JACK WHITAKER, *essayist for ABC Sports, in his eulogy for Jim*

Photographs

Jim Murray plays around in Dodger Stadium, circa the early 1970s

"I've never been unhappy in a ballpark."

Top: Jim visits Steve Garvey, left, and Jerry Reuss in the dugout during the Dodgers' home opening game in 1980. Left: Jim and Dodger announcer Vin Scully at the 1997 Richstone Family Center's Caritas Award dinner. Jim, who won the award in 1992, never forgot to wear his medal to the yearly event. Scully, who won the award in 1993, accidentally left his at home.

Top: Jim visits with baseball legend Yogi Berra in 1995. Bottom: Jim and wife, Linda, with former Dodger owner Peter O'Malley and his wife, Annette, in 1997

"Baseball is the last stand of another America in this century. It's as American as the pumpkin. Or stud poker. A game where you always have a hole card."

"Arnold Palmer didn't make golf, he just put it on Page 1."

Above: Jim interviews Arnold Palmer in 1980. Right top: Jim with race car driver Mario Andretti and actor James Garner in 1996. Right bottom: Jim shares a few laughs with comedian Milton Berle.

"Murray had a God-given talent that was out there for the world to enjoy, whether he was covering the fields of entertainment or sports. And yet, with all of the honors he received, he remained every humble, somewhat shy and self deprecating." —VIN SCULLY, at the September 26, 1998, memorial tribute to Murray

"Picture an Olympic procession. Every group would parade around the stadium; the roar of the million fans would be deafening. Leading the group of sports writers would be Jim Murray." —Al Davis, at the September 26, 1998, memorial tribute to Murray

In February, 1998 Jim was honored with the Lifetime Achievement Award by the Southern California Broadcasters Association. Joining him that day were four other sports media greats, from left, Laker broadcaster Chick Hearn, Dodger broadcaster Vin Scully, NBC Sports broadcaster Dick Enberg and, on Jim's left, ABC Sports broadcaster Keith Jackson. (Photo by Jon SooHoo. Courtesy of the Los Angeles Dodgers)

In 1990 Jim was awarded the Pulitzer Prize for outstanding commentary. He picked up the prize at Columbia with Linda by his side, top, and below, celebrated the announcement in *The Times* newsroom with Sports Editor and long-time friend Bill Dwyre.

"I never thought you could win a Pulitzer Prize just for quoting Tommy Lasorda correctly."

Graham Hill in 1966 but Hill was not really a rookie either, except here. He was a blooded, longtime Formula One driver who had won a world driving title. The last real rookie to win it was George Souders—in 1927.

7. Don't necessarily expect the pole sitter to win it. In 77 runnings, it has been won only 14 times from the pole, by 11 drivers. Rick Mears won it three times from there and Johnny Rutherford twice.

8. Don't think you're safe in a seat or behind a fence. Four spectators have been killed by flying wheels or flying cars, not counting firemen in the pit or pit crewmen. Spectators also have been burned by crashing cars spewing flames through homestretch fencing.

9. You have to know the Indy qualifying rules are by Rube Goldberg out of the Red Queen in "Alice In Wonderland." In 1974, Johnny Rutherford won it from the 25th position. But he had qualified faster at 190.446 m.p.h. than everyone but the pole-sitter! On time posted, not on day of the week, he would have been in the front row instead of the ninth.

This year, Bobby Rahal starts from the 10th row—but he qualified faster than the next 21 cars in front of him! Don't ask me to explain it. I get a headache.

10. Don't look behind the third row for the winner. Since Rutherford won from Row 9 in 1974, only two winners, both Unsers, have come from behind Row 3. Al Unser won from 20th, the middle of Row 7, in 1987 and his son, Al Jr., won from 12th position, outside in Row 4, in 1992. In fact, of the rest, only Danny Sullivan in 1985 started as far back as the third row.

11. Is the race really as American as apple pie? Uh-uh. More like fish and chips. With the Offenhausers long gone, most of the successful power plants in Indy cars have been made in England, including the "Chevy" engines of recent years, the Ford-Cosworths and even this year's highly touted Mercedes-Benz machines.

12. Are the fans just a lot of morbid thrill seekers waiting for an accident? Nah! Of the quarter of a million people there, most will be frying

chicken or drinking beer during the race. They used to have an infield club that fined anyone caught so much as looking at a race car. It's a holiday.

13. Are race drivers great athletes? The ones who weren't are dead.

14. Where's the best place to watch the race? Los Angeles or New York. Channel 7.

15. Do race drivers have a death wish? No, they have a money wish. There's $7.5 million put up for this thing. They want to live to enjoy it. People with death wishes don't get in race cars, they get on bridge railings.

16. Are race drivers brave? Would you do it?

Gentlemen, start your imports!

JULY 18, 1994

Hokey Finish Can't Cheapen Value of Prize

Oh, dear! Or, rather, oh-oh!

The two best soccer teams on the planet struggled through three periods of the game Sunday and neither could score.

Brazil won the World Cup, 0-0.

Brazil won it from the free-throw line, so to say.

It was like watching two woolly mammoths struggle in a tar pit all afternoon and end up gumming each other to death.

It's kind of embarrassing. What they do in situations like this is, after 22 guys run and kick and dribble and trip each other for 120 minutes, they put the ball at point-blank range and give each team five kicks at it. Even then, they miss. It's only 12 yards into a goal eight yards wide, but the World Cup went flying down to Rio when the guy who is supposed to be one of the two best strikers of the soccer ball in the world, Roberto Baggio, kicked the ball over the goal.

If you can picture a World Series scoreless tie in Game 7 in which they decide the championship by a home run derby with key players or a base-stealing contest, you get the picture.

It's the first World Cup final decided this way. It's really a kind of crapshoot. Like cutting the cards or maybe deciding a heavyweight championship fight after regulation by having the fighters held by someone and letting the opponents see who can score the most knockdowns.

As unclassical as it was, it was exciting. You can bet Brazil likes it just fine.

So, strike up the marimbas! Get Carmen Miranda to put a bunch of bananas in her hat and give us a chorus of Chicky-chicky-boom-boom. Get the conga line going. Tell the gang at Copacabana beach to break out the rum and Coca-Cola for all hands.

As for the forces from Forza Italia, hold the fettuccine. Nobody feels like eating. Tell Pavarotti to forget "Funiculi, Funicula." Maybe "Laugh, Clown, Laugh" would be more like it. Sorry, paisan.

I don't know if they have "goats" in World Cups like World Series, but if they do, I hate to say this, but I have to feel Roberto Baggio must fill the bill. Poor guy! He came up to the postgame showdown with his team down 3-2 in penalty kicks. If he makes it, he at least forces the fifth Brazilian kicker to make his shot to win.

He kicked it clean over the top of the goal. That's 8 feet high. He had just kicked the Cup to South America.

His chief rival for player of the tournament, a flamboyant Carioca who, like Picasso and Napoleon and Madonna and Cher, goes by one name—Romario—made his penalty kick. But I have to say it hit the post first.

If it was inartistic by football purists' standards, it was probably better than the alternative. The way these two teams were going, they might have gone the rest of the year without scoring.

You know how that announcer became famous in Cup contests shouting "G-o-o-o-o-l!" Well, Sunday, he would have had to yell "S-a-a-a-v-e!"or "O-o-o-ps!" Even uncontested from the 12-yard line, four of nine missed.

It was like having a putt-off to decide the U.S. Open. But you have to say the Great Soccer Experiment was a crashing success. You know, we export our national sports to other countries. But not the World Series. Not the Super Bowl. Not the Final Four.

We export exhibition games, demonstration sports. These guys gave us the whole enchilada. The United States got the greatest soccer spectacle in the world. We got the greatest players, the greatest teams and an event that occurs only every four years.

It was a great party. More than 3.5 million spectators jammed nine venues. The gross, figuring an average of $100 a ticket, was $350 million not counting TV receipts.

For that, you cheerfully do penalty kicks. Penalty kicks ordinarily are awarded for infractions in the penalty area.

Even the victorious goalkeeper, Claudio Taffarel, described the postgame kick-off as "a lottery." He blocked only one of the three shots Italy missed.

Does this now mean Brazil is the best team in the world? Well, you play by house rules whether it's in a Vegas casino or a floating crap game. After all, Brazil penalty kicks went in the goal. The one miss was blocked.

In the history books, it goes down as a victory. Same as 5-0 even though FIFA will list the score as 0-0. Brazil won; it is the World Cup champion by house rules. As the golfer Lloyd Mangrum, when criticized for not playing classic golf from tee to green but proceeding to one putt his way to victory, asked sweetly: "Are we playing how or how many?"

Brazil can say the same. It was playing how many—and it had the most. Can't wait till 1998.

••••••••••••••••••••

AUGUST 21, 1994

Game Is Too Young to Die

Once upon a time in this country there was a game called baseball.

You would have loved it.

Green grass, bright sunshine, hot dogs, Cracker Jack. The cares of the world you left at the door. "Outta the lot, Hack!" "We're wit ya, Carl, baby!" You were a kid again. No matter what age you were.

You brought the kids. It was an heirloom sport. Passed on from fathers to sons. Generation after generation. The baseball gene ran in families.

And the ballparks! You should have seen the ballparks! Lovely old Fenway Park. That left-field fence! The Monster! The Creature that ate pitchers. Ted Williams hit here.

You ever been to Fenway Park? A pity! Everyone should spend an afternoon at Fenway Park. It's a part of Americana.

Then there was Yankee Stadium. The house that Ruth built. Opera lovers had La Scala. Balletomanes had the Bolshoi. Playgoers had the Old Vic. We had Yankee Stadium. There's a monument to Babe Ruth in the outfield. "How about that!" Mel Allen would say.

The game had stars. Walter Johnson had a fastball you could only hit by Braille. Ruth hit more home runs himself than any team in the league some years. Nolan Ryan threw two no-hitters a year.

You loved to hear the infield chattering. "No hitter up there, Sandy! Throw him the deuce! Make him be a hitter, babe!"

Some of the best afternoons of your life were spent in a ballpark. The poet said the time spent in a ballpark, like fishing, didn't count against your life span. No one could age in a ballpark. You got younger, not older. You could live forever in a ballpark. Someone once complained the game was too slow. Not for us. I never went to a ballpark in a hurry in my life.

If you're in a hurry, go to an airport, I'd tell them.

It was a game that Yogi Berra—ah, Yogi Berra!—once said ain't over till it's over. Not so dumb, at that. It's a game without a clock, is what he's saying. A football game can be over before it's over. Not a baseball game. The gun doesn't go off on you. You never run out of time, just outs.

What happened to this happy hunting ground, this magic isle in life? Where did all those summers go?

Well, it might have died in the summer of 1994. By its own hand.

No one could ever figure out quite why. It was the picture of health to the end.

It didn't run out of sluggers, southpaws, speed burners, shortstops. It ran out of love. It didn't die of old age, lack of interest, neglect. It died of a disease for which there is no known cure—stubbornness.

They all said they weren't trying to kill baseball, they were trying to save it. Meanwhile, the patient died on the operating table. The tombstone should read, "Here Lies Baseball—Negotiated to Death." It was an inglorious end for such a glorious tradition.

It was the victim of the oldest feud in the annals of sport—owners vs. players. It doesn't matter what the issue is—salary cap, pensions, revenue sharing. If the owners are for a salary cap, the players are against it. If the players are for revenue sharing, the owners are against it. If the owners were against the man-eating shark, the players would be for it.

It's nothing new. It's as old as the game.

Owners were always rich men. Ownership was a hobby. But they couldn't help applying business principles—if that phrase is not an oxymoron—to their hobby. They tried to make a profit. They were, after all, capitalists.

They managed to move the game outside the Constitution of the United States early on—1876, to be exact—when they instituted the "reserve clause," which bound the services of five players to the parent club in perpetuity. Eventually, they expanded it to include all players.

The players' resistance was token at first. After all, it wasn't considered a profession then. Most of them kept their day jobs.

But the players countered by trying to form a new league—in 1890 and again in 1914. Both leagues went spectacularly broke.

The owners held unbroken sway from 1920 to the mid-1960s when the players brought up a can't-miss rookie.

Marvin Miller couldn't hit the change-up, couldn't bat .300, field .900, throw, catch or hit the curve, but he had what all the great ones from Cobb to Robinson had—a searing resentment of the Establishment verging on hatred.

The game was never the same after he joined it. Baseball's were probably the last workers of the world to unite. Miller put together a union equivalent of the '27 Yankees. They never lost a strike. Or a lockout.

Other factors played a part—most notably binding arbitration, which the owners put in themselves—but the bare facts of the matter are that, when Marvin Miller undertook to organize the players, the average big league salary was $19,000. Today, it is $1.2 million.

The even stranger truth is, even though it cost them astronomically more money to run the game, the owners ended up making more.

Most of them anyway. A whole cannot be greater than the sum of its parts and baseball is no exception. Historically, whenever a part began to threaten, the whole had a solution: Move it. There were always bright-eyed, bushy-tailed new towns slavering for big league baseball.

A lot of them have since managed to make do with pro basketball or pro football franchises. And moving doesn't always prove a solution in the long run. The portable franchise started with Boston, which moved to Milwaukee in 1953 after its attendance bottomed out at 281,276. The Boston Public Library drew more.

The Braves went to Milwaukee, where they were to draw 2,131,488 two years later. However, 13 years later, after new ownership had announced a move to Atlanta as soon as was legally possible, they bottomed out at 555,586 and headed southeast. And there were times in

Atlanta when that franchise was put in the window with a "make-offer" tag on it.

It was a great game. It's too young to die. But those who love it were not consulted, the ones who collected the bubble gum cards, peeked through knotholes, bought the jackets, ate the Wheaties, waved the pennants and said, "Say it ain't so, Joe," and introduced sons to the game. Who cared about them?

But what's October without a World Series? Italy without a song? Paris without a spring? Canada without a sunset?

Once upon a time in this country, we had World Series. You would have loved them. Ruth pointing. Sandy Koufax curving. Pepper Martin stealing. Kirk Gibson homering.

You shoulda been here.

•••••••••••••••••••

DECEMBER 11, 1994

Arnie Will Always Be the King

LA QUINTA—We always knew Arnold Palmer would be playing golf till they had to cut the shoes off him, or have an iron lung waiting for him at the 18th green. Even if there weren't a senior tour, Arnold would be on a golf course.

Palmer and golf were synonymous. Arnold American, I used to call him. Arnold without a golf club in his hand was as out of place as John Wayne without a horse, Ruth without a bat, Carl Lewis on a bicycle. An offense against nature.

He turned golf into a heavyweight fight. He didn't play a course, he slugged with it. Toe to toe. Sometimes, it was Dempsey-Firpo. The thing about Palmer was, he kept getting up. Other golfers had failures.

Arnold had catastrophes.

Anybody can hit a golf ball off a fairway. Arnold hit 'em off rocks in the Pacific Ocean, out of parking lots, over trees and through jungles. There was no such thing as an unplayable lie for Palmer.

Watching him play golf was like watching Dempsey fight, Kelly dance or Mays go after a fly ball. It wasn't that he had a gorgeous swing—he slashed at the ball like a guy beating a carpet.

But he was as strong as truck-stop coffee. He had forearms like a blacksmith's, wrists like wagon tongues. And he never saw the golf shot that could make him flinch. Arnold would try to par Rhode Island. No, birdie it.

He went after a course like a caveman. He made a two or a 12. He hit the ball in places where he had to chase the seals to play it or lift tree limbs and beer cans off it.

He was at his most dangerous from off the pace. You never wanted Palmer in your rearview mirror.

He never lagged a putt in his life. He never laid up or used an iron off a par-five tee. Palmer never tried to outsmart a course, he just charged it. He didn't want to win on points, he wanted the knockout. He wanted to hang it on his wall. He was like Dempsey with his man on the ropes, Tilden at match point.

He was the greatest long putter I have ever seen. He treated 40-footers as though they were tap-ins.

"When he got it within 20 feet, you felt like saying, 'That's good,'" Dave Marr used to say.

The truck drivers loved him. The public loved him. Other golfers had galleries. Arnie had an army. If he goes to Heaven, God better have a handicap. Or Arnold might not stay.

He didn't make golf. Golf made him. But he lifted it out of the stockbroker-banker constituency and opened it to the public. He came along just as television did and it was a marriage made in golf heaven.

Hogan would have sold cars in any era. So would Snead. But Palmer brought in the people who sat in center-field bleachers at Ebbets Field or in the balcony at St. Nick's Arena. And they didn't come to see Good Housekeeping golf by some meticulous ex-Walker Cupper or Brigham Young graduate. They came to see Palmer with his shirt out, cigarette smoking, ball in the high rough and needing a three to tie for the lead.

You wouldn't put his swing in copy books. It was a wild slash, the kind you see at midnight at the driving ranges, but it hit the ball long and straight. Arnold won the U.S. Open at Denver in 1960 by driving the par-four, 346-yard first hole. He won 60 PGA tournaments and two British Opens. A guy's a superstar today if he wins a dozen tour events.

The 40-foot putts don't go in anymore. Sometimes, the four-footers don't go, either. He has to hit a four-iron where once he hit a six. The holes get longer, the greens get smaller but the magic is, he's still Arnold American, Captain Golf. Maybe not the leader in the clubhouse anymore but the leader in the marketplace.

Americans cling to their icons, probably because we have so few. We get our royalty from sound stages and playing fields.

When they set up the Diners Club Matches down here at the PGA West Nicklaus Resort course this weekend, they chose 32 playing pros from the regular tour, 16 from the women's tour and 16 from the senior tour.

But when they paired Arnold Palmer and Jack Nicklaus on a seniors' team, they immediately relegated the rest of the cast to extras. The galleries, the autograph hounds, the guys with notebooks and microphones crowded around. It was a pairing made in golf heaven. It was 1960 again.

Golf permits the preservation of legend this way. It was like seeing Ruth and Gehrig again, watching Dempsey and Gene Tunney climb into the ring, cheering the 1959 Bob Cousy-Bill Russell Celtics.

When Arnold and Jack teed it up, they represented 130 tour victories between them, to say nothing of five British Opens and three U.S. Amateurs. They towered over their sport as few athletes have in history.

Arnold Palmer didn't make golf, he just put it on Page 1. He made it as exciting as a "Rocky" movie. Arnold on the charge on a golf course was cut-to-the-chase stuff. The public adored him. It still does.

Even though he has to say "what?" a lot. Even though the eyes need bifocals to read the greens and the hair is white and the old familiar slash looks like a window shade going up, Palmer is as charismatic as any American hero from Buffalo Bill to Sitting Bull. There might have been better players, but don't bet on it.

Arnold is as famous for his megafailures as his 60 triumphs. Once, in a final round of a U.S. Open, he had a seven-shot lead with nine holes to play. To lose that takes concentration.

The next day, no one wrote about the winner. "How I Lost the Open" was going to be the title of my essay. I thought it was terrible but it wasn't. It was Palmer. Part of the mystique.

He hit a ball in the water on No. 18 Friday, which seemed typical. Arnold out on a rock again. But Nicklaus saved the par and, when the match went into overtime, the team of Nicklaus and Palmer won.

The tournament organizers were overjoyed. Television promptly rescheduled the next day's competition to put the seniors' event on. The word spread. The galleries grew. We were all young again.

When Nicklaus and Palmer won again Saturday, dismissing Chi Chi Rodriguez and Jim Dent, 4 and 3, the Diners Club four-ball had a chance to become a historic event, which is already a Palmer specialty. If he and Jack can eliminate Raymond Floyd and Dave Eichelberger today, there should be a plaque on the 18th green commemorating the event.

Only three personalities rated the description "the King" in our generation. One was Gable, the actor. Another was Elvis, the singer. And the other was Palmer, the golfer.

Arnold in the water or in the trees is still a bigger story than anyone else on the green.

Golf is lucky there was a Palmer, and Palmer concedes he was lucky there was golf.

But in his new book, "A Personal Journey," Arnold writes, "Some people think of me as just plain lucky and I can't argue with them. I would like to say, however, that a man might be walking around lucky and not know it unless he tries."

Palmer tried. He gave luck two shots a side. And still won four ways—the nine, the 18, the match and the life.

1995

• • • • • • • • • • • • • • • • • • • •

FEBRUARY 16, 1995

As I Was Saying Before I Was So Rudely Interrupted . . .

BERMUDA DUNES—Hi, there!

Remember me? Yeah, that guy.

Thought I'd gone away for good?

I almost did.

Went under the knife at Cedars Sinai a bigger underdog than the San Diego Chargers. You got me and 40 points. Vegas wouldn't even post a line.

But I had a great lineup, a great draft. Drs. Aurelio Chaux and Jack Matloff with Gary Sugarman, Jeffrey Helfenstein and Rex Kennamer coming off the bench. I mean, we're talking about the '66 Green Bay Packers of the medical league here. We beat the spread. Shucks, we won the game.

It wasn't easy. Game went into sudden-death overtime, I was told. Had to have a great second half.

A lot of people from Eugene thought I ducked out to escape facing the Oregon fans in the Rose Bowl. But I had my own bowl game going. Five quarters against an opponent that made the 49ers look sluggish. I might have set the record for goal-line stands.

It all began when I started running out of breath. I mean, I didn't mind when I ran out of breath going uphill, but when I ran out of breath going downhill, I knew something was wrong. When I ran out of breath just sitting down, I figured I had finally booked passage on the Titanic. I better learn the words to "Nearer My God to Thee." Icebergs everywhere.

"You've sprung a leak, you're throwing oil," Dr. Sugarman told me.

Now, any race driver knows what that means: Get off the track. Pit before they black-flag. I needed a valve job. They had to overhaul the whole engine. I lost a lot of laps.

That's not all I lost. I lost touch.

For example, where the hell are the Rams? Anybody see them lately? They were here a minute ago. They were in Anaheim when I went under anesthesia.

What'd they do—go back to Cleveland? It was only yesterday that they came out here from Cleveland with their hats in their hands, wiping their feet and bowing and scraping and begging to be allowed to play in the Coliseum. And now I come out of the anesthesia and all that's left is a note on the door and their closet is cleaned out.

Of course, that's one of the troubles with L.A. Turn your back for a minute and everything's changed. You can't find your way home anymore. New freeway. The bank you went to for 20 years is suddenly a parking lot.

I'm told the Raiders are all packed and studying road maps. You'd think L.A. was a hotel fire or a sinking ship. Everyone's jumping off. I mean, what are we, Sheboygan?

Also, the memory plays tricks after an operation of this kind. For instance, anyone remember who won the World Series last fall? I can't for the life of me call it up on my memory screen. They try to tell me there wasn't one but I say, C'mon! Baseball couldn't be that stupid! What's America without a World Series? Latvia? France without wine? Germany without parades? Italy without music? England without poets? I know there was one. Had to be. We've had one every year since 1905.

There's always been a Pepper Martin running wild, a Babe Ruth calling his shot, a Grover Alexander striking out Lazzeri when the bases were loaded and so was Grover. There's Gibson's home run. Willie Mays' catch, the Red Sox, the Black Sox.

How could there be no World Series? Who would believe owners or labor leaders would let that happen? I'm not gullible enough to buy it. Next, they'll be telling me George Foreman won the heavyweight championship.

The World Series and opening day are baseball's two big showcases. No way they let them die. They're as American as harvest moons. Fireworks.

Guys who go down in the mines strike. Guys who get $7 million for standing out in right field for six months, blowing bubble gum and scratching, don't strike. You strike to get 35 cents an hour more. I've done it. You don't strike when you get $40,000 a day. For two hours a day. And no heavy lifting other than a 32-ounce bat.

No, these guys must think I was born yesterday to try to tell me baseball is going to disappear in a union dispute.

So, if I'm going to go back to work, I'm going to expect to see the Rams west of the Tehachapis, opening day in Dodger Stadium with Mike Piazza batting cleanup and a World Series every October. With big leaguers. If I'm going to cover a sport with players who might as well be wearing masks, I'll cover wrestling.

I grew up in a business in which the World Series was as certain as a sunrise and boxing had a saying, "They never come back." The hockey season began in October and Army-Navy was the Big Game, not one between a couple of football factories in Florida.

I'm down here this week to cover the 36th annual Bob Hope Chrysler Classic golf tournament. My kind of sporting event. Thank God golfers don't worry about salary caps, strikes, lockouts, reserve clauses, antitrust exemptions. They pay their own money to play, believe it or not. They win the money they get. They don't get paid whether they bat .230 or .330. If they bat .230, they get cut. They're out the entry fee, the hotel bill, the air fare. And there's no pension. There'll be a U.S. Open, a Masters—and a Hope Classic—every year.

The President doesn't throw out the first ball, he hits it. He plays it. Two other Presidents join him.

It's nice to know some things are immutable. It's nice to know the sport of Jones, Hogan, Snead, Nicklaus, Nelson and Palmer respects its traditions.

It's nice to have something to write about you can count on. These guys aren't going to move to St. Louis or picket the British Open or get guaranteed contracts. And just remember, when they hit a foul ball, they have to go out and play it. And not even Jack Nicklaus gets a no-cut contract. The only thing they strike is a Titleist.

••••••••••••••••••••

FEBRUARY 26, 1995

Don't Tell Him Golfers Only Drive for Show

It's easy to see why the American public loves John Daly.

The American people always love the John Dalys. They worship power. They want their heroes not merely to win but to crush the other guys. Split decisions and tiebreakers bore Americans. They want one-round knockouts.

Look at all the fans the Yankees had in the years they were winning World Series with scores like 18-4, 13-5, 12-6, 16-3, 12-0 and 10-0.

The fans like movies titled "The Terminator," "Rambo," "Superman." Sir Laurence Olivier was the superior actor, but John Wayne sold tickets. They like movies—and fighters—named "Rocky." We're not a subtle people. The coaches were right—winning isn't everything, it's winning big that is. The "Hitless Wonders" don't get it. "Murderers' Row" does.

We go for Babe Ruth, Jack Dempsey, tennis players nicknamed "the Rocket," not "Bitsy" or "Bunny." We want "the Sultan of Swat," "the Manassa Mauler," "the Brown Bomber," "the Astoria Assassin," not guys named Evander or Ezzard. The 1940 Chicago Bears' winning the championship, 73-0, feeds the group esteem. "We will rock you!" is the real national anthem.

We want Secretariat winning by 31 lengths, not a nose. We like fastball pitchers, not junk throwers. We want 7-foot dunkers in basketball, not point guards. We want hat-trick hockey players, not penalty killers. Power might corrupt—but that's all right with us.

Golf is no different. We don't want guys who putt their way to the championship. We don't brag about short games. We want guys who take the course by the throat.

You ever know a golfer who dreamed of becoming a great putter? You ever go to a driving range and see a truck driver practicing his nine-irons? Nah! He's got a wood in his hands. He doesn't want to be a chip-shot artist. He wants to be John Daly. Jack Nicklaus. Arnold Palmer.

He wants the guys who hit the ball so high and so far two groups could play through before it comes down.

No one has hit the ball as far as John Daly does. Nicklaus came closest. Hogan hit it as far as he wanted to.

But golf is a funny game. It's really two games. Schizophrenic. It's one game from tee to green and another one when you get there. Golf is a discipline. Control is critical.

The reality is, there have always been big hitters in golf. George Bayer, Jimmy Thompson, Mike Souchak. They haven't mattered in the long run. They really had to scale down their sweeps at the ball to be competitive. It's an anomaly of the game that the bombers have to throttle back their distance to score and be competitive.

That's the beauty of John Daly. He hasn't yet given in to the demons of golf who punish you for cannonading it. He still has that awesome 380-to-400 degree arc where the club almost hits the ground on the backswing. And the ball heads for the ionosphere.

The public loves it.

There's an old saying in golf, "Drive for show but putt for dough." You win money on the green, not on the tee.

John Daly gives the lie to the adage. He drives for a lot of dough. He has won only three tournaments, but he's only 28 and he drives for dough, big dough.

Take the second round of the Nissan L.A. Open at Riviera on Friday. Daly teed off behind a threesome that included a guy, Kenny Perry, who was tying the course record, 62. But he was doing it with putts. He had only a handful of stragglers following him. But the crowd behind him was elbowing for position, trampling one another to see Daly. They might have stumbled across Perry and asked, "Pardon me—did you see John Daly come through here?"

They don't really care if he hits the ball out of bounds. They would rather see him hit a 325-yard drive over the fence than see any other golfer make an eagle. After all, there's nothing dramatically enticing about a well-hit six-iron. It's a golf version of a left jab.

Daly will not compromise with the grand old game. He shows no inclination to cut back on the horsepower. He is almost the only golfer on tour who carries only one wood—a driver. It has a seven-degree loft. To give you an idea, the Empire State Building probably has a seven-degree loft. There's little margin for error there. Your friendly discount-store driver probably has 11 or 12 degrees. If you had a seven-degree driver, you would probably not get the ball in the air.

He's not even carrying a one-iron this week. He doesn't need it. If the driver is too much (i.e., if the hole is less than 320 yards), he uses a two-iron. It's almost like spotting Riviera the first draw.

If you've never seen Ruth bat, Koufax pitch, Dempsey punch or Jordan soar, you probably should see John Daly tee off.

That notion occurred to about half the crowd at Riviera on Saturday.

He was hardly shooting a course record. In fact, on the back nine, he was busy defending himself from the course.

He began the day by knocking Riviera around for eight holes. He had moved from six under par to nine under.

The wheels didn't exactly come off, but they began to flatten. A six at the par-four 15th hole turned the tournament back to the guys who carry three or more woods and a one-iron, the guys who romance the course, not scare it to death.

It won't matter to the crowd. American galleries aren't into bunters, jabbers, clinchers, guys who say, "I'll play these." They like the guy who swings for the fences, wouldn't clinch with a leopard and with 16 showing says, "Hit me!"

They used to say watching Ruth strike out was more exciting than watching anybody else hit a triple. Watching Daly make six can be more memorable than a lot of guys making two.

The hope is, nobody talks him into adding a four-wood or five-wood, practicing layups and adding three degrees of loft to his driver. That would be as big a national calamity as if they kept Babe Ruth a pitcher. Or taught Dempsey footwork. It might be good golf, but it ain't big box office. It'll never play in Peoria. Or at Riviera.

• • • • • • • • • • • • • • • • • • •

April 6, 1995

Fittingly, a Legend Rides One

Whether you're a horse owner, horse trainer or horse player, you're all right if you have Gary Stevens riding for you.

Go bet.

Whether it's the Kentucky Derby or a $5,000 claimer in Juarez, you get the same impeccable trip around the track. Gary rides your horse as if he were Man O' War.

You know how baseball managers like to say of their players, "He's my professional"? Casey Stengel always referred to Whitey Ford as "my perfessional pitcher."

Well, Gary Stevens is your professional race rider. You get the same all-out, intelligent, dedicated performance every time. Not flashy. Not headlined. Just there in the winners' circle. Lou Gehrig, if you will. Not the Babe.

Riders hate to see him coming. It's like getting an Unser in your rearview mirror. Stevens rides to win. But he has no reputation for using up a horse, asking him for more than he's got.

He sits on a horse the way the horse should be sat upon. Not scratching all over the place like a Hartack or an Ycaza. Not busting through a wall of horses like a Cossack. Looking for the hole, saving the run for the psychological moment. He has the concentration of a diamond-cutter, the peripheral vision of an NFL quarterback.

He doesn't always get the best stock. When he arrived at Santa Anita more than a decade ago, that went to other riders. The track was still known as "Shoemaker Downs" or "Pincay Park." Those were the jocks who got the 3-to-2 shots.

Stevens won anyway. By 1986, he was the leading rider on the circuit, winning meet titles at Santa Anita, Hollywood Park and Oak Tree. He was a money player. His horses won $13,881,198 in 1990, first in the nation.

Stevens was born near Boise, Ida., where Dad saddled horses at the three-quarter-mile track (Le Bois), and he proved early on that horses ran for him, not from him as they did with so many other riders. "There's a telepathy between horse and rider," Stevens says. "You can't teach it. It's there. Or, it isn't."

With Stevens, it was there. He took the act, not to the big time, but the bigger time—Longacres in Seattle. He immediately became leading rider. In a jockey colony that was as good as most, he set the meet and stakes record—168 victories in 1983, 232 in 1984.

Great riders had come out of Idaho before, most notably the elegant Laverne Fator, who had been leading money-winner in the 1920s, when the storied Earl Sande and Mack Garner and Sonny Workman were also in the irons. By the time Gary came to Santa Anita in 1984, he was hailed as a new Fator.

"I came to California in October of '84 intending to ride a weekend and go back to Seattle," he says.

That was a long weekend. Stevens is still here.

Every jockey wants to add a Kentucky Derby or two to his dossier, the way a golfer wants to add a Masters, a ballplayer a World Series or a driver an Indy 500. One Triple Crown victory is computed to be worth 20 or more ordinary firsts.

One of Stevens' strengths as a rider was his ability to have a calming influence on younger horses. His success with 2- and 3-year-olds is legendary. He won his Kentucky Derby on his fourth try on the filly Winning Colors.

Fillies are supposed to have their minds on other things in the spring, but Stevens kept her mind on business, kept her head straight and gave her a masterful ride to prevail by a nose. Stevens had done something Laverne Fator never could—win a Kentucky Derby.

Stevens' record in Kentucky is noteworthy. In his last four Derbies, he has never been worse than fourth and has been second twice. A first, two seconds and two fourths in nine Kentucky Derbies is pretty impressive. They write poems about riders who do that.

Stevens' record in the Santa Anita Derby, which will be run this Saturday, is even more extraordinary. He has won the last two, three out of the last five, and five out of the 10 he has ridden in. He has been second twice and never worse than fourth.

He rides Larry The Legend in the Santa Anita Derby on Saturday, a Horatio Alger horse bought out of a bankruptcy sale for $2,500. Owner-trainer Craig Lewis didn't want the horse exactly, but he was the only collateral the debtor had left. It was either that or a truck.

Gary Stevens is not distracted by Larry The Legend's penniless beginnings. "He looks like a very professional horse to me," he says.

That would be a happy coincidence. Two professionals for the price of one. A true daily double.

Stevens' professionalism was proved to be recognized worldwide this January, when he received a call from the Crown Colony of Hong

Kong offering a contract he couldn't refuse to come ride there. He went.

He returned for one weekend to win the Santa Anita Handicap—on board a British horse who had never run in this country or on dirt before. Urgent Request had been described as "strong-willed" and "unmanageable," which around a racetrack means he is the next thing to a serial killer. Stevens had him as mannerly as a butler by the clubhouse turn.

If Stevens can do that on a rogue, what comfort can the competition take in the fact that he will be riding a "professional" horse Saturday? Even a horse they got, so to speak, out of a remnant barrel is a threat with Stevens aboard. He may wind up with more Derbies than Parliament on a rainy day, but before he's through, you know one thing: Larry The Legend better keep his mind on business or Gary The Legend will remind him of it. If there's one thing he can't stand, it's unprofessionalism.

APRIL 30, 1995

At Least There's Justice in Baseball

One of my favorite novels—and movies—is Somerset Maugham's "Of Human Bondage." In it, there's a medical student, Philip Carey, hopelessly addicted to an unrequited love for a sluttish waitress, Mildred, who keeps scorning him, cheating on him, abusing him, throwing things at him until you couldn't bear to look. Nothing deters him. He's hopelessly obsessed. He keeps coming back for more.

Baseball fans can relate. Baseball fans are a million Philip Careys. They keep after their two-timing love, the erstwhile national pastime, the game they love. Their Mildred. Their bondage is inhuman.

Look what the game has done to them: Canceled a World Series. Interrupted a whole season. Delayed another.

I don't know whether you know it, but baseball's appeal is decimal points. No other sport relies as totally on continuity, statistics, orderliness of these. Baseball fans pay more attention to numbers than CPAs.

To interrupt them is to trifle with the fan's love, to cuckold him. You wipe out part of a season, you show you don't care about his affection. What he holds dear, you don't.

Yet here he comes again, limping up the front stairs anew with a bouquet of flowers in one hand, a box of candy in the other and hope in his heart, praying you won't do this to him again. And Mildred—er, baseball—will probably be standing there ready to throw his gifts at him. "Dimwit! I told you—not roses! And I hate chocolate!"

You don't think so? Check the opening-day attendances. In the first nine home openers, the American League had 330,041, or an average of 36,671 a game. The National League had 332,746 for eight home openers for an average of 41,593.

That'll teach 'em not to mess with us! We cut the attendance by 58 people in Toronto. We actually had 18,230 more people at Cincinnati.

Philip Carey is alive and well and sitting on the third-base line with a hot dog in one hand, a Coke in the other and wearing a warm-up jacket with the home team logo. You think he wants to press charges?! Buy him some peanuts and Cracker Jack. He don't care if he never gets back.

I went out to Dodger Stadium the other night to check the relationship between Philip Phan and Mildred Major Leagues. See if either side needed to get into counseling.

Forget it. Philip is still batting his eyes and looking adoringly on his beloved, while Mildred is still figuring on taking him for all she can get. He's as smitten as ever. It's business as usual. So, butt out!

Someone once said trying to wise up a sucker is the most thankless job in the world; so we might as well find something good about baseball.

One of the things good, it seems to me, is the Atlanta team. With a three-time Cy Young Award pitcher, a two-time Cy Young runner-up and a promising closer on the staff and a lineup of .300 hitters, this club is armed and dangerous.

And the right fielder has Hall of Fame written all over him.

When David Justice was coming up in the Braves' organization, he was universally conceded to be the "best-looking young player to come along in a long time."

They didn't necessarily mean his (1) swing, (2) arm, (3) bat, (4) speed, (5) power.

They meant his looks. David Justice looks like the pro from Central Casting. Movie star good looks. Matinee idol stuff. The Great Profile.

He's 6 feet 3, 200 pounds, nice smile, big brown eyes, and if you wanted a poster boy for Baseball '95, David Justice should be it. He's a poetic Justice.

He was rookie of the year in 1990. He drove in 120 runs in 1993. Pitchers curse when they see him up there with men on base and no place to put him. A free-swinger, he nevertheless walks almost as often as he fans.

But what really titillates the scholarly fan is, he comes, if not exactly in duplicate, at least in tandem.

He follows Fred McGriff in the batting order, and this means big trouble for the National League East.

You see, throughout history, great sluggers have come in partnership. Look it up. Take the greatest sluggers in history—Babe Ruth and Henry Aaron. Ruth was part of that middle-of-the-lineup crash attack—Ruth and Lou Gehrig. Aaron came with Eddie Mathews attached. Between them, they had 1,267 home runs—Mathews had 512 of them.

Ruth and Lou Gehrig had 1,207 home runs between them. Mickey Mantle had Roger Maris hitting alongside and, while their joint lifetime total, 811, is not so high (Maris had 275), they have the one-year record, 115 in 1961.

Willie Mays and Willie McCovey had 1,181 homers between them

(Mays had 660).

Two big bats in the middle of the lineup take a lot of weapons out of pitchers' hands. They dare not, for instance, flirt with walking their man. They usually have to make "good" pitches. And good pitches frequently end up as gopher balls.

Justice and McGriff have been frustrated by baseball unrest. In the truncated '94 season, McGriff had hit 34 home runs, Justice 19. The year McGriff joined Atlanta, he hit 37 home runs (18 in San Diego before the trade); Justice hit 40.

Is Atlanta on a path to deja vu —i.e., another Mathews-Aaron? McGriff has 264 big league homers, Justice 132.

David Justice doesn't look for it. On this case, Justice may be blind. But this Justice for all doesn't think so.

"Look at it realistically," he said as he stood in the middle of the Dodger Stadium locker room the other night. "I'm not your basic home run hitter. Fred is going to get his 30-35 homers a year. I'm more of a line drive hitter. I go up there looking for the hit, the opposite-field hit—whatever works.

"I'll give you at least your 20 or more homers a year, but I'm not looking for the seats on every pitch."

What about the 40 homers he hit in 1993? That's more than McGriff has ever hit in a season.

"Well, yes, I hit 40. But Fred is still more apt to hit it out than I am," Justice insists. "He has more of a home run stroke than I do. I concentrate on getting a hit."

Oh, well, he's still better-looking. And he can hit, field and run. As Shakespeare said, thrice is he armed who hath Justice on his side.

••••••••••••••••••••

JUNE 25, 1995

Al Proves Them Wrong: You Can Go Home Again

Well, goodby, Al. Turn off the lights when you leave. I'm sorry it had to come to this. Come back and see us sometime. Write if you feel like it.

Leave the key under the mat. Don't leave mad. But take your team with you, will you?

Sorry it didn't work out. But you know how these things are. Win a few, lose a few.

Going back where you came from, hey? That's new! How interesting! What happens now? Do the Washington Redskins go back to Boston? That's where they started. Do the Arizona Cardinals become the Chicago Cardinals again? That's what they were before they became the St. Louis Cardinals, then the Arizona ones.

Do the Indianapolis Colts become the Baltimore Colts again? Or do they become the Dallas Texans? You remember, that's what they were. And before that, the New York Bulldogs. Ted Collins' team. You remember, Kate Smith's manager. And husband.

Where do the Rams go back to? Cleveland, where they originated? Anaheim, where they moved in 1980? Or Los Angeles, where they moved in 1946?

The NFL has been a federation of Bedouins from the start. Heck, the Chicago Bears were the Decatur Staleys, if you want to go back that far. Their purpose on earth was not to go to a Super Bowl but to sell starch.

Things haven't changed much. The goal of football today is to sell luxury boxes, right, Al?

We in the Los Angeles area have now lost two professional teams in a span of a few months. A shocking state of affairs, Al, but not your concern, eh?

It used to be, they would be bucking a trend. The rest of the country was trying to get to Southern California, not out of it. If you don't believe it, just look at the record: When I came to this state all those years ago, the population was a little over 8 million. Today, it's 32 million. One of the great mass migrations of history.

You have to ask yourself, are the Dodgers next? The Lakers want out too?

Of course, Al, you are the first one to go back to square one, your roots. And the author Thomas Wolfe, no less, warned "You Can't Go Home Again." But what does he know?

A lot of guys are going to say "Good riddance, Al. And take all those motorcycle gangs and tattooed ruffians with you, with their black leather jackets and jackboots."

But the departure of a sports franchise is like a death in the family, Al. Particularly to a sportswriter with a deadline. Particularly to the hotel or restaurant industry. A TV network. A concessionaire. The limousine business. Ticket scalpers.

On the other hand, Al, we have to ask ourselves, did we ever really have the Raiders? Or want them?

The evidence is overwhelming. The Raiders were in Los Angeles but not of it. They weren't disliked. They were merely tolerated. You never crept into our hearts, Al. I don't know whether you ever noticed it.

You see, every other carpetbagging team that arrived here was coming into a vacuum. We never had pro football here till the Rams arrived from Cleveland. We never had major league baseball till the Dodgers arrived from Brooklyn. We never had pro basketball till the Lakers came from Minneapolis.

The Raiders were, in a sense, interlopers. They were never truly accepted. Their fan base was modest to low. When they contested for the title in a playoff game, 90,000 showed up. When they played Tampa Bay, 30,000 came.

Their image was hardly reassuring, Al. A police presence had to be beefed up for Raider games. Raider paraphernalia all across the country came to be the costume of the scofflaw. Every hooligan in the country caught beating his brother or holding up a 7-Eleven seemed to be wearing a Raider jacket. A Raider end zone fan once kicked into a coma a fellow spectator incautious enough to wear a Pittsburgh Steeler jacket. That was embarrassing for laid-back Los Angeles. Not our style.

The Raiders could hardly be held accountable for fan behavior, Al, but look at it this way: The reality was, the Raiders kept a light in the window for on-field renegades too. Raider lineups were so full of guys who had been thrown off other teams, guys whose very sanity was suspect, that rival coach Chuck Noll, no less, referred to your Raiders as the "criminal element" of the league. He thought they belonged not in Oakland but in Folsom.

To leave Los Angeles bereft is one thing for the Raiders, quite another for the league. I mean, resentment of and dislike for Los Angeles was a powerful motivator for ticket sales in other communities. To shout "Beat L.A.!" is one thing. To say "Beat St. Louis!" or "Beat Oakland!" does not have quite the same ring. Like, who cares? "Beat L.A.!" means "Make my day!"

The league—and the networks—will not long want the 20 million people south of the Tehachapis to be unrepresented in the scheme of things. We'll get a team, whether we want one or not.

Too bad it had to turn out this way. Nobody's fault, really. I'm glad Oakland is willing to take you back. Shows great forbearance on their part. Still, I'd kind of watch my back if I were you. Cut the cards, if you know what I mean.

But, what am I telling you? Nobody messes with Al Davis, right? Not unless they want to find themselves out in the cold, wondering what happened to their pants.

You might want to tell Oakland some things have changed. They may be in for a shock there when they see that this Raider team is not the one that went over the wall on them in 1982.

I mean, don't look for Jim Plunkett, Snake Stabler or Mad Bomber

Daryle Lamonica. Cliff Branch won't be split out there. Art Shell won't be ripping open holes for Clarence Davis. No Gene Upshaw, Dave Casper, Dave Dalby. Just a bunch of Hollywood types who can't get open anymore. Six-yard Sitkos.

They may think somebody made a mistake and sent them the Rams.

This time, try to keep them there, will you? Not our type, Al. You understand. But don't think it hasn't been fun! Just win, baby!

•••••••••••••••••••

JULY 19, 1995

You Heard It Yelled Here First

ST. ANDREWS, Scotland—This is where it all began. This course saw Sarazen, Vardon, Bobby Jones, Hagen. Nicklaus won here. Twice.

This is golf's shrine. Its fountainhead. Its Garden of Eden.

This is where a guy first yelled "Fore!" at a slow-playing group ahead. This is where the first guy said, "That's good, take it away!"

This is where they first pressed the bet, where a guy three down first said, "You're pressed—four ways!"

This is where a guy first clapped his hand to his head after a tee shot and groaned, "No! Not over there again!" This is where a guy first said, "What am I doing wrong?" This is where a guy first said, "Anybody see where that went?"

This is where the handicapping system took form. Made golf the only sport this side of horse racing that tries to level the playing field. This is where a guy first said, "I'll play you for tuppence if ye'll gie me three strokes a side." This is probably where the first hustler with an 18-handicap shot a 69 when he had to. This is where a player first begged, "Get legs!" or, "Bite! Bite!" depending on whether his ball demonstrated a tendency to quit on him or to take off like a moon shot. This is where a mis-hit shot became a slice or a hook, where the first golfer said, "I topped it!" This is where sand traps came from because the whole original course was one giant sand trap.

This is where a five-iron was a "mashie," a three-wood a "spoon," a two-iron a "cleek" and a nine-iron a "niblick."

The whole story of golf is enclosed here on this eccentric series of tees and green on the North Sea littoral. It is 6,933 yards of contrariness and stubbornness. If it were human, it would smoke a pipe, have a white walrus mustache and stride around with pink cheeks and an imperious look in a tweed suit that smelled of tobacco and had patches at the elbow. And he'd be prone to say, "Here, here! We'll have none o' that!"

It would be sad to him that "gowfers" didn't still have to use the tradesmen's entrance and know their place and not be getting airs. And they'd have to change their shoes at their cars and not be cluttering up the members' quarters where gentlemen were and not people who putted for money.

He would be Lord something-or-other and would wear a bowler, carry a brolly and vote Tory.

In some ways, this is the last stand of the British Empire. The sun not only doesn't set on St. Andrews, sometimes it doesn't rise on it either. Rain gear probably made its first appearance on this course too.

You kind of get the bends when you walk on St. Andrews if you're a golfer. It's like a Catholic entering the Vatican for the first time, a Muslim reaching Mecca.

It has reason for its haughtiness. You're not really a champion till you've won at St. Andrews (pronounced sin-TANDREWS). Ben Hogan never won here. Hogan won a British Open, but he never confronted the remorseless contours of St. Andrews. Which is a pity because Hogan and St. Andrews were made for each other. It would have been Dempsey-Tunney, John Wayne and the Indians. They were alike in many ways. Asking and giving no quarter. Hogan stalking, probing for weakness, St. Andrews dancing out of reach.

At first glance, St. Andrews appears under-equipped. There's not a tree on it. It's as wide open as a waterfront saloon. Its defenses come largely from the weather—and its own dottiness. It relies on its attackers' overconfidence.

It's wide and inviting. It seems a little like a guy strolling through a crowd with his wallet sticking out and a $25,000 Rolex on his wrist. Pickpockets fight to get near him.

That's the way golfers are at St. Andrews. The first time. They get less reckless with each succeeding 18 and get downright cautious after they've been embarrassed by it a few times.

You can win some British Opens from the parking lot. Seve Ballesteros did in 1979 at Lytham. You can't win on St. Andrews from anywhere but the fairway.

The course is like the Brits themselves, cheerfully ignoring the way the rest of the world does things. They both generally proceed at their own pace and to their own drummer.

You know how the Brits pronounce words any way that suits them? They take the position it's their language. Well, they and St. Andrews take the position that golf is their game too. They blithely ignore abnormalities like double greens and merely smile indulgently when a Tommy Bolt comes along, spots these double greens—such as the one that is a terminus for either the third hole or the 16th—and inquires whether he can choose the closest one to putt into.

If you say, "We don't have double greens in America," they murmur, "What a pity!"

The fairways are so close together that a sign is posted: "Homeward players have the right of way."

St. Andrews stands alone among golf courses. It has since 1744. Golf is 18 holes a game because there were that many at St. Andrews—after they pruned four others out of the rota because maintenance was too steep.

It used to be watered by God and mowed by sheep. But now, it has the modern contrivances. Somewhere, Old Tom Morris must be gnashing his teeth.

Americans used to skip this tournament. You couldn't make expenses, receipting for a few hundred quid and having to meet a transatlantic steamship cost.

Australian Peter Thomson or South African Bobby Locke won it annually—till Arnold Palmer decided to add it to his dossier in the '60s. Americans won eight out of 10 in the 1970s. But, since 1984, only one American has won it. Mark Calcavecchia survived a three-man playoff with two Aussies in 1989. It has been won in the last decade by two Brits, two Aussies, a Zimbabwean and a Spaniard, besides Calcavecchia.

St. Andrews doesn't care. It has seen its game grow since it was played by a couple of shepherds wielding tree limbs and balls made of goose feathers. And now that it's a worldwide game of such consummate architecture, the practitioners consider St. Andrews quaint.

St. Andrews considers them quaint. I mean, whose game is this anyway? Shut up, Yank, and just don't get in any of those pot bunkers and get on the right side of those double greens.

• •

AUGUST 20, 1995

Mantle's Life Was Hit and Myth

Show me a hero and I will write you a tragedy.

—*F. Scott Fitzgerald*

Scott Fitzgerald never knew Mickey Mantle. Or did he? He may not have known the man, but he knew the type. He knew the fate.

The lives of the celebrated are seldom what they seem. "Success" is often just the opposite. We often envy those we should pity. It was Lord Bryce who said of Napoleon that "his life would be the funniest comedy of modern times were it not caked in human blood."

I suppose Mickey Mantle thought he had the world by the tail. After all, he was the toast of New York; his very name comprised some of the most recognizable syllables of the era.

The name, of course, helped. You wonder if Mickey Mantle were Frank Rogers or Alvin Babbitt if even his athletic feats would carry him to fame. But Mickey Mantle was probably the most felicitous collection of vowels and consonants this side of a Frank Merriwell novel. The Mick. Perfect! Had a nice headline ring to it.

He played in New York, which was just right also. Meant a parade of World Series. He did what he did in prime time. He played the Palace, so to speak. Broadway. The Big Apple. If you can make it there, you make it everywhere.

But did he belong there? Was that really his kind of town?

New York had the highest concentration of media, electronic and print, in the Western world, and they held their athletes and politicians and other newsmakers to a standard Joan of Arc would have trouble meeting.

The word "flawed" is probably the most-used word in the Mantle obits. In his case, it simply meant he drank.

Drinking is a classic defense against feelings of low esteem. With a bat in his hands, Mickey Mantle was the equal of anyone in the annals of his sport. But in societal confrontations, the evidence is it was a drink Mantle needed in his hands. It's entirely possible the haut monde of Manhattan frightened the young Mantle. Or gave him feelings of inadequacy. He contracted a destructive habit very early in the game.

I often wonder what turn the Mantle legend would have taken if Texas were in the big leagues when he came up and if he had signed with one of its clubs. Or even if he had played out his career in, say, St. Louis or Kansas City. Minnesota. California. The boy from Commerce,

Okla., might have been more comfortable in those places.

Unfortunately, Mickey was a "good" drinker. English translation: not a mean drunk. He drank to get happy and relaxed, not aggressive. Mickey didn't have a mean bone in his body. He was mischievous but never malicious. I can't think of a single instance where The Mick attacked an umpire, a fellow player, a fan.

I got an inkling of the size of his problem when I attended a celebrity golf tournament (put on by Harmon Killebrew) in Sun Valley, Ida., one year. By chance, I flew back with Mantle and his son and an acquaintance. As luck would have it, we had a long layover at a connecting stop in Salt Lake City. On a Sunday.

Mickey was frantic. He needed a drink. But Salt Lake City on Sunday is no place to get one. The bars were closed. So were the state liquor stores.

I volunteered to phone the president of Western Airlines, Art Kelly, to see if the hospitality room could be made accessible. It was. Art phoned in the authorization. It was the kind of thing we did for Mickey Mantle. We were eager to oblige. Wish we hadn't.

Several bottles of vodka later, I wondered if I had done the right thing. Not that Mickey got belligerent. He just got in one of his giggling moods.

The thing I remember clearest about Mickey Mantle is, he didn't have a jealous bone in his body, either. You learn very early in this business that superstars frequently resent one another. After all, Ruth and Gehrig didn't speak for years.

But, I first got to know Mantle fairly well the famous year (1961) when Roger Maris broke Babe Ruth's home run record. Roger hit 61 homers that year. And Mickey hit 54.

There was a historical inequity at work here. It should have been the other way around. Maris hit 40 or more home runs only that one time in his life. Mantle did it four times. Maris hit 275 home runs lifetime. Mantle hit 536.

But Mickey was as genuinely delighted for his teammate as anyone. I remember once waking Mickey in his hotel room at 8 o'clock in the morning. My New York colleagues were stunned he didn't abusively hang up on me. The secret was, I wanted to talk about the fact Mantle and Maris, together, were about to break the all-time tandem home run record. Ruth and Gehrig topped out at 107 their best year.

Mickey liked that approach. He had no trouble at all sharing a spotlight with Maris.

Interestingly enough, it was that season that made Mickey Mantle a true Pride of the Yankees. Before that year, Mickey had been perceived by many Yankee fans as the hick who tried to take Joe DiMaggio's place. But that season made the Mick a sympathetic character. Mickey used to hit these gorgeous 550-foot home runs. Maris hit mostly these 310-foot shots that barely cleared the right-field wall. Mickey was seen as the real Pride of the Yankees who had been cheated. It would have been considered fitting for him to have broken Ruth's record, not Maris.

Mickey never took that position. Mickey never wept for himself. But he was brutally honest with himself. When he finally sobered up and took a look at what he had done to his life, he didn't look for someone to lateral the blame to. He signed for it himself.

The thing about Mickey Mantle is, he never got old. Even ravaged by illness, his face still had that eager, happy look of a kid seeing his first Christmas tree. He was a hero. And a tragedy.

• • • • • • • • • • • • • • • • • • • •

AUGUST 31, 1995

Old School Is Fine, Thank You

Writing in the Sporting News of recent issue, Pat Jordan got it all wrong.

Wrote he: "Am I the only person in America who finds Cal Ripken's mind-numbingly plodding pursuit of Lou Gehrig's consecutive-game record a bore? I mean, this is supposed to be the highlight of the season, the day or night Ripken breaks Gehrig's record? Is this what the game has been reduced to? Awards for perfect attendance?"

First of all, before we go on, let me tell you where I'm coming from: To begin with, I've had it up to here with tabloid America. The glorification of the rebel, the outlaw, the guy who makes up his own rules. And makes you live by them. You know what I'm talking about: tennis players who get famous not for their own forehands but because of the one their wives plant on the jaw of officials, basketball players who make millions and don't show up for team practices and make magazine covers, scofflaws whose very criminality gives them celebrity, the whole sorry, sick panoply of sports in the '90s.

Forgive me, but I want to tell you about my grandfather. I don't think he ever got his name in the paper. Till he died. He worked 54 years as a millwright in a factory. He was due at work every morning at 7. So he was usually there at 6. He sat on the steps and smoked a "paper of tobacco" before he went in and put the smock on. When he got injured on the job, he went right back to work with cotton stuck in the hole in his head. Off work, off the payroll. There was no company-paid sick leave in those days.

He raised eight children. He went to church every Sunday. He worked 14 hours a day.

Dull? No hero? In my book, he was. No one ever writes any songs about a guy who shows up for work every day, who pays his bills, feeds his family, who makes the tools that build the country. He was not "colorful." He never robbed any stagecoaches, wrecked any cars (he never had one to wreck). He never went into rehab, never had to be forgiven or paroled. He was even taken for granted by his own family.

I don't want to finger Pat Jordan, a journalist for whom I have respect. It's just that I deplore the worship of the splashy and the trashy that has taken over in this country. It is when it is accompanied by sneering at the accomplishments of the dependable, the reliable, the guys who show up for work every day because that is the way they were brought up, that I rise to make a point of order.

Grandpa! Meet Cal Ripken. You have a lot in common.

Cal has been pursuing his record, Lou Gehrig's 2,130 consecutive games, to a claque of abuse. Critics derided him. They periodically called for him to abandon the chase. They demeaned it and him. Pat Jordan even reprises the derision heaped on Ripken. "Haven't there been times when he should have been benched for an injury or a slump, rather than play merely to sustain his bogus pursuit of a record that for all intents and purposes is meaningless?"

If you're asking me, Pat, in a word, No. I mean, it isn't as if he has been up there sitting on a flagpole all these years.

Cal Ripken is the fourth-best fielding shortstop who ever lived. Look it up. He once went an entire season (161 games) with only three errors. Some shortstops make that in an inning.

He has hit 322 home runs, driven in 1,241 runs, scored 1,252. He has 2,340 hits. If you don't think those numbers are legend-makers for a shortstop, you don't know baseball.

But for much of his career, you'd think Cal Ripken was doing something reprehensible. Like showing up for work on time. Doing a day's work when he got there.

He has never broken any barroom mirrors, gotten into a scuffle with the cops, missed the team plane. I don't think he even chews tobacco. He has batted over .300 four times, has gotten over 200 hits twice. Yet every time he'd go two or three games without a hit, out would come the detractors. He was being selfish, they would scream. Or, they would recommend brightly that he stop his streak one day shy of Lou Gehrig's. Or stop it at 2,130, right on Gehrig's.

Let me ask you something: If you were running a business and someone came to you and said he could bring you an employee who would not only show up for work every day for 14 (or 20) years not only ready and in condition but would also be one of your most productive workers, would you start thinking of ways to get him out of the lineup? Put some no-talent goldbrick in his spot? Or would you do a little dance and buy some more shares of company stock?

I can understand some of the frustration of the press boxers. After all, I'm one of them. They like the guy who pitches two no-hitters in a row—even if that's just about all he did in his career in which he ended up a .496 pitcher. They like the guy who hits 61 home runs one year, even though he never hits over 40 any other year in his career and is over 30 only twice.

The 9-to-5 guy doesn't inspire the superlatives. I think, in a way, it's what happened to Henry Aaron. Aaron felt he never got his due for breaking Babe Ruth's all-time homer record. And he probably didn't. Aaron, like Ripken, simply did what he was supposed to do, quietly, efficiently, constantly. The kind of steady contribution that gets you a gold watch and a dinner. Willie Mays would have set off more dancing in the streets. Mays did things like hit four homers in a game and over 50 a season. His hat flew off as he caught 480-foot line drives. And, of course, he did a lot of it in New York.

Still, no one suggested Aaron quit one homer shy of Babe Ruth or retire when he hit 714.

Baseball lineups used to be full of guys like Ripken and Aaron—and Gehrig. There were Charley Gehringers, Tommy Henrichs, Earle Combses, Terry Moores by the dozen. What?! You never heard of any of them? Of course, you didn't. But you've heard of tantrum-throwing and racket-throwing tennis brats, you've heard of guys who had to be bailed out to be suited up, substance-abusers, wife-abusers, no-shows, no-autograph, no play-today. You've heard of guys who didn't have the self-discipline of a hound dog.

They make good copy. But you can have them. I'll take Cal Ripken. I'll take Grandpa.

•••••••••••••••••••

SEPTEMBER 14, 1995

What They've Done To Game Is a Crime

If you didn't know who the defending national champion college football team was, you'd probably be able to make a pretty good guess about now.

Nebraska, right?

And how would we know? Well, for a start, one guy on the squad is charged with attempted murder and two others are charged with assaulting former girlfriends and another with carrying a weapon.

How's that for a "Dream Team?"

But it sounds like a national champion, all right.

The year before Nebraska won it, Florida State was the reigning champion. Half a dozen players were illegally treated to a $20,000 clothing shopping spree by wanna-be agents.

Miami used to win it all with personnel such that a national writer once suggested the team photo should be taken front and side and the pictures hung in post offices instead of national magazines. Then, a rap artist and a big backer of the team insisted he be able to pick the starting quarterback—a pal of his—or he'd "blow the whistle on the whole program."

Colorado won the title with a team that had a worse arrest record than the Mafia.

And so on.

Now, I'm sure there are thousands of fine young men playing college football. I mean, they're nice to their mothers, eat with their hats off, even kneel in the end zone after a score (if the administrators of the game let them, that is). There are plenty of fine young men.

There are a lot of thugs too. I can never forget my first introduction to the new breed when Coach Bear Bryant at a clinic in Santa Barbara once said something like: "If you got any milk-drinking, church-going, book-learning, suit-wearing students who can throw the football, you send them to Stanford. If you got any whiskey-drinking, women-chasing, fist-fighting a-tha-letes who can knock your jock off, you send them to ol' Beah!"

Deke Brackett, longtime assistant at UCLA, once confided, "If you've got one kid who's a pretty good player and his grades are all good and got no record and you got a kid who just beat up three cops in a nightclub, maybe one football coach will go see the first kid but the cop-beater's front doorstep will be so lined with coaches they'll have to take numbers."

The character, or lack of it, of their football teams never seems to deter the fans who show up with their faces painted red, their hair shaved with the school letter and yelling, "Hit 'em again—harder! harder!" They wouldn't seem to care if it was Jack the Ripper out there playing linebacker for them. They'd love it. They'd like nothing better than to get his sweaty jersey with the bloodstains still on it to hang in their rec rooms. They don't care what he does in his spare time.

Somebody's got to start caring. About the university's image, the game's image. I thought our colleges were supposed to be educational institutions, not halfway houses.

The Nebraska back apparently had "Heisman" written all over him. Lawrence Phillips has gained more than 2,500 yards in his career. In another era, he'd be a Galloping Ghost or a Pony Express or some such.

He has been a troubled young man. His mother, unable to control him even at age 12, turned him over to a youth center in Covina.

When Phillips showed up at Lincoln, Neb., in a new Mustang convertible, the NCAA launched an investigation. They were told the group home had bought it for him as a gift.

Oh, sure.

This is the third time this year he has been hauled up on charges. In the other two, charges were dropped or fines paid.

The latest incident had Phillips breaking into an apartment at 4:30 a.m., grabbing his former girlfriend whom he is alleged to have hit and then dragged down three flights of stairs before neighbors could call 911.

Coach Tom Osborne has been making some familiar noises, dismissing Phillips from the team, then changing the punishment to an indefinite suspension.

"I'm not giving up on him yet," the coach told the press bravely. "We will do everything we can to help him get his life back together. I'm certainly going to continue to support him in every way that I can emotionally and academically."

English translation: You think I'm going to let go a guy who made me four touchdowns last week?! Are you outta your gourd?!

Prediction: Look for the charges to be dropped. And the apartment door to be fixed.

After all, they've got a national championship to defend.

• • • • • • • • • • • • • • • • • •

October 15, 1995

He's Still Big Dodger in Dugout

News Item: "Manager Tommy Lasorda Hired for Another Year at Dodger Helm."

What would baseball be without Tommy Lasorda? You don't want to know. A meal without wine, a day without sunshine, a dance with your sister. Any cliche you want. A life without song.

Not to see that wonderful character bounding out of the dugout, belly first, fist pumping, bowlegs churning, throat yelling on his way to the umpire to straighten him out and tell it like it should be one more time? Never!

Who will speak for baseball when Tommy's gone? One of those tight-lipped, monosyllabic bores who manage those Midwestern teams or sit glaring from the corner of the dugout as if they were watching the fall of France? Gimme a break!

I've been lucky I've had Thomas Charles, pride of the Abruzzi, and Norristown, Pa., Lasorda to deal with all these years. You never come away with an empty notebook. Tommy loves baseball and has a keen eye for the drama of it. Nobody understands it the way he does.

He is lovable to the fans. A cartoon character. Casey Stengel and Yogi Berra rolled into one. Ring Lardner would have loved him. Every guy with a deadline always does. Disney would have drawn and animated him.

He can handle men. He has a strong sense of right and wrong, and even a locker room full of millionaires don't faze Lasorda. He was a left-handed pitcher who didn't like you crowding the plate and he manages the same way. Get out of line and the ball, figuratively, is whizzing by your ear.

He didn't have much of a pitching career, but those are the guys who figure out what the game is all about. Not the guys who figure you can solve everything with a home run. Guys who know the game is a struggle make the best managers.

He was typecast for the job. He was to his role what Clark Gable was to Rhett Butler or Tracy to Dr. Jekyll.

A manager has to be part father figure, part sidekick and all man. Lasorda slid home safely on all counts.

Baseball is the last stand of another America in this century. It's as American as the pumpkin. Or stud poker. A game where you always have a hole card.

It's a game played by little boys in big men's bodies. It's corporate America. It's also sandlot America. It's a link with our past in a way no other sport is. Its critics say it's too slow. What are they in a hurry about? If you're in a hurry, go to an airport. Baseball is to savor, to make last, like a pheasant dinner in a Paris restaurant.

Lasorda revels in it. It's not just a time clock to punch for him. He's never too busy to promote baseball. I caught him one time on his way to Nova Scotia to make a speech extolling the grand old game.

The game is Ruth pointing, Ty Cobb coming in with spikes high, Willie Mays' cap flying off as he pulls in a triple—or what should be a triple. There was no such thing when Willie was out there.

But it's also Connie Mack standing in a dugout in a celluloid collar and tie wig-wagging a program at his outfielders where to play and it's John McGraw, feisty, glowering, willing his team to the pennant.

It's kids playing in a corner lot with rocks for bases and it's the Dodgers playing in the seventh game of the World Series in sold-out Yankee Stadium.

It's the citadel of the second guess, and Tommy has been prey to his share of them. Why didn't he walk Jack Clark before his home run in 1985? On the other hand, who put Kirk Gibson up there in the ninth inning against Dennis Eckersley's slider when Gibson could hardly walk? Lasorda, who knew Gibson got rich on sliders.

It was all part of great, good fun. Old? Tommy will never get old. He doesn't know how. And Casey Stengel was managing till he was 75 and Connie Mack till he was 88. There's no heavy lifting involved. You just have to know when to bunt. And how to recognize a great talent from the window of a moving train. And who to put in the lineup.

God is a Dodger fan, Lasorda will tell you. He plans to bring an autographed baseball to heaven for Him. So he'll get a good table. When the Dodgers are home, the best Italian restaurant in town is Tommy's locker room.

Tommy is full of harmless hokum like that. But not when it comes to his country. Tommy will tell you the world is lucky there's a United States of America in it and if you don't think so, the conversation is over.

He's never said "No comment" or "That's off the record" in his life. Tommy is on the record and full of comment. Sometimes, it's X-rated.

Baseball needs a lot of things this Year of Our Lord. And one of the things it needs is a Tommy Lasorda in a dugout. Not sign him to a new contract? Are you kidding? Might as well do away with the infield fly rule. It's guys like T. Lasorda who have made baseball what it is.

Dodger Stadium without Tommy Lasorda?

1996

••••••••••••••••••••

JANUARY 2, 1996

Wildcats' Tale Not a Stretch

So, the glass slipper didn't quite fit. The clock struck midnight. The prince wanted her just to do the laundry. There was no happy ending. The carriage turned back into a pumpkin, the horses into mice.

But was that fairy tale enough football for you? Palm-sweating, heart-pounding football, was it? Did "Cinderella," i.e., Northwestern, come close enough to making fairy tales come true? They don't, you know. Only in Disney movies.

They almost came true in the Rose Bowl on Monday.

Northwestern is supposed to be the scullery maid of Big Ten football. The Wildcats get to eat with the family only occasionally. They're supposed to know their place and keep out of the way of their stepsisters, i.e., the other members of the conference. You know, shut up and mop the floor. That is, lose eight of 10 games a year. Go do windows.

So no one took them completely seriously when they came out for the Rose Bowl. They were ranked No. 3 in the country and USC was ranked No. 17—but the gamblers had the Wildcats three-point underdogs. Prevailing opinion was they were doing it with mirrors and wands. A fairy godmother at work.

Can I tell you something? It makes good copy, but Northwestern is nobody's Cinderella. I'm not sure the better team won.

Northwestern came west with a reputation of being a bunch of scholars who got lucky.

Well, I can tell you all you need to know about Northwestern. It is the close of the first half. The Wildcats have had some bad breaks. A guy catches a pass for them for a good gain, but the ball falls loose. An SC player, considerably to his surprise and with a look-what-bounced-into-my-hands expression on his face, scoops it up and runs it in for a touchdown.

With 12 seconds left in the half, Northwestern is down, 24-7. And SC has the ball.

Time to say "Wait till next year!" eh?

Not Northwestern. It forces a fumble, recovers it—and in only 10 seconds, it has moved to a field goal.

It is a terrific morale booster. Northwestern comes out in the second half, marches the kickoff back for another field goal. Now it's 24-13. Then it completely makes a patsy out of SC with an onside kick. SC players are peeling back to block for the returner. So Northwestern gleefully recovers almost unopposed. And in six plays the Wildcats have a touchdown. It's now 24-19 and SC is like a guy who hears a noise in the attic. Trying to look over both shoulders at once. Eyes big, nerves on edge.

But now comes the play that might have been the game.

All afternoon, Northwestern was the equal of any player on the SC team. Except one.

Keyshawn Johnson is one of the few pop-off guys you will ever meet who is as good as he says he is. With Johnson, this is pretty good. Usually, a guy pops off to conceal hidden insecurities. Johnson doesn't have any of those. Johnson doesn't have an insecurity in his system. He thinks football is lucky to have him.

The USC Trojans are. Because, just as the team was about to become unglued, hearing footsteps, Johnson caught a pass from Brad Otton, eluded the whole Northwestern team and danced in for an answering touchdown. With six minutes to play in the third quarter, Johnson has put SC up a critical 12 points, 31-19.

Johnson, of course, was the least surprised guy in the Rose Bowl. Johnson is surprised when he doesn't make a touchdown. All Johnson requires is that the ball be in the air. He catches balls behind him. He catches them in crowds of four. He catches them at his shoe tops. He caught 12 passes for 216 yards Monday. Almost every one of them was a dagger in the heart of Northwestern.

Without him, the Cinderellas live happily ever after. The slipper fits, the band plays, the prince takes her to Camelot.

They didn't do it with mirrors, wands or tricks. They even came to Planet Hollywood and sportingly joined in all the hoopla, hype and fun at Disneyland, where they rode cups and participated in gags with their distinguished alum Charlton Heston. Unlike the old Woody Hayes bowl teams, they smelled the roses.

This was supposed to be fatal to football. When Pittsburgh teams came out here in early years to lose, 47-14 and 35-0, the whisper was, they had spent all their time on the Sunset Strip.

Well, Northwestern never missed a dance. But the Wildcats didn't leave their game in a nightclub. SC was like a fighter hanging on and looking at the clock when the game ended. Sure glad to hear the final gun. Northwestern scored almost at will, as the final 41-32 score attests. The clock just hit 12 on this Cinderella team.

The Wildcats probably brought more IQ to a Rose Bowl game than it has had since Harvard was last out here. The game had been advertised as a game between brain and brawn—and it was. Even the halftime show featured grand opera tunes. Usually, you get "Waiting for the Robert E. Lee," and the band is a steamboat. Northwestern gave you "Turandot."

The Wildcats also gave you alert football. They were slower than SC, but they were smarter. They might even have been stronger. Speed is not essential if you are in the right place at the right time. They usually were.

The game was what the fight mob calls a "crowd pleaser." Like a bar fight between two drunks—all offense. But it was exciting. The kind of game every Rose Bowl should be. One of the best ever.

You hope Cinderella gets a sequel. If the Wildcats get one without Keyshawn Johnson to chase, they might even get one that can live happily ever after.

• • • • • • • • • • • • • • • • • • • •

FEBRUARY 29, 1996

She'll Run With Best of Them

I'd appreciate it if you'd keep this from Gloria Steinem, Bella Abzug or any of those other fire-breathing women's activists, but a female has never won the Santa Anita Handicap. I mean, talk about runaway sexism. Why, they've had 58 of those over the years. And 36 fillies and mares have tried to win it. And failed.

Talk about politically incorrect. Male chauvinism. The Santa Anita Handicap ranks right up there with Henry VIII.

Fillies have won the Santa Anita Derby. They've won the Kentucky Derby, the Preakness and the Belmont.

The best they could do in 36 tries in the Santa Anita 'Cap were two seconds, two thirds and a couple of fourths.

They haven't been legislated out of the winner's circle. They segregate themselves.

It's not that they can't run against the clock. The girls are as speedy as the boys. It's the infighting. It's not the male horses that give them the problems, it's the male riders. Johnny Longden, Ralph Neves and Eddie Arcaro never let anybody get by them, much less a female horse.

It wasn't the distance. Miss Grillo finished third in the mile-and-a-quarter Santa Anita 'Cap in 1949. Then she won the mile-and-three-quarters San Juan Capistrano Handicap two weeks later.

In the early '50s, Alfred Gwynn Vanderbilt, no less, came out here with two gorgeous, sweet-striding fillies, Next Move and Bed O'Roses. Next Move was second in the 'Cap in 1951 and Bed O'Roses was fourth a year later. Vanderbilt left in a huff. Also a Rolls-Royce.

In 1950, Calumet brought the beauteous filly, Two Lea, out here along with the great Citation. Two Lea promptly romped in the fillies-

and-mares Santa Margarita Handicap, and the stable put her in the 'Cap as a kind of rabbit for Citation.

It didn't work. Noor ran both of them down. But the railbirds were impressed when Two Lea failed to fold and ran a gutty third.

Still, the results have been so emphatic, no female has even tried this race in five years.

But none of this seems to faze owner Bob Lewis or trainer Wayne Lukas. This year's Big 'Cap was so resolutely all-male it was supposed to be won by a horse called Cigar. But they have a plucky little lady named Serena's Song who plans to be where the boys are this Saturday at Santa Anita in the 59th running of this bastion of male dominance.

If you looked at the Racing Form chart, you would be hard put to know Serena's Song was a she. She is the Cal Ripken of thoroughbreds. Barely 4 years old, she has been to the post 25 times already in her career. Man O'War made it only 21 times. So did Secretariat.

She never misses a race. She's disgustingly healthy. As they say around a racetrack, "Never had a pimple on 'er!" She's what they call in shed row a "good doer." English translation: She eats like a truck driver. She's an athlete, not an Amazon. She's small for a racehorse—15 hands, 900–1,000 pounds. She can corner like a hockey player, change leads without breaking stride. She's as easy to ride as a merry-go-round.

If she were human, Lewis says, she'd be a movie star. "Oh, she's beautiful!" he tells you. "Prettiest horse in any paddock." She had a chance to be America's Sweetheart last May when she led the Kentucky Derby all the way to the far turn before tiring. She came out of the gate as if the sheriff were after her and set such blistering fractions clocks were breaking all over the backstretch. Then she faded to 16th. Thunder Gulch won. Tejano Run, a horse Serena's Song had beaten four weeks before in the Jim Beam, was second.

Ordinarily, an experience like this is devastating to horses of any gender. They begin to doubt themselves. Animal psychiatry is indicated. At least, a long layoff to rebuild self-esteem.

Serena's Song (and Lukas) weren't having any. She went out 13 days later and tow-roped a field of fillies at Pimlico in the Black-Eyed Susan Stakes.

Any married man can tell you resiliency is a female characteristic. Most male horses are faint-hearted, easily intimidated and the likelihood exists a 16th-place finish would demoralize even a Man O'War. Serena's Song acted as if it never happened. She even beat males again in the Haskell Invitational.

The first time Lukas spotted her at the Keeneland sales, he thought he was looking at an equine Babe Didrikson. Remembers Lewis, who purchased her for $150,000: "Wayne said to me, 'She's so athletic we could take her right now, as a yearling, and run her at Santa Anita against 2-year-olds.' "

Maybe in this era when you can't call a female performer an actress anymore or a female heir an heiress, Serena's Song thinks she's a colt. Owner Lewis laughs. "No, she's just a consummate professional. She loves to compete. The sex of the competition doesn't matter to her. Even after a race she doesn't win, she's kicking down the stall by Wednesday wanting to get back out there in front of an audience."

So, she didn't become the fourth filly to win the Kentucky Derby. Can she become the first to win the Big 'Cap? It may not be the ladylike thing to do—but is there any such thing anymore? Shoot! You don't even have to take your hat off in an elevator anymore when a lady gets on. And if you get up to give her your seat on the bus, she might whack you over the head with her purse.

Anyway, a filly better win it soon. Five years from now it may be illegal to mention gender, and the headline story may read "The Santa Anita Handicap was won by a horse today, one formerly known as a filly." Serena's Song might be our last chance to make it news.

• •

MARCH 24, 1996

Legend Of Legends Is What Power Begat

LA QUINTA, Calif.—For 30 years, he was the most recognizable silhouette on a golf course. Also its most dominant force.

He was always the one to beat. The path to the championship ran through him. Lee Trevino had him to beat to win the Open at Oak Hill in '68 and again at Merion in '71. Tom Watson had him to beat to win his Open at Pebble Beach in '82. Tom had him to beat to win his British Open at Turnberry in '77. Trevino had to chip in to beat him by a shot at the British at Muirfield in '72. De Vicenzo beat him by two shots at Hoylake in '67 and Gary Player beat him by two at Carnoustie the following year.

Even in Arnold Palmer's lone win in the Open at Cherry Hills in 1960, he was second—at the age of 20—and Ben Hogan himself, who played the final 36 holes with him, said later, "I played the last day with a kid who, if he had a brain in his head, would have won the Open by four shots."

No one was ever to say that about Jack W. Nicklaus again.

What Babe Ruth was to baseball, Dempsey to fighting or Tilden to tennis—and what Bobby Jones and Hogan had been to golf—Jack Nicklaus was to his sport.

Never mind the perfectly astonishing 20 "majors" he won. Or the 70 tour tournaments. You get the true measure of the man when you know he was second—take a deep breath!—59 times in his career! And that's only in this country. He was second in the British Open a record seven times.

It's easy to see where Jack Nicklaus could easily have won more than 100 tournaments (he thinks maybe he did—the PGA totaling system is whimsical at best). He could have won, conservatively, five more "majors."

Winning more than 90 tournaments (counting European, Australian and other Asian wins) is mind-boggling enough, but being runner-up, the man you had to beat, more than 70 or 75 times staggers the psyche.

Oh, yes! He was third on the U.S. tour 35 times.

The greatest player of all time? Only Hogan and Jones could dispute it.

When Jack Nicklaus first came on the golf tour, he was, well, "fat" is the only word that comes to mind. He was so overweight, the tour seers predicted a short career, a diminishing role.

So, he slimmed down to movie-star dimensions. It was our introduction to the spires of will power and determination Jack Nicklaus could ascend to.

Jack was the greatest there was for looking a fact in the face. His career was meteoric: The first tournament he won was the U.S. Open. That's like winning the heavyweight championship in your first fight. He was 22 at the time. Hardly anybody wins a U.S. Open before he's 35, maybe 40.

Watching Nicklaus stare down a fairway was like watching a predator peeking out of the bushes at his prey. You felt the golf course should at least be blindfolded, given a last cigarette.

He didn't assault it with boots on and guns out and charging at it like Arnold Palmer. He surrounded it where necessary. He was like a general who would accept its surrender.

He wasn't the first to use a one-iron, but he was the best. He was the first, really, to make multiple use of it. I cannot remember his ever hitting a fairway wood. Too imprecise for Jack. The ball ran too much off a wood club for scientific golf. Jack didn't like to leave the ball on its own. He wanted it disciplined.

No one ever saw him throw a club or kick a ball-washer or heard him cuss a caddie. And no one ever saw him smoke on a golf course although off it he did (not anymore). Jack never tarnished the game of golf for an instant.

When he first came on tour, no one had ever seen shots the distance Nicklaus hit them. They were the longest, straightest drives in history. The famous quote on them came from Bobby Jones, no less. "He plays a game with which the rest of us are unfamiliar."

He was of the "What elephant?" school of concentration. ("Didn't that elephant bother you running across the green as you were putting?" "What elephant?")

Yet his career was never gaudy. He wouldn't let it be. He hit that ball 350 yards on occasion—and about 300 yards any time he wanted—with a steel shaft and a persimmon head.

But idolatry rolled right off him. Bear in mind that no golfer, much less a great one, likes to admit to any shortcoming at all in his game. A Cary Middlecoff would never admit he was a poor sand player, though he was. A Lloyd Mangrum would never confess to being an erratic driver. ("Are we playing how or how many?")

But listen to Jack as he sits in a press tent at the Liberty Mutual Legends of Golf this week at PGA West.

"My game was power golf," he admits readily. "That was my strength. Sure, I hit the ball far, where I could drop a short iron in on the green close to the hole. The short game was never my strong suit. I was an adequate short-game player, never more than that. But I was a more-than-adequate putter. I made my living off par-fives."

He sure did. Most guys try to make birdies on par-fives. Nicklaus was always trying to make eagles.

Hearing him put down his short game is like hearing Muhammad Ali say there were hundreds of guys with a better left jab.

Jack doesn't even think he's being modest, just honest. Jack is like that French general who said, "There is no use getting angry at facts—it is a matter of indifference to them."

Imagine going to a ballpark today and seeing a Joe DiMaggio batting against a Bob Feller and both of them being within a reasonable facsimile of their old selves and you get a clue on what it's like to see a Nicklaus in a tournament like the Liberty Mutual.

Nicklaus supplanted Palmer as the definitive golfer of his age. But no one replaced Jack. Lee Trevino and Tom Watson came closest. Johnny Miller, Seve Ballesteros. But they fired and fell back.

Jack admits he has lost 25 yards off his tee game. But if he had today's equipment 30 years ago, he might be driving the greens.

It may be your last chance to see a true legend, a player the golf fan of the 2000s may have difficulty believing existed. He's still meticulous. He believes the short-game artists—Raymond Floyd, Dave Stockton—may have passed him by.

Don't you believe it. He's still the one to beat.

JUNE 8, 1996

The Eyes Have It, And Chavez Shows He No Longer Does

LAS VEGAS—It wasn't a fight, it was an execution. As one-sided as an electric chair. If you liked that, you should get a collection of Stalin's home movies.

It was an Oscar night. It wasn't Cesar's Palace this night. De La Hoya rendered to Cesar the things that are Cesar's—but didn't used to be. A bloody eye, lumps in the ribs, ringing in the ears. Julio Cesar Chavez used to pass out those things, not get them.

It was one of the pugilistic anticlimaxes of all time. It was over before it was a little more than a minute old. Oscar De La Hoya slammed in a straight left over Chavez's left eye, which burst open like a melon dropped from a truck. Cascades of blood streamed down Julio's face. A few seconds later, the right eye added to the stream of blood.

To the advantages of height, reach, speed and power that De La Hoya held was now added eyes.

It looked like a mismatch even before that. Chavez couldn't fight Oscar with a ladder. It looked in some light like a lion fighting a sheep. De La Hoya has had tougher fights in the gym.

Chavez trained as fervently as though he were getting ready to fight the German Army. Turned out all he needed was an eye doctor.

You wonder how Chavez thought he could fight this guy. Most of the night, he couldn't even find him.

For Chavez's information, Oscar De La Hoya is a 5-foot-11, dark-haired, 23-year-old man. He's got brown eyes and a nice smile and all his teeth and ears and was wearing white trunks when last seen.

Chavez must have wondered who was causing all the bleeding, because there were times he must have thought De La Hoya didn't show up. He kept missing him, not by inches or feet but by time zones. Chavez kept aiming punches where De La Hoya had been earlier in the evening.

Julio Cesar Chavez brought a new technique to the ring with him. He backed up from the start. It was a good idea. A better idea would have been if he backed out of the ring altogether.

There is a well-worn boxing adage that a good big man will always beat a good little man. This is what happened at Caesar's Palace on Friday night. Julio Cesar Chavez made his fight as best he could, but first he had to find his opponent. And then he had to climb him. The only thing the fight really proved was that Julio is Type O.

But he was fighting through a mask of blood, and he was calling on skills that were there only months ago but deserted him now. Happens to all of us. One day you're running up the stairs, chinning yourself on the hall bar and opening cans with your teeth. The next thing you know you have to stop three times to climb the stairs, you can't jump over a half-dollar and all your teeth are good for is to eat Jell-o.

When you spot your opponent age, height, reach and eyes, the issue is pretty much wrapped up.

So, does this make Oscar De La Hoya the second coming of Sugar Ray? Well, his advantages meant he could fight this battle at longer range than a battleship. He could reduce the target to rubble without suffering much real damage himself. Oscar didn't get his hair mussed. Chavez most of the night looked like a guy fumbling for a keyhole in the dark. He did briefly go on the attack in Round Four. It was not only too little too late, it was foolhardy. He shortly thereafter looked as if he had been hit with a falling safe.

It was not a test for De La Hoya in the real sense of the word. He won't be tested till he fights someone who can look him in the eye—and not bleed from that eye. Face it, the only thing Chavez could do better than De La Hoya was bleed. Chavez ended up the night at the hospital, where the medics will probably need a picture to stitch him properly. Two more rounds and his face would have looked like a baseball the rest of his life.

You wouldn't have thought Chavez would back up from an oncoming express train. But he must have sensed that De La Hoya was a railroad gun.

Chavez had no resources. George Plimpton once said when you get in the situation he was in where you call up reserves that are no longer there, it's like an admiral calling down instructions from the bridge of the ship but the crew is drunk and they don't do what he tells them. Chavez's troops betrayed him Friday night. De La Hoya's muscles do exactly what he tells them to. It was the difference.

• •

JULY 18, 1996

A Hall of Fame Pitch for Rose

I bring this up not to brag—it's no big deal—but I'm in the Baseball Hall of Fame at Cooperstown, N.Y.

To be sure, I'm in the writers' wing, not the players'.

But, the point is, I'm in it.

And Pete Rose is not.

Think about that for a minute. I mean, I have a lot of difficulty juxtaposing those two ideas.

I mean, I never slid home with the winning run in an All-Star game, I never played in seven league championship series and six World Series.

But why pick on me? There are lots of guys in the Baseball Hall of Fame who never did any of those things. There are guys in the Hall of Fame who hit .258 in their careers. Rabbit Maranville. There are guys in there who never got 2,000 hits. Lots of them.

Pete Rose got 4,256 hits—in 3,562 games. Pete Rose had more hits than anyone who ever played baseball. He's one of only two guys in history who had more than 4,000 hits. Ty Cobb, no less, is the other.

Ty Cobb is in the Hall of Fame. On the very first ballot they had.

Pete Rose had more than a hit a game. He holds the National League record for consecutive games hit in: 44. He had more than 200 hits in a season 10 times. He is second all-time in doubles. Tris Speaker is first. But Rose is ahead of Stan Musial (third), Cobb (fourth) and Napoleon Lajoie. They're all in the Hall of Fame.

Rose didn't have a career, he had a parade. He's fourth in runs scored. He almost never struck out—26 times one year, 27 another, that kind of thing. Mickey Mantle struck out that many times in a week.

So why is Rose out in the cold, barred from Cooperstown, a Valhalla he richly deserves admittance to? He's almost a one-man Hall of Fame. You name it, he did it. He played wherever they wanted him to. He hit all kinds of pitching with equal degrees of skill and enthusiasm. He played the game with such boyish skill and zest they nicknamed him "Charlie Hustle." You think anyone is ever going to nickname Albert Belle "Charlie Hustle"?

Maybe the public demands Rose be banned from the game he loves? Well, I watched with amazement the other weekend at the City of Hope Victor Awards at the Las Vegas Hilton when a blase audience full of skilled athletes, surgeons, financiers, lawyers, scientists and show biz types stood and applauded for five minutes when Rose was introduced. Earlier, a comedienne drew thunderous applause when she remarked that the next time she stood there she hoped to see Pete Rose in the Hall of Fame.

Why isn't he? It's like the Pope being locked out of the Vatican.

So why is Rose a pariah? Well, it's hard to fathom. The rap against him was largely compiled by the late commissioner Bart Giamatti. So far as I know, it was never properly adjudicated. You know, with DNA, eyewitnesses, whereases, cross-examination, all the legal jargon. The only really damning point is that Rose never fought the banishment with any vigor. Uncharacteristically, for once in his life he just kind of stood there with his bat on his shoulder.

He acted against the best interests of baseball, the commissioner ruled. But it was a little like Nathan Detroit rolling the dice in his hat and calling out the results. Giamatti was judge, jury and executioner.

Rose did go to jail. He was sentenced for income tax evasion, which is the other great American pastime. But so did Darryl Strawberry. Rose was sentenced to prison in Marion County, Ohio. Strawberry was sentenced to Palm Springs. His own home.

Rose was adjudged to have besmirched the game of baseball. Giamatti decreed that he was not to be employed, indeed declared unemployable, by any team or broadcast organization associated with baseball. He could not even participate in any old-timers game. He could not set foot in any clubhouse, dugout or front office. He could not even attend a baseball dinner. He was a non-person to baseball. If it could be enforced, he would even have been barred from even attending a game.

His sin was, he dishonored the game. But Darryl Strawberry and Steve Howe were banned from the game for cocaine abuse, which hardly honored the grand old game. Howe was reinstated seven times. Strawberry is currently a member of the pennant-bound New York Yankees. He can step in every clubhouse in the game. So can Dwight Gooden, who also was reinstated by that great rehab center in the Bronx, otherwise known as Yankee Stadium.

Rose bet. That's an addiction. But so is cocaine.

Did he bet on the game? Probably. Rose bet on the color of the next car coming down the street. Rose was an addict. But odds were his addiction, not street drugs. Rose doesn't even drink.

But betting on games is hardly fixing games. The only other players banned for life from the game are the 1919 Black Sox. They were crooks, not addicts.

I caught up with Rose after the Victor Awards. Was he bitter? Did he feel he had been mistreated, singled out where others were forgiven? Rose wasn't having any. "Nah, I'm not bitter," he said. "Listen! I made some mistakes. I know it. I got in with a bad crowd. You tend to do that when you gamble. Not many saints in that game. I was friends with Bart Giamatti. I saw his side. I was dumb. I should have known better. No one should think he's untouchable."

Not even when you get more hits than anyone who ever played the game. Does he plan to sue for reinstatement? "To whom?" Rose asks. "I got to wait till there's a commissioner in place. In the meantime, I got my radio show. It's nationwide. I got my restaurant in Boca Raton and I'm opening one in Las Vegas soon. I'd love to be in the Hall of Fame, but I'm not blaming anybody because I'm not."

Maybe so. But I wish he'd come join me there. I feel very uncomfortable being in a Baseball Hall of Fame where Pete Rose is not. So should Rabbit Maranville. Shucks! Rose can have our place.

• •

JULY 28, 1996

Plenty of Bread In NBA's Circus

You know, it was not too long ago—I'm old enough to remember—when, if you were 7 feet tall, the best you could do with your life was join the circus. Or get a fur hat and open cab doors for rich folk outside a New York hotel. Now you get $17 million a year and all the Rolls-Royces you need. People open cab doors for you.

And you get it while you're young and can enjoy it. It's not as though you have to work your way up the business ladder or plug away at Wall Street as J.P. Morgan had to do. You don't have to invent the elevator or electric light. All you have to do is post up, whatever that means.

I can remember when if you were 7 feet, you couldn't play basketball. For one thing, you had to bounce the ball on the floor if you went to the basket, and 7-footers were too slow and too clumsy to do that. Today, you can go to the basket like a guy running for a bus and everybody scatters out of your way. Also, 7-footers aren't pituitary freaks anymore. They're perfectly proportioned.

Dr. James Naismith invented basketball precisely so you couldn't carry the ball like a fullback. He wanted a sport in which brute strength didn't count so much as finesse and grace.

You think Naismith ever envisaged the dunk shot? You think he ever envisaged anyone signing a $120-million contract to play his game?

Of course, it's the oldest con in the world, as old as the Roman

Empire. Juvenal first called attention to it in the 1st century A.D. when he wrote, "Two things only the people require—bread and circuses." The Roman emperors gave it to them. Chariot races, Christians vs. lions. Only, the best the Christians could get was their freedom; the best the lions could get was a Christian for lunch.

Nothing changes. To keep the citizenry from becoming mutinous, you give them the circus—something that lets them paint their faces blue or red and jab their forefingers in the air and scream "We're No. 1!" on television. Nero would have understood.

You think basketball fans aren't high-fiving each other over the capture of Shaquille O'Neal by the Lakers? Get real.

You think the public cares what Shaq cost? They think it's somebody else's money. Television's, maybe.

It isn't. It's their money. Even if they don't pay the $600 per game for the courtside seats, they pay for the dunk shots, the sky hooks, the fastbreaks. "Free TV" is an oxymoron. Every time you buy a Ford or Toyota or can of Pepsi or pair of Nikes, you're paying for what they sponsor. The cost of the ad is factored in the cost of the car. You're paying for your circuses.

Sometimes it's difficult for us old-timers to comprehend what's happening in the countinghouses of sports these days.

I'm also old enough to remember when Bob Short first brought the Lakers to Los Angeles. They were going broke in Minneapolis, where the games were played in relative privacy.

They didn't exactly have SRO here, either. Basketball was far from a sports-page staple. Baseball was America's sport of choice. Football. Boxing. The highest salary in the NBA those days was $19,000 a year. Plumbers did better.

I went to a playoff game once—a playoff game!—at which there were 2,800 paying customers.

All that changed. I helped. I had the sport almost to myself. And what a sport! Bill Russell, Bob Cousy, Jerry West, Elgin Baylor, Wilt Chamberlain. The Big O. I was like a kid in a candy store. I traveled with the Lakers. What a cast of characters! They almost wrote themselves.

But modesty dictates I must confess it was Chick Hearn who did the most to make the Lakers household names in L.A. First on radio, then on TV. Television was slow to pick up on the sport, but basketball, like football, was uniquely suited to the TV screen, a rectangular sport with a large ball.

The pro game didn't even have a radio contract at first. Teams played league games in places like Sheboygan, Morgantown, Peoria. A league game was a prologue to a Harlem Globetrotter exhibition. The Globies drew the people, not the Knicks or Lakers.

The graph grew. Smart entrepreneurial owners such as Jack Kent Cooke moved in. Jack knew what sold tickets—stars. The Lakers had an Academy Award lineup. What they didn't have was the clincher—the big man in the pivot. Jack twisted arms till he wound up with Wilt Chamberlain. When Wilt left, Cooke angled to get Kareem Abdul-Jabbar. Jack didn't want playmakers, point guards, sixth men. Jack wanted the marquee players, guys nicknamed "Magic."

Now, Jerry Buss has joined the owners' wing of the Hall of Fame. He has done what Cooke did, brought the Big Man to town, put the team on Page 1 again.

The circus is in place; the bread is somebody else's problem.

Will O'Neal be a tumble-down Shaq? Or are Michael, Olajuwon, the Admiral Robinson, Patrick Ewing ready to yield their positions?

Is even a championship circus worth that kind of bread? Do you know how much $120,000,000 comes out to? Well, if you spent $1,000 a day for the next 300 years you'd still have almost $11 million left.

But there's only one Shaq. And Buzzie Bavasi, the baseball man, said it best. "You don't mind giving all those millions to a Babe Ruth. But where does it say you have to give $3 million to a second baseman hitting .230?"

Exactly. It's the other guys on the coattails who boggle the mind. Chris Childs is getting $24 million for six years? Who, pray tell, is Chris Childs? Antonio Davis is getting $38.5 million for seven years? I wouldn't know Antonio Davis from Bette. Dale Davis is getting $42 million for seven years. Allan Houston is getting $56 million for seven years. He played for Detroit last season, in case you didn't know.

Don MacLean is getting $12 million for four years and you almost feel like taking up a collection for him. Alonzo Mourning is to get $112 million for seven years. Gary Payton gets $85 million and nobody ever called him "Mr. Clutch" or "The Big G."

I'm always happy to see a kid move up in the world. But I can't help but feel sorry for all those earlier-day giants who had to bend crowbars or tear telephone books or sit in the sideshow with the bearded lady or the tattooed man to earn a living. One sure thing: Dennis Rodman could handle it either way. And bite the heads off chickens if you wanted.

•••••••••••••••••••

SEPTEMBER 22, 1996

Slugger's Statistics Becoming Ruthian

Mark David McGwire as Babe Ruth II? Well, you have to crunch the numbers a little bit, but a case could be made.

Mark has sent 50 baseballs into orbit this year. Only 12 other players in the long history of the grand old game have done that. Babe Ruth did it four times, Mickey Mantle and Willie Mays, twice.

But the stat on Mark McGwire you have to pay attention to is the fact he got his 50 home runs this year in only 390 official times at bat. Mathematics was never my long suit, but I make that a home run every 7.8 times at bat. That stat is Ruthian.

In 1927, when he hit 60, Babe Ruth went to bat officially 540 times. Home run every nine times at bat, right? In 1961, when Roger Maris unaccountably hit 61, he struck a homer every 10 times at bat.

The stats take into account only official at-bats. A bit misleading. It discounts bases on balls. The notion is, since they are unofficial and don't count on your batting average, they shouldn't count on your homer average, either, since you had no chance to hit a home run off, say, Ball 4.

Well, not necessarily. The truth is, many a home run has been hit off Ball 4—or Ball 1, 2 or 3. Lots of home runs have been hit on balls outside the strike zone.

The presumption is, if Ruth had waited for strikes to hit, his home run totals would be halved. Or, anyway, lowered. When he hit 60, you have to believe, based on old umpires' recollections, that he hit a considerable number of them off high-outside or low-inside pitches.

Ted Williams might have insisted on a strike to hit, but Ruth almost never got one. He led the world in walks—2,056 of them lifetime. He regularly led the game in bases on balls—11 times by actual count. He walked as many as 170 times a season.

With Ruth, a walk was a victory for the pitcher. You will note in the record books, Ruth was not among the all-time leaders in intentional walks. This is preposterous. It is unthinkable pitchers did not try to walk him almost every other time at bat. You have to assume he wouldn't let them. You can only conclude that many a pitch the pitcher thought was outside the strike zone really was when Ruth got through with it. It was in the center-field seats.

You have to be careful comparing a hitter to Ruth for another reason: When Babe Ruth hit 54 home runs in 1920, that was more home runs than any other team in the league hit. There were 369 home runs hit in the American League that year. Washington hit only 22, for instance. Ruth hit 54, his Yankee teammates and the rest of the league 315.

That meant only one thing: The ball was not jacked up in those years. It was still a comparative beanbag. Knocking it out of the lot still requires the basic hand-eye coordination and strength, but in those days you got no help from the ball. It took massive strength to propel it out of the park.

In 1921, Ruth hit 59 home runs. The seven other teams in the league got 402.

Know how many home runs the American League had hit this Year of Our Lord as of Wednesday last? 2,578 is all.

So, it's a tricky business, comparing a hitter today to Ruth's day—although the practice of juicing up the baseball apparently originated with him and even Ruth had a missile to swing at in his later years.

But the Babe—even with his plethora of walks—had his 500-plus and 400-plus at-bat seasons. Mark McGwire went to bat only 84 times in 1993, only 135 times in 1994 and only 317 times last year. McGwire is troubled by bad feet. Ruth missed games but not parts of seasons and mostly from suspensions for high living, not physical ailments.

McGwire looks the part. Beneath all that curly red hair, those alert blue eyes is the body of the born hitter. The powerful arms, the sloping shoulders. Sloping shoulders seem made for hitting something hard. Joe Louis had sloping shoulders. So did the Babe. He had a sloping everything.

You have to be around 6 feet 5, 250 pounds to keep hitting a five-ounce baseball into orbit with a 40-inch, 35-ounce bat as October rolls around. McGwire qualifies—when his feet let him.

He misses at-bats for another Ruthian similarity too: He has walked 108 times this year, fourth most often in the league. He led the league in walks in 1990.

I went down to the locker room at Anaheim the other night to see how the Ruth-chasing was coming along.

"Are you proudest of the 50 homers or the .322 batting average?" I ask him. Mark has never hit .300 over a full major league season.

"I'll take the 50," he says. "It's a first for me. I had 49 and 42, never 50."

Did he ever feel he had Babe Ruth in his sights as the season wore on? McGwire shakes his head.

"I can say I never thought about that. I just tried to get a hit. You never try to hit a home run. If you do, you won't."

What's his secret? Eyesight? See the craters on the moon on a clear night, can he? Got 20/15 vision? McGwire smiles.

"My vision without contact lenses is about 20/500."

Without contacts, he says, he not only couldn't see the ball, he couldn't even make out the pitcher. With contacts, he says, he does have 20/15.

Will he hit 60?

"Oh, someone could," he begins. "Oh, you mean this year? Naw. Got what? 10 games left? But some year? It's possible."

In a sense, he's fortunate. The man who goes into mid-September with 55 or more home runs would soon seem to be leading a parade. An army of photographers, TV cameramen, reporters, talk-show recruiters, sponsors, advertisers, fans and agents would be marching behind his every move. Roger Maris' hair fell out under the onslaught.

Still, if a man can hit a home run every 7.8 trips to the plate, he can expect to be noticed. If he ever got to bat 600 times—Pete Rose had more than 600 at-bats 17 times, Maris had 590 his year and Willie Wilson had 705 one year—that would work out to 75 home runs for the year.

Even in a year when there were 2,500 others, that would get attention. That would work out to "Babe Ruth? Who was he?"

• •

OCTOBER 27, 1996

N.Y. Gets What It Deserves

NEW YORK—Awright! You got 56,000 people singing "Noo Yawk! Noo Yawk!" Every one of them thinks he's Frank Sinatra.

You thought the world championship was going to go back to have those little town blues?

Fergitaboudit! Eat yer heart out, rest of America!

The Yankees are back where they belong. Babe Ruth can rest easy.

Joe DiMaggio can show his face in public again. Reggie Jackson can put the logo on his cars. It's over, Yogi.

Wade Boggs is riding around on the back of a police horse, waving to a delirious crowd. New York's finest line the field. The big town hasn't been this happy since Jimmy Walker was mayor.

You thought Atlanta was going to win this? Gidouddahere!

A world championship is New York's legacy, its birthright. It's as much a part of New York as a mugging in Central Park.

I'll give your regards to Broadway, remember you to Herald Square. They're dancing in the aisles, spraying champagne in the locker room. They're blowing horns on Park Avenue, the Battery, Bowery, Tribeca, Flatbush, SoHo, Harlem.

It used to be old stuff to this town. This is the Yankees' 23rd world championship, their 34th appearance in it—far more than any other team.

So, the title is back on Broadway, the Great White Way. They're going to have the biggest ticker-tape parade since Lindbergh came back.

They had a world championship in this stadium the year it was built and had one about three or four times every decade since.

But not lately. Not in the '80s or the '90s. This is the first world championship in 18 years for the once-mighty Yankees—and their first pennant in 15. The town was getting kind of cranky.

This wasn't the Big-Inning Yankees, the ones who used to score more runs in nine minutes than the other team scored in nine innings.

They won really because they returned to their roots, danced with what brung 'em here. They had a lineup that scuffled for runs like a bag lady, beat you with the small skills. When the Yankees start talking about "beating you with the glove," you know they have trouble. But they finally put big boppers in the lineup, long-ball threats like Cecil Fielder and Darryl Strawberry. The old Yankees had nine guys like that, but now they looked like one of the teams they used to score 18 runs on in Series games.

Old-time Yankee Series were more executions than contests. This one was desperate, a knife fight in a dark alley.

For the Yanks, it started out like a horror movie. Atlanta won the first game, 12-1. They shut out the Yankees in the second game. In the old days, the Yankees would go whole seasons without being shut out, never mind only two games into a World Series.

Then, they did what Yankee teams always used to do: won four in a row. Only, the old Yankees were never down 0-2 when they started the string.

Atlanta had a lineup of Cy Young pitchers when it started. But baseball history shows you that great pitchers, for some reason, struggle in World Series. Greg Maddux, who lost Game 6 after winning four Cy Young Awards in a row, is in good company.

In the 1929 Series, Philadelphia Manager Connie Mack, who had a staff that included the storied Lefty Grove, George Earnshaw and Rube Walberg, knew the series hex and elected to start a 35-year-old pitcher who had won only seven games and pitched only 54 2/3 innings all year. And all Howard Ehmke did was strike out a then-record 13 batters and win, 3-1.

Recall what happened to Sandy Koufax in the last game he ever pitched. He had won 27 games that year and had an earned-run average of 1.73. Nevertheless he lost that 1966 Series game to Baltimore, 6-0, helped by a three-error inning by his center fielder, Willie Davis. Sandy also lost the first World Series game he ever pitched, although he pitched brilliantly in a 1-0 loss to the White Sox in 1959.

It goes on like that. Is Tom Seaver your idea of a masterful pitcher? Of course. But he lost his Series debut, to the Orioles in '69, 4-1. It was the only game the Mets lost in that series.

You like Bob Gibson, Cardinal legend? OK, but he lost Game 7 in 1968 (he won Game 7 the year before) and he lost (to the Yankees) in Game 2 in 1964, 8-3.

So, Greg Maddux, trailing his Cy Young ribbons, was supposed to stop the bleeding for the Atlanta Braves on Saturday night. He had already shut out the Yanks in Game 2.

The jinx was waiting. Old-timers could have told him. Even Christy Mathewson, Walter Johnson and Grover Cleveland Alexander lost World Series games. Lefty Grove was 31-4 one year and still was only a .500 pitcher in World Series.

Greg Maddux was his usual self, which is to say he made a specialty of getting the batters to hit them where they ain't. He had only one careless inning, which is to say he threw pitches the batters were expecting. Paul O'Neill hit a double, Joe Girardi hit a triple, Derek Jeter and Bernie Williams singled and that was the old ballgame and the old World Series. One inning undid him. If it wasn't quite the Big Inning pioneered by Ruth and Gehrig, it was a big inning by present Yankee standards.

Maddux's teammates didn't help him. Some audacious, not to say ill-advised, baserunning killed a couple of key rallies.

After years of being able to say Yankee Go Home, baseball has to deal with the haughty pinstripes again. Putting home run hitters at the corners makes pitchers sweat and fidget. The three-run homer or the threat of it still takes the opposition out of its game. Fielder and Strawberry made the '96 Yankees at least an unreasonable facsimile of the '27 ones.

So, start spreading the news. The Yankees are back, New York still has them, Yankee Stadium is the Vatican of baseball once again. They almost killed the game with their ruthless excellence once, but this time they may have saved it. For one thing, Yankee haters will have someone to hate again. And that's good for business.

• • • • • • • • • • • • • • • • • • • •

NOVEMBER 10, 1996

Evander Proved Us Wrong

LAS VEGAS—Are you sitting down? Ready for this?

Do me a favor. See if the sun rises in the west tomorrow. See if the oceans run dry.

You're going to think I've been drinking. You'll think I'm making it up. But, honest, Evander Holyfield beat Mike Tyson Saturday night. Knocked him out!

It was supposed to be an execution, not a fight. Tyson, one of the most awesome creatures you ever saw when his opponent is paralyzed with fear, was supposed to leave Holyfield in a pile in a corner within a minute.

They even insulted Evander by selling the fight by the round in the expectation that he might hit the floor immediately and the buying customer would feel cheated.

They needn't have worried. As this is written, a chastened Mike Tyson, his eyes hollow with stunned disbelief, is standing in the ring trying to answer questions.

Fighting Tyson with a boxing glove was supposed to be as forlorn an adventure as hunting a tiger with a switch. The implements were ill-suited to the purpose.

People not only feared for Evander's safety, they feared for his life. Not too long ago, a fibrillation appeared to have been detected in Evander's heart. It proved a false alarm, but in the ring with Mike Tyson seemed as bad a place for a guy with a bad heart as the top of Mt. Everest.

There's nothing wrong with Evander Holyfield's heart. Before the fight, we knights of the press asked him if he intended to box with Tyson. You know, stick and run, stay out of his way, try to pile up points. "Naw," said Holyfield, "I'm going to knock him out."

There was a short pause while we smothered our laughter.

But, Evander had spotted the flaw in Tyson's grandeur. Tyson makes his fight like a guy chasing a bus, about as scientific as a cop busting up a crap game in an alley. Evander makes his fight like a guy hanging drapes. He's methodical.

He knew Tyson would come to him. And when he did, Evander smashed him in the mouth. He floored Tyson in the fourth round but Mike didn't learn the lesson. He continued to charge.

There were times when Evander seemed able to turn the fight into what the fight mob calls an "agony" fight, i.e., one in which the contestants labor at long distance or in frequent clinches without inflicting any discernible damage on each other.

But Evander has never been in an agony fight in his life. And he was determined this would be no exception. He pounded respect into Tyson, who, by the fourth round, was even paying respectful attention to his corner, something he usually scorns.

Evander made Tyson respect him, but not enough for Tyson to change his reckless style, which gradually undid him.

Before the fight, someone asked Evander if he didn't feel the fight was coming too late in his career, that he would have been more ready when it was first staged five years ago. Evander shook his head. "I'm smarter now," he said.

He was. He fought a smarter fight than Tyson.

They said he was crazy to take this fight. Over-age and under-dog. He was only going to ring down the curtain on a distinguished career, bloody and beaten. In the end, it was the younger, feared over-dog who ended up bloody and beaten.

Evander knew he was a better fighter than the world viewed him. Saturday night, he proved it to everybody. He was St. George bringing home the dragon on his shield. It was a victory for the white hats, but it was in sum a victory for a guy who was not resigned to being just another heavyweight champion but a guy to whom attention must be paid by history.

• • • • • • • • • • • • • • • • • • • •

DECEMBER 8, 1996

Rozelle Was Super Man for the NFL

Some years ago, when he retired, I wrote of Pete Rozelle:

"The Super Bowl is his monument. It exists because of Pete Rozelle. He built it from scratch. Michelangelo had his David, Da Vinci, his Mona Lisa—and Rozelle, his Super Bowl."

A little overblown, perhaps. But not all that much.

Pete Rozelle defined the position of commissioner. Baseball should have one like him. Basketball does.

I also wrote of Pete Rozelle: "This is the supreme Organization Man. Madison Avenue times two. As a PR man, he is without equal. He could have made Castro President of the U.S.

"His great strength lay in appearing to compromise without really doing so. He made everybody feel is if he was their best friend. He understood public relations as few did in our generation.

"Few people remember that the first Super Bowl was almost a disaster. It fell 30,000 short of selling out as it was, but it might have been much worse if Rozelle hadn't come to town, rolled up his sleeves and put it on Page One and the 11 o'clock news.

"The World Series was the great American hype when the Super Bowl came along. That, or a heavyweight championship fight. A 'Bowl' game was the Rose. Or the Orange. Basketball was hopeful but rudderless and unfocused. It used to have to play doubleheaders with the Globetrotters to attract crowds. But Pete made Super Sunday into the single biggest sports event of the year. Not since Dempsey-Tunney had the whole nation come to a halt around a single sports event."

It's impossible to fix exactly Pete's impact on his game. As I noted, it was a kind of cult game before he came along. People liked it kind of the way they developed a fondness for escargots—or old silent movies. Pete, so to speak, took it out of the art houses and onto Broadway. He hooked up with television the way no one had before or since. The old commissioner, Bert Bell, whom he replaced, had sort of worked out of his back pocket. He ran the game the way you might run a cockfight. Pete put the business on Park Avenue. Literally. That was the NFL office address in Pete's years.

Pete had television eating out of his hand. He got the idea for "Monday Night Football"—NFL in prime time—and didn't let go of it till he sold it to Roone Arledge at ABC and there wasn't a bar in America that didn't have it on. Pro football became an American tribal rite.

Pete knew he had the product. And he didn't let it go cheaply. But he did it all with an urbanity that offended no one.

The only time he locked horns with any of his people was when he tried to stop Al Davis from moving his Oakland Raiders to L.A. It was a forlorn battle. Pete was actually on the side of the angels—Oakland had supported the Raiders lavishly. But, while large areas of professional sports are outside the Constitution, the right to move a business, any business, from one location to another was not negotiable. In its history, the NFL had moved from Boston to Washington (the Redskins), Chicago to St. Louis (Cardinals), Cleveland to Los Angeles (Rams). And, the Rams had just finished moving to Anaheim with impunity. Pete was tilting at windmills.

Pete never held grudges. He considered that a waste of time. And energy. He also knew that, in this business, today's enemy was tomorrow's ally.

Pete handled Capitol Hill as deftly as he did Madison Avenue. He had to get the leagues' merger OK'd and large elements of antitrust law overlooked before he could even think of a Super Bowl, revenue-sharing and the other refinements that made his administration one of the most successful in sports history.

I have known Pete Rozelle, man and boy commissioner, since he was a young PR person, first with the Rams, then with Qantas Airlines, then back to the Rams. I was a young magazine reporter then, and, when he was on his second stint with the Rams, he picked me up one night in New York to go to dinner with then-Ram owner Dan Reeves and his family. I even remember the name of the restaurant—the Iroquois. The dinner became contentious. With Dan, it often could. As we got home, I asked Pete if he didn't think football was too shot through with outsize egos to prevail. Pete smiled. "Nah," he said, "everything responds to sweet reasonableness."

Death, as it must to all men, came to Alvin "Pete" Rozelle this week. There isn't a game, there isn't a man in it who doesn't owe him a debt of gratitude. He never threw or ran for a touchdown, kicked a field goal or intercepted a pass. On the field, that is. In the league offices he regularly did all three. He did it without ever losing his temper, doing an end zone dance, gloating, whining, complaining or being vindictive. If football really wants a role model, they have one in Pete Rozelle.

1997

• • • • • • • • • • • • • • • • • • • •

JANUARY 7, 1997

A Tip of the Cap for Putting L.A. in the Big Leagues

I never saw Walter O'Malley in a locker room. I played poker with him, drank Irish whiskey with him on St. Patrick's Day, but never saw him on the field or in a dugout. He never fancied himself an expert on the grand old game. He hired people who were.

He himself provided the environment—and the money. The skeptics said when he built Dodger Stadium, it would just be a flimsy facade that would soon come down and be replaced with the skyscrapers of commerce, hotels, maybe even casinos.

Dodger Stadium is a ballpark. Period. It is as clean and wholesome today as it was on opening day in '62. I know. I was there.

In a funny way, it was the day when L.A. was certified as a major player in the complex of American cities—no longer just the place where Charlie Chaplin waved his cane, Pauline had her perils, and the cowboys and Indians chased each other down Gower Gulch while a director shouted "Action!" No longer just Flicker City. Goodbye Tinseltown.

The stands were powder-blue and filled. The sun was high and hot. The Cincinnati Reds were the opposition and we had Koufax and Drysdale and Maury Wills. Pennants waved, Wally Post hit a mammoth home run and Vin Scully explained it all to us.

O'Malley had brought it off. The Dodgers had found a real home. We were big league.

When the O'Malley family patriarch, Walter, bought into the Dodgers in the early 1940s, he was hardly a baseball man and the Dodgers were hardly the icons of baseball they were to become.

In fact, they were at times the laughingstock of the game, identified by an irreverent press as the "Flatbush Follies" and "Dem Bums," a team so eccentric on the field that once when a fan called down to an associate outside the park, "The Dodgers have three men on base," the cynical retort was, "Which base?"

O'Malley at the time was general counsel to the Brooklyn Trust Co., which was the repository of 50% of the team stock. O'Malley's job was to try to improve its value. The Dodgers had a ratty, rundown relic of a ballpark with 32,000 seats, no major local newspaper and the sad happenstance of trying to sell tickets in a town that also had the New York Yankees and New York Giants.

"The trust company had a sick dog on its hands with that ballclub," O'Malley was to say.

In those days, Walter was a bottom-line man and no fan of the dotty Dodgers. But, when 25% of the stock came on the market, he invited two associates—John Smith and Branch Rickey—to go in with him, and they bought the 25% for $200,000.

The next year, the Brooklyn Trust Co.'s 50% came on the market and O'Malley, Smith and Rickey bought that for $720,000. Jim Mulvey, president of Samuel Goldwyn Movie Productions, owned the other 25%.

O'Malley and Branch Rickey detested each other. Walter was a festive man, Rickey a preacher-type who didn't drink or smoke. And disapproved of people who did. So, when Rickey sold out, he demanded $1 million, and if he couldn't get it from O'Malley, he threatened to sell out to William Zeckendorf. O'Malley screamed blackmail but had to pay it because the last thing he wanted in the world was the acquisitive Zeckendorf as a partner.

Whatever their personal relationships, there was no doubt Branch Rickey, knowledgeable and single-minded, was good for their business. Rickey brought off one of the masterstrokes of baseball history when he signed Jackie Robinson. He integrated the game, raided the Negro leagues generally and made the Dodgers America's Team overnight. It's possible that he undersold at a million dollars.

O'Malley had to raise the money to buy him out and rival owners were only too happy to oblige. They would advance O'Malley the money—if they could have Roy Campanella, Don Newcombe and Duke Snider for it.

"I can't play bags of money," O'Malley sniffed—and raised the money elsewhere.

Walter O'Malley left the running of the team to baseball men. But he chafed at the conditions under which the Dodgers had to compete.

He is reviled to this day by New Yorkers for absconding with a community treasure, but it is, in some ways, a bad rap. O'Malley, at first, wanted to move no farther west than the intersection of Atlantic and Flatbush avenues. He proposed to build his own ballpark there and it would have been the first stadium privately built in a quarter-century. It would also have had a dome, another first.

Before condemning property for the new ballpark, the Brooklyn Sports Center Authority required that O'Malley put up $4 million, a gulping sum in those days. But he promptly sold Ebbets Field for $3 million and his Montreal and Fort Worth minor league parks for $2 million and posted his money in escrow to await the land clearance.

It never came. The Sports Center Authority, as it were, died on third. The project withered and left O'Malley sitting there with his $5 million, short-term leases and no domed ballpark of his dreams. He began a slow burn.

That was in 1955 and O'Malley began to turn his attention to Los Angeles. It was a place where two minor league franchises were drawing better—more than a million fans a year—than most major league teams. Including the Dodgers.

In December of 1956, he secretly traded his Fort Worth territorial rights for the rights to Los Angeles, which were held by Phil Wrigley. Less than two years later, he arrived in California with Horace Stoneham and the Giants in the duffel with him.

It would be a little overblown to say the move saved major league baseball. But it certainly didn't hurt it any. The Dodgers became only the second franchise in the history of baseball to draw more than 2 million fans, and they became the first to draw more than 3 million. They were as successful on the field as they ever had been under Rickey.

It became probably the most successful—and valuable—sports franchise in history.

Peter O'Malley inherited the team when Walter died in 1979. He was, really, the proverbial chip-off-the-old-block, the son everybody wishes he could have. A replica. When you called him a clone, he was flattered. Like his father, he was educated at the University of Pennsylvania. Like his father, he was a formal man who showed up in a suit and tie. Walter even played poker in a business suit.

The odyssey of the O'Malleys and the Dodgers is over. Son Peter announced Monday that he is putting his legacy up for sale. The team that Walter O'Malley more or less found in his lap 55 years ago will go to the highest bidder.

It may be a sad day for baseball. It could be a sad day for Los Angeles. You would only hope another O'Malley gets it. Whoever gets it should not expect to get 25% of it for $200,000—or 50% of it for $720,000. Whoever buys it may have to make up his mind whether he wants the Dodgers—or Rhode Island.

• •

MARCH 6, 1997

Up Lanes and Down Aisles

Look! If the Masters golf tournament were to be played in the L.A. area this week, would you be scrambling all over the brokers' row, trying to find tickets?

If Michael Jordan were in town for a playoff game, would his picture be all over the paper?

When Tiger Woods was here last week, the cops on Sunset Boulevard turned you back from Riviera because the lots were all full.

Well, the greatest players in the world in the nation's biggest participant sport—enjoyed by 40 million to 50 million—are in town for a major showdown. And there are plenty of good seats left.

Tiger Woods and Greg Norman may not be here. But Walter Ray Williams Jr. is.

Walter Ray is only the best bowler in the world right now. And he's no better than a co-favorite to win the AC Delco Classic at the Cal Bowl in Lakewood this week.

That's because Mike Aulby, David Ozio, Bob Learn Jr. and Tom Baker, the defending champion who had nine strikes in a row in last year's title match, are on hand. A blue-ribbon field for a blue-ribbon event.

Not all of us have golfed, played tennis, shot baskets or tried to hit the breaking ball, but I dare say, most of us have bowled. It's as American as Rip Van Winkle, as ancient as the Bible, and a winter's night in the East would be more bearable because the friendly neighborhood lanes would be packed with everyone from a stenographers' pool to the hustlers waiting on the sidelines for some pigeon to come along for the plucking.

It's a happy sound, that of a bowling alley. The crash of pins, the thud of the ball starting its 60-foot journey to the pins—or the gutter—means fun, recreation, a happy, noisy night out for weekend rollers. Americans love noise.

It's a far more difficult proposition for the 120 or so contestants in the AC Delco. First of all, these are guys for whom a nine is a disastrous score. In fact, a nonstrike is like bogey to a great golfer. This is not league night at Laurel Lanes. There are millions of dollars at stake here.

Fred Couples never lined up a shot or a two-break putt with any more care than a bowler. First of all, there are the lanes. The lanes are the adversary.

"Sometimes, you have to test them with a bad shot," Williams warns. "It may tell you more than a good one."

The lanes are oiled like a race car. Cal Bowl has an aluminum sheaf under them and, if you are to succeed, you have to calculate what that—and the oil residue—does to the speed and location of your ball.

You think Greg Maddux has a good curveball? You haven't seen a curve till you've seen a 16-pound ball go from one side of the lane to the middle of the pins. Stan Musial couldn't get a bat on one of those.

Williams' repertoire runs more to the fastball. He wants to get those pins flying. (There are no knuckleballs or changeups in bowling. You want the ball to come in hot and destructive.) If he were a golfer, Williams would be said to have one of the great swings on tour, a long, fluid sweep of the arm and extended follow-through. Sam Snead with a bowling ball.

You know how you and I go up to the lane and pick a ball out of the trough and throw it? Not these guys. They travel around with 20 or so bowling balls in their trunks or trailers and they calibrate them as carefully as Wernher von Braun did a ballistic missile. The first suspicion they're out of round, out they go and the bowler must drill new ones. If your thumb wobbles in the hole, you must tape it—or redrill the ball. Tolerances are minimal when you are trying to make every game perfect.

Williams has bowled 40 perfect games in competition—Bob Learn has 58—but it's consistency that has been his hallmark. He averages well over 220 and probably will become the first bowler to go over the $2-million mark in lifetime earnings. First prize this week at Cal Bowl is $48,000.

Williams has had a bowling ball—or a horseshoe, he's also a champion at shoe pitching—in his hand since he was 11. He is the reigning PBA player of the year, a title he has won twice before.

The only trouble with Williams is he wears this beard. Makes him all too recognizable. I mean, you have this dream of being hustled in a bowling alley some night by this con man and he'll invite you to pick a partner and you'll say, "OK, I'll take that guy with the beard over there."

And the hustler will smirk sweetly and say, "Oh, no, you don't!

That's Walter Ray Williams, the best there is!"

While I've got your attention—I do, don't I?—I'd like to interject a personal note if I may. Team Murray underwent a roster change, a line-up revamp last Monday. The beauteous Linda McCoy signed on. We got married.

Federal Judge Mariana Pfaelzer performed the ceremony at the home she shares with her husband and our old friend, Frank Rothman. Frank is general counsel for the NFL, no less.

A word about the new recruit, the bride. First of all, she'll bat cleanup. I'll move up in the order where I'll mostly bunt and take. She goes to her left as well as anybody in the game, bats right, fights out of a crouch, has a great jump shot and is a Gold Glove fielder.

We were both free agents—12½ years—and came in well under the salary cap. She outdrives me on the golf course, but I'm better at emptying the dishwasher and we're about even when it comes to vacuuming. She'll be sending in the plays, I expect. But, of course, I have the right to audibilize at the line of scrimmage (I think).

Jerry Reinsdorf thinks he pulled the coup of the year signing Albert Belle for the White Sox?

Fergetaboudit! I signed the real pennant winner. The Unreal McCoy. I wish I could have invited you all to the wedding, but home plate at Dodger Stadium was busy.

• •

March 16, 1997

Chang Survives Champions Purge

INDIAN WELLS—Wait a minute! WHO ARE THESE GUYS?! What's going on here? What is this, the "WHERE IS EVERYBODY" Open?

Look, when you start out with a tournament draw that includes most of the Who's Who of the game—and end up with most of the Who's He—you had better check around and see which tennis god you've offended.

The Newsweek Champions Cup tournament at Hyatt Grand Champions resort this week looked on paper like Wimbledon West at the start of the week. It looked like a clay court at Indianapolis by the quarterfinals.

Look whom they had. Want to start with Pete Sampras? The best player extant and one of the best ever?

Gone. Eliminated not by another candidate for the tennis Hall of Fame but by somebody named Bohdan Ulihrach. The Bohdan Ulihrach.

Well, now, you've heard of Andre Agassi? Right! Brooke Shields' significant other. The "Image is everything" spokesman. Winner of the Australian and U. S. opens and Wimbledon. That Andre Agassi. Well, he was kicked out of here, image and all, by Mark Philippoussis, a player whose serve has been likened to a Scud missile but the rest of his game is more like bow and arrow.

How about Jim Courier? Winner of the French Open twice, the Australian Open twice, finalist in a U. S. Open. Courier couldn't handle Francisco Clavet.

Hey! You've heard of Goran Ivanisevic. Big server. Leads the world in total service aces with more than 1,500. Plays the game like a guy who dares you to beat him. Goran got tumbled by the immortal Jonathan Stark. You know Jonathan. Sometimes makes it clear to the second round at Wimbledon.

The ribbon clerks have taken over this poker game. When you've got a tennis tournament that could have Pete Sampras, Andre Agassi, Jim Courier, Goran Ivanisevic, to say nothing of a Thomas Enqvist, in the quarterfinals—and you end up with Jonas Bjorkman, Alberto Berasategui and Bohdan Ulihrach, you wonder where you can go to get your money back.

It's anarchy, is what it is. On the other hand, it's kind of heart-warming. If you don't have to sell tickets.

Fortunately, Charlie Pasarell doesn't have to sell tickets. His tournament finals are sellouts annually. The players could presumably play in masks.

This year, they might as well have, but for one thing: the presence of Michael Chang.

The great survivor, Michael Chang, as usual, found a way to creep through the draw, as hard to get rid of as a mosquito in a hot room. And right along with him was the stubborn Austrian, Thomas Muster, the most underrated player on tour.

It would probably not surprise you to know that the current ATP rankings list Chang as No. 3. But it should shock you to know that they list Muster as No. 2.

In a game that's been taken over by the home run hitters, the serve-and-volley terminators, finding a Chang and a Muster listed as closest to Pete Sampras looks like a typo. It isn't. In an era of 140-mph serves and volleys that flatten the ball when it hits the court, Muster and Chang play more of a shell game. Chang comes out of a match as if he had crawled under barbed wire and through bombardment and machine-gun fire for 2½ hours. When Chang plays, you bring a lunch. Or a good book. He never goes quietly. He keeps returning the ball until the other guy is ready for a straitjacket.

Muster is craftier. He is like a gambler with his own deck. Playing him on clay is like fighting a jaguar in a tree. He is like a guy who pulls a quarter out of your ear. He doesn't overpower you, he outsmarts you. If he were a baseball player, you would say he hits 'em where they ain't.

Poetic justice would have had these two to meet in today's final. It would be fitting for No. 2 to play No. 3.

Alas, tennis doesn't deal in poetic justice.

The trouble with tennis is it's match play. There's no tomorrow.

Golf used to be largely match play—until television came along. Match finals were OK so long as they had Hogan in them—but when they came up Chandler Harper v. Henry Williams IV, TV pulled the plug.

A double-crossing by the draw deprived the Newsweek of a face-saving final between Chang and Muster. Instead, they played each other in one semifinal Saturday.

So, instead of a final pitting the world's No. 2 vs. the world's No. 3, we're going to get one featuring a mystery guest.

Because, the other semifinal pitted the world's No. 35 vs. the world's No. 43. Jonas Bjorkman vs. Bohdan Ulihrach. Only a few spectators knew which was which.

Not that it matters. One of them won, 6-3, 6-2. I'm not sure which. The blond one.

Michael Chang, of course, we knew. But the way this tournament is going, he'll doubtless lose today to Bohdan Ulihrach. Or whoever that guy was who won the other semi in the Who-Are-These-Guys? Open, the Massacre at Indian Wells.

••••••••••••••••••••

May 4, 1997

A Memo to Shaq: Now Is the Time

All right, Miss Kelly B., let's take a memo to Shaquille O'Neal. That's right. Shaq, himself. Slug it "urgent." Also, "personal."

Dear Shaq,

I know we've been over this before, old buddy, but in the middle of the playoffs, it bears repeating.

It's about the championship, Shaq. You know, the top of the NBA heap.

Shaq, I don't know how to broach this to you, but I have to reemphasize it in case you've forgotten about your responsibility in this matter.

Look, Shaq, it's imperative L.A. win this title. As they say in other sports, this is what it's all about. No compromise. This is one case where winning is everything.

Remember when they had that first America's Cup yacht race and the U.S. won it and Queen Victoria asked her sailors who was second and their captain said, "Your Majesty, there is no second."

Well, that's the case here, Shaq. Look! They gave you all that money—what was it, 40, 50, 100 million? Something like that. Enough to buy a railroad.

They figured they were buying something else. They figured they were buying the championship, Shaq. It's a Laker tradition.

Check your history, Shaq. Back in 1968, the Lakers were tired of finishing second every year to the Boston Celtics because they didn't have a big man in the pivot. So Jack Kent Cooke went out and got the biggest—Wilt Chamberlain himself.

Now, Wilt had ricocheted between the Philadelphia and San Francisco franchises and had one championship to show for it—Philadelphia, 1967. But he had Bill Russell to try to dunk over in those days. And Russell had won 12 championships, eight in a row.

Wilt had these great stats. Threw in 50.4 points a game one year, led the world in rebounds. But no flags on the roof. You get my drift here, Shaq?

Well, Russell was in his final season by the time Wilt got to L.A. and Wilt finally paid off. He led the Lakers to a crown in 1972.

By that time, Wilt had figured something out. His point total dropped from 2,500-3,500 a year—he had a high of 4,029 in 1961-62—to 1,200-1,600. But his assists went from a low of 148 a year up to a league-leading 702 one year.

Something to think about, right, Shaq?

By that time, Cooke was casting eyes at the new kid on the block—a fellow named Kareem Abdul-Jabbar. He had won a championship at Milwaukee (with a little help from a fellow named Oscar Robertson), but he wasn't happy there. Jack twisted a few arms and got Kareem to L.A. in 1975.

That resulted in five championships for the Lakers. To be sure, Kareem didn't pay off immediately. Not till a rookie named Magic Johnson showed up here in 1979.

Beginning to see a pattern here, Shaq?

Now, in terms of 1960-1970 values, Cooke spent a lot of money for Wilt and Kareem. But, the top salary in the league in 1960 was only $19,000. Chamberlain had left much more than that on the table when he left the Globetrotters because he didn't care to play Barnum & Bailey basketball for a living.

But Cooke didn't hypothecate the huge dollar package you got, Shaq.

So, I think what we have here is a simple case of quid-pro-quo, Shaq.

I mean, we're not talking in terms of "doing our best," or "the old college try," or any other malarkey. We're talking "Show me the money!" here or, "Show me the championship, Shaq!"

It's implicit in that contract of yours. Jerry Buss wants that title flag hanging from the rafters.

They got lots of guys "doing their best." The Clippers got guys doing that.

Your "best" is not good enough, Shaq. We're talking championships here, not solo art.

You ask me how to do it? How should I know, Shaq? I just set policy here. Implementation is somebody else's problem. Yours, for instance. As Al Davis says, "Just win, baby!"

It isn't as if you said, "Well, I got my 35 points, too bad about the team." Your stats are impeccable too, Shaq. But, what we're looking for here is not "Nice try!" but "Take that!" In-your-face stuff. You're the "go to" guy. Attract a crowd, then go to the open man, maybe. You figure it out. Earn the money.

I'm glad to see you're paying attention to your free-throw shooting, at last. Sixty percent from the line in the playoffs is better than your 48%. Or your 39% of last year's playoffs. You can't let these guys put you on the line, knowing they're trading a sure two-point basket for a one-pointer. Or a no-pointer. Wilt was about a 50% free throw shooter most of his career—.380 in 1967-68. Abdul-Jabbar was in the 70s in free-throw percentage. Lord, Shaq, can't you almost touch the basket from the foul line?

So, to sum up, Shaq, let's make no mistake about it. You're supposed to come with that old gonfalon attached. How you do it is your problem. As that shoe ad says, Just do it! Never mind the Mailman, the Admiral, Hakeem the Dream, the Worm or even mighty Michael the Archangel. You the Man, Shaq!

Now that you've eliminated all those 6-2 dudes from Portland comes the fun part—Utah. No matter. You have to beat them. Period. Down the line, here comes Mr. Jordan. Piece of cake! Right, Shaq? Better be.

You come home wrapped in the pennant, Shaq. Look at it this way: You don't have any Bill Russell to get by. Michael Jordan? Pshaw! Michael Jordan would have had to shoot from midcourt all night to score over Bill Russell.

You got the shadows of Wilt and Kareem looming over you in the media guide. You want to be the one who didn't win the championship? I don't think so. You want a guy to be saying some day, "Who was that guy who came after Wilt and Kareem? The one who couldn't get the championship?" And you want the other guy to say, "I don't remember. Hack O'Hara, or something like that."?

I don't think so. So, cut to the chase, Shaq. We're tired of the Chicago Bulls and the Houston Whozits around here. It's time order was restored. You can do it. You have to. That's what they gave you all the money for.

Yrs. Insincerely,

JUNE 29, 1997

Tyson's a Two-Bit Fighter

LAS VEGAS—Well, Mike Tyson didn't need a new referee. He needed a rabies shot.

He has been hailed as having the fighting style of a wild animal.

He sure has. He proved it here Saturday night.

He tried to bite Evander Holyfield's ear off Saturday. Twice. Referee Mills Lane disqualified him before he tried to bite his nose off.

America's Wolfman made a mockery of the Marquess of Queensberry rules. He made a mockery of sportsmanship. He took pugilism back to the cave.

He is one disturbed young man. He should not be allowed to fight again. Unless it is against a hungry grizzly.

It had to be seen to be disbelieved. We've all heard of a "hungry" fighter. But never one who tried to eat his opponent.

The funny thing is, they might have spotted Tyson the first bite. Even though part of Holyfield's ear was missing, the ref just deducted a couple of points. But when Tyson chomped down again in the next round, they decided to get him out of there before he bit off more than he could chew.

It was such a shocking bit of cannibalism, they decided to halt the proceedings before Tyson tried to put him in a pot.

I guess people in the dawn of history settled matters that way. But today only dogs and mosquitoes get forgiven for biting. Prizefighting has rules. No kicking, choking, shooting, knifing—or biting.

Mike Tyson was unregenerate to the last. He had been butted, he insisted. "My career was on the line!" he exclaimed. He was entitled to retaliate, he felt. Removing an ear seemed to him to be a suitable reaction. For a mad dog, perhaps. But for a licensed pugilist?

Even Tyson's manager didn't seem to get the point. "A little nick on his ear don't mean nothin'," he screamed at the press. "My fighter had a three-inch cut."

Even Evander Holyfield was incredulous. You encounter a bear, a leopard, you protect yourself against a bite. But how do you stop a clinching opponent? "I thought my ear had fell off! Blood was all over!"

It was boxing's lowest moment. There are many things wrong with the manly art of self-defense, but we always thought those mouthpieces were in there to protect the teeth of the wearer, not the ear of an opponent.

"He spit the mouthpiece out when he bit me!" Holyfield revealed.

The heavyweight championship was awarded once in history on a disqualification, is our recollection. But that was when Max Schmeling lay on the floor and refused to get up after being hit low by Jack Sharkey. He was awarded the title even though the low blow was unintentional.

Tyson's foul was so intentional, he repeated it. Maybe he liked the taste of Evander's ear.

We are at a low point in our history. Our prizefighters bite each other, our ballplayers spit in your face.

Mike Tyson has been suspended "temporarily" by the Nevada State Athletic Commission. He gets a hearing as to whether his purse—a mere $30 million—should not be held up.

That may be the most expensive dining-out in history if the commission tries to make the "fine" stick.

Why did Mike Tyson do it. Well, that may be like asking a Doberman pinscher why it does it.

As this is written, newsmen are asking principals whether Holyfield will give Tyson a return match. Give Tyson a return fight?! What would Evander have to do—put ketchup on his ears?! Mustard on his nose?!

Mike Tyson should be allowed to fight only a thing that can bite back. His fighting days should be over.

Biting is a tactic of the overmatched. Mike Tyson was getting properly beaten up. Defeated partisans think up horror weapons. They bring in secret weapons. That's what Tyson did. He burst his moorings and began to assault the world in the ring.

I don't know what he could do to restore his dignity and professionalism. Become a vegetarian, for starters. But, I would think, given his history, he is the last guy in the world I would want to bite back.

It's not funny, it's a sad story. Ask Evander's plastic surgeon.

JULY 3, 1997

The Mike Tyson He Knew Showed Humor, Not Bite

All right, Miss B., take a letter to Mr. T. That's right, Mr. T., the quondam heavyweight champion. Boxing's Dracula. Half-pug, half-vampire. The Tooth Fairy.

"Dear Mike,

"I guess I go back with you as far as any other journalist. You remember, we rode to the Roy Firestone show in a stretch limo a few years ago. You were the up-and-coming heavyweight hope and you poked me in the ribs as we got in the car and you grinned 'You know, if I were around a limo like this five years ago, I'd be stealing the hubcaps.' You seemed to have an appealing sense of humor behind that frightening exterior and those bulging muscles.

"I don't want to say I defended you to many of my friends, but I did tell them I saw another side to the brute they perceived in mid-ring.

"I knew your co-manager Jimmy Jacobs well. He had been world handball champion and a world-class fight buff who collected boxing films all the way from the days of Thomas Edison's early kinescopes.

"I knew your other co-manager, Cus D'Amato. A man of dignity and probity, he also was the most paranoid fight manager I ever knew. I drove him and Floyd Patterson to the Olympic Auditorium one night (Floyd fought a man named Jimmy Slade) and I thought Cus was going to have a heart attack when I made a wrong turn. He suspected me of being Sammy the Bull. "Who are you?! Where are you taking us!? I have told the police to be on the lookout for our kidnapping!" he shrieked before I could calm him down.

"But, in spite of these derangements, you were in good hands, Mike. Cus kept you on a pretty tight leash. Because he knew you needed it. Jacobs inculcated a love of boxing history in you and you were the only guy I ever met who knew more boxing lore than I did. (You stumped me on Mickey Walker-Pete Latzo, remember, Mike?)

"When Jacobs and Cus died, you put your career in the hands of guys who would let you do anything you wanted. They were afraid to say no to you. They were as scared of you as Peter McNeeley was. Afraid of offending by offering even good advice you didn't want to hear. "Sure, Mike!" was their idea of guidance. You were a cash cow to them. Jimmy Jacobs never needed cash and Cus D'Amato had almost no interest in it.

"You were on top of the world, Mike. Or thought you were. Don King used to chortle you were 'the baddest man on the planet Earth' and if you weren't, you were getting there.

"The rape of Desiree Washington was the signal to the world you were out of control. You thought you were a law unto yourself. Athletes get that way. All the adulation, the publicity, the hype. You get a false sense of your own importance. It's called 'How dare you turn me down?! Don't you know who I am?!'

"Yeah. You're about 87 cents worth of zinc, iron, calcium and water like everyone else. A ranch mink is worth more than you skinned.

"Prison is supposed to be about rehabilitation. There are social scientists who think you could put a man-eating shark in prison for a year or two and, with 'help' (buzz word for therapy), he will come out a goldfish. Maybe so, but don't get in a pool with one, especially if your nose is bleeding.

"I don't know how you came out of prison mentally, Mike, but it looks as if you went right back to the same sycophants, leeches and manipulators with which most fighters surround themselves.

"The inevitable happened. The one dignity you had left was your athletic prowess. When Evander Holyfield robbed you of that, you couldn't deal with it. You became obsessed with revenge. It would make everything all right. I mean, how dare Holyfield? Didn't he know with whom he was dealing?

"When it became obvious by the second round you weren't going to make everything all right, that it was deja vu all over again (as Yogi says), you burst your moorings. Your eye was bleeding, you couldn't hurt Holyfield, I think you would have killed him if you had a knife. You did the next worst thing, something that was the most disgusting thing I have ever seen, not only in a prize ring but anywhere else. Maybe Jeffrey Dahmer did it, but they didn't sell tickets. It wasn't on pay-per-view.

"I don't know whether you couldn't handle fame or fame couldn't handle you. You want to be allowed to fight again? Why, Mike? So you can get the rest of his ear? So you can punch out more cops, spit at more customers, encourage more lobby riots?

"I don't think so, Mike. We've kind of lost the capacity for indignation in this country. Forgiveness is the 'in' thing.

"But, boxing shouldn't forgive you. You made it seem like a citadel of depravity. As a student of its history, let me ask you—do you think Joe Louis would ever behave like that? Rocky Marciano? Dempsey? Jack Johnson? Ali? Lord, even Sonny Liston? I don't think so.

"Letting you back in the ring would be like letting Hannibal Lecter in a prom. If you fight Holyfield again, what are they going to release it as—'Jaws, the Sequel'?

"If we want to see things get bitten, we'll go to a cockfight. So, wipe the blood off your teeth. I wouldn't go to see you and Evander Holyfield again even if you wore a muzzle and he wore earmuffs."

• • • • • • • • • • • • • • • • • • • •

JULY 26, 1997

Ben Hogan Dies, But Not the Mystique

Ben Hogan was more than an athlete to me.

Hogan was mythic. Hogan was my idol. "Charisma" doesn't begin to describe the hold Hogan had on our imaginations, on the golfing public's.

We held Hogan, who died Friday at the age of 84, to a higher standard than we did the rest of the sports world.

To us, he was like the cowboy hero of a thousand Saturday afternoon serials. He could do no wrong, could never let you down.

The golf game is awash with Hogan stories. My favorite is the time Hogan was playing Riviera. Now, Hogan never asked a caddie anything except maybe what time it was. But after his drive on 15, he looked at the ball, the green in the distance, and turned to his caddie and said, "What's the shot?" And the caddie squinted at the green, threw grass in the air, and said, "Mr. Hogan, it's 146-147 yards." Hogan scowled at him. "Make up your mind!" he ordered.

How good was he? The latest book about him ("Hogan" by Curt Sampson) notes that he teed it up in 292 lifetime tournaments and he finished in the top ten 241 times—and in the top three 139 times! Are you paying attention, Tiger?

Even his losses were epic. Jack Fleck beat him in a playoff for the U.S. Open in 1955, but Fleck was never the man who won the Open that year; he was the man who deprived Ben Hogan of his fifth U.S. Open championship, who committed an offense against nature. He might have come to wish he hadn't.

Hogan was quite simply—with apologies to Jack Nicklaus, Arnold Palmer and even Tiger Woods—the best striker of the ball who ever played.

It didn't come naturally to him; he mastered it, subdued it, as he did every challenge in his life. Hogan was grim, stubborn, stable and relentless. He practiced till his hands bled. He didn't worry about being long off the tee, although he was. He hit the ball where he wanted to, not where it wanted to. Where it left the best next shot.

I worshiped him, revered him. My finest hour in the game came once in a practice round Palmer was enduring at Rancho. On one hole, he hit the ball dead left, into a buried lie underneath beer cans, pine cones, fallen branches, even squirrels. Arnold spotted me, hitched up his pants and growled, "OK, wise guy, what would your idol Hogan do here?" I smiled. "Hogan wouldn't be here," I told him. Arnold laughed. Hogan had all the trouble shots. He just didn't need them much.

I never could understand why Ben didn't call the cops when I came into view in his life. I was bad news to him. It began when I did principal work on the cover story we ran on him in Time magazine in 1949. I had followed him for five days. I grew to respect him more than anyone I had ever interviewed. The night the story was closing, we had a chart illustrating Hogan's "average" distance with a driver, a four-wood, seven-iron, etc. Hogan frowned. "There's no average distance!" he exclaimed. "It depends on the time of day, the temperature, whether it's cloudy or foggy, the lie, the composition of the grass!"

"Ben!" I screamed. "They're holding the presses at Donnelly in Chicago at $40,000 a minute!" No matter. We had to get it right or no Hogan OK.

The point is, after the Time cover appeared, Hogan got hit by that bus on his way home in Texas, giving rise to the "Time cover jinx." (Sugar Ray Robinson was later to lose his first fight after appearing on our cover, solidifying the hoodoo.)

Next, I was sitting with Ben in the locker room at the Olympic Club in San Francisco just after he had apparently won the '55 Open when over the transom above our heads began to trickle announcements of birdies by someone named Jack Fleck. A black day. Fleck tied him and was to win the playoff the next day. I was beginning to feel around Ben like that guy in "Li'l Abner" who goes around with a cloud over his head.

I wrote about him extensively over the years, all aspects of the Hogan mystique. His name, for instance.

"Throughout the history of civilization, there have been syllables of terror handed down from generation to generation. 'Geronimo,' for example, could be counted on to empty one fort after another in the old West. 'Attila' would strike as much naked fear as the plague. In the littler world of golf, 'Hogan' elicited much the same effect. Nothing could paralyze a field of golfers as much as this whispered collection of syllables. Strong men bogeyed when they heard this dreaded name. Sam Snead once said the only thing he feared on a golf course was lightning—and Ben Hogan."

When he couldn't putt any more (he was in his 50s), I wrote about that sadly.

"I never saw any of man's baser acts of inhumanity to man. I never saw screaming 'witches' burned at the stake, Christians tossed to starving lions, maidens pushed over the edge of active volcanoes. I never even saw a man going to the electric chair. But until I do, watching Ben Hogan walk up to a five-foot putt is my idea of cruel and inhuman punishment, only a Hitler would enjoy. You feel like saying, 'Go home to your wife and kiddies and don't look upon this terrible thing!' "

What did he do to engender these kinds of lyrical outbursts? Well, in 1953, one of his last productive years on the greens and fairways (limited after his bus accident because he lacked a vena cava and had to stand on his head in the morning to get the blood flowing), he teed it up in six tournaments. And won five of them. And what five! The Masters, the U.S. Open, the British Open, the Colonial and Pan-American Open. It's as close as anybody has ever come to the modern Grand Slam. And Hogan didn't tee it up in the PGA because it was match play in those days and you had to walk 36 holes the last two days. His legs couldn't.

In 1956 he almost won his fifth Open again and inspired a rival, Mike Souchak, to blurt one day, "Ben Hogan just knows something about hitting a golf ball the rest of us don't!"

In 1960, at the age of 48, he again could have won his fifth Open. He hit 34 consecutive greens on the last day, all 18 in the morning. He later told me he really hit the 17th in the afternoon but the ball had so much backspin it trickled back into the water. "I had to put the ball close 'cause I couldn't make any putt over six feet and I fine-tuned it too much."

What kind of man was he? Well, they said he was cold, aloof and a loner. A boy whose father shot and killed himself in front of his family when the boy was 9 years old is not apt to be a cutup. He kept the world at bay. But he could be fun-loving, a wonderful dinner companion to share a pre-meal martini with. Hogan didn't care whether you liked him or not, just whether you respected him.

Hogan played micrometer golf. He was a man of uncompromising integrity. He was married to the same woman, the marvelous Valerie, for 62 years. It was a great love story. Valerie lived because Hogan threw himself in front of her in that bus accident in 1949. They took care of each other.

Some years ago, Tom Laughlin wanted to do a new Hogan picture and said Ben wanted me to do it. I was thrilled. I spent a magical week with the Hogans and the Laughlins in Palm Springs. But I couldn't make the cut. I couldn't lick the script.

After all, it was Hogan, wasn't it? When someone said he wanted "warts and all," I said, "What warts?"

•••••••••••••••••••

AUGUST 14, 1997

Return to the Scene Of the Crime

MAMARONECK, N.Y.—In 1973, Johnny Miller, the golfer, committed a terrible crime. He shot a 63 in the final round of a U.S. Open to win by a shot.

Now, to the doyens of all golf, the United States Golf Assn., this was an unpardonable sin on a par with voting Communist, painting mustaches on the Mona Lisa, eating with your hat on.

Drastic action was called for. Order had to be restored. Punishment was in order.

So the USGA took the venue for the next year's Open, Winged Foot, and carved it into a proper Hall of Horrors so no other golfer would be able to demonstrate such callous disregard for the hallowed traditions of the game.

What did they do to Winged Foot in 1974? Well, let me begin with Jack Nicklaus, who is probably Numero Uno among all who have ever played the game.

Nicklaus had won three U.S. Opens and 11 majors and about 50 tournaments in all when he teed it up at Winged Foot.

Nicklaus was probably one of the 10 best putters who ever lived. But as he lined up a 25-foot putt on the first green of the opening round that year, he looked like you and me. He putted that 25-footer. And he ended up 25 feet past the hole.

That was really all we had to know about Winged Foot that year. They had made those greens like spun glass. When Jack Nicklaus rolls a putt 25 feet past the cup, you know what you're in for.

It wasn't a tournament, it was a death march. Hale Irwin didn't win it, he survived it. The fairways were littered with the bones of competitors who didn't.

The course was lengthened, the greens were shaved. The fourth hole was 25 yards longer and the 18th was 25 yards longer than they had been when the Open had last been played there (in 1959, when Billy Casper had won). It was demonic. "Who was the architect—the Marquis de Sade?" the writer Bob Drum demanded as we got our first look at the unputtable undulations.

The USGA needn't have worried about anyone shooting a 63 over this tapestry of terror. The average score for the first round was 77.

Now, that might be OK for the Truck Drivers' Local member-guest. But these were, certifiably, the greatest players in the world. Winged Foot leveled them to the stature of guys whose foursomes you'd want to get into and bets you'd want to take at Montalvo Municipal.

The cut was a lusty 153—13 over par.

There were 104 (count 'em!) scores in the 80s. And 26 guys couldn't break 80 at all. Even of the guys who made the cut, 13 had rounds in the 80s, and 41 guys couldn't break 300.

Five former Open champions (Tony Jacklin, Gene Littler, Casper, Lee Trevino, Ken Venturi) missed the cut. One player, Bill Erfurth, shot 32 over par, which meant, effectively, that he had bogeyed every hole but two in each of his two rounds.

The carnage was so total, Dick Schaap was to write a book titled "Massacre at Winged Foot."

It was such a miasma of missed putts, buried lies and non-negotiable sand traps (the USGA cut in enough new traps to make some holes look like the outskirts of Casablanca) that Johnny Miller, he of the 63, stood in a trap on the seventh hole and three times his explosion shot hit the lip and trickled back down to his feet. He took a quadruple bogey.

Somewhere in the clubhouse lounge, you surmised the USGA types were smiling broadly.

Miller made the cut (narrowly) but not only couldn't fashion another 63, he could barely make a 74 (76-75-74-77—302).

Now, ordinarily, your reporter here is a big fan of double bogeys. A 63 offends me almost as much as it does the USGA. But even I began to feel the pangs of pity. I used to walk the fairways of an Open in those days hoping to stumble upon a player having to hit left-handed out of a tree trunk or faced with an unplayable lie in a clump of poison ivy, but I began to feel like Florence Nightingale abroad in a No-Man's Land of the dead and dying.

I came upon Nicklaus on one of these forays as he was throwing a little 76 at the course one afternoon and he spotted me and stopped. "How can you stand to watch this—I can hardly stand to play it!" he said, shaking his head. Nicklaus had 136 putts over the four days, the most of anyone in the tournament.

But it had its moments. In the middle of all those bogeys, there was this young player from Missouri who looked as if he had just stepped out of the pages of Mark Twain. It was here Tom Watson (who looked more like Tom Sawyer) first served notice he was to be reckoned with. Two weeks later, at the Western Open, he was to win his first tournament.

He could also have won at Winged Foot. Tom had to claw his way into the Open that year via sectional qualifying, but he led the Open after three rounds with a 213 to Irwin's 214. But Watson faltered to a nine-over 79 on the last day, troubled with a few smother-hooks and putts that lipped out while Irwin kept the wheels on for a creditable 73. He beat Watson by five and Forrest Fezler by two.

Fezler might have won, but, on two holes, with a sand trap between him and the green, he hit the ball short and into the trap, leaving this kind of mistake shot known to the press as "fezzling" or a "fezzle."

A golf tournament is never one golfer against another. Your foe is the course. Hale Irwin got the cup. But Winged Foot won the tournament.

The 63 had been avenged. Incredibly, there were two more 63s on Open scoreboards—Nicklaus and Tom Weiskopf shot 63s at Baltusrol in 1980—but the USGA took that in stride. The Open the next year—at Merion—was not as punitive and not one of the players surviving the cut shot in the 80s.

And, in 1984, when the Open returned to Winged Foot, only four players couldn't break 300. Instead of seven over par, Fuzzy Zoeller and Greg Norman were four under, Zoeller winning in a playoff.

Winged Foot is still nobody's palooka. It still may have the unkindest cut of all this week at the PGA. But the golfers will not all feel as if they have been tied to a stake and the sticks at their feet set ablaze. Or as if they should leave word with their loved ones what to do with the remains as they tee it up. Winged Foot '74 was the Titanic of tournaments. The ultimate victory of nature over man on the golf course.

•••••••••••••••••••

SEPTEMBER 28, 1997

90 Years of Ridin' The Range

They called him "The Cowboy" and everybody loved him.

He never went anywhere without a 10-gallon hat and snakeskin boots. A string tie, if it was formal. He was a legit son of the pioneers, born on the lone prairie of Tioga, Texas, where the deer and antelope play and the skies are not cloudy all day.

He was always a happy sort. He was a telegrapher by trade in Oklahoma in his youth and, one day, as he was sitting between wirelesses, playing his guitar, fate walked in. It was the greatest cowboy of them all, Will Rogers, and he was wiring in his daily newspaper column.

Rogers listened to a cowboy lament sung by the young man and he said, "Son, you're wasting your time sending copy. Go to New York and get yourself into show business."

So, Gene Autry did. Only he went west instead of east and became one of the most beloved show business figures in the history of the movie industry. He made 94 feature films as the original singing cowboy.

His pictures were a staple of Saturday matinees all over the world. He never killed anybody in his pictures, just lassoed the varmints and, at the fade-out, rode off in the sunset, singing about home on the range.

He never got an Academy Award. They usually gave that to some artiste whose picture lost a million at the box office. But the exhibitors loved him and complained that they wanted a Gene Autry picture instead of one of those costume dramas where everyone went around saying "Forsooth!"

Everything he touched turned to platinum. He was a canny businessman whose handshake was as good as a 100-page signed contract. He went away to war, even though his producer, Herbert Yates, threatened to make Roy Rogers a star in his stead if he went through with his enlistment.

He wrote blockbuster songs with collaborators. "Back in the Saddle Again" became almost as famous as "Home on the Range." He wrote "That Silver Haired Daddy of Mine" and the whole country cried. He was grand marshal of the annual Hollywood Santa Claus parade and he wrote "Here Comes Santa Claus," which almost rivaled "White Christmas." In fact, Irving Berlin stopped him on stage one night and told him he wished he could write cowboy songs too.

Autry pioneered what has become country and western music. But he was not infallible. One day, they brought him a Christmas song he didn't think had a chance and he proposed to put it on the flip side of a record he deemed better. But his late wife, Ina, protested.

"It's the song of the ugly duckling! It's beautiful!" she told him.

So Gene Autry recorded "Rudolph the Red-Nosed Reindeer." It only became the biggest-selling record of all time.

Gene bought radio stations, TV stations, bankrolled movies. He had parlayed a guitar and a saddle into megamillions and, in 1960, when baseball was going to expand, he and his partner, the late Bob Reynolds, traveled to the winter meetings to see about a radio contract with the new expansion team in L.A.

Instead of the contract, he got the team. Baseball was overjoyed to have such an immensely popular and impeccable character. And Gene, a lifelong baseball fan, became not only the Angels' owner but No. 1 rooter.

He was in the locker room as often as the trainer. In a way, Gene remained a little boy all his life. I don't think anybody ever saw him mad. In all the years I knew him, I never even heard him curse. He never acted rich. He always acted as if he had just left the bunkhouse.

He was the first owner to move his team out of L.A. But he went only 36 miles down the road to the suburbs, Anaheim. He really just wanted to get out of Dodger Stadium, where his team was like the sister with the buck teeth rooming with her beauty queen sibling.

His baseball team didn't break his heart. Gene didn't deal in heartbreak. He was as optimistic as a kid on Christmas morning all his life.

But real disappointment struck on Oct. 12, 1986. In the pennant playoff against the Boston Red Sox, the Angels, leading three games to one, had two outs and a 5-4 lead in the ninth inning—Boston had a man on base—and needed only one strike to win the '86 pennant and get into the World Series.

Alas! The batter, a slumping journeyman named Dave Henderson, hit a two-run homer that gave the Red Sox the lead—and ultimately the pennant.

It was one of the few unhappy endings of Gene's career. Even that day, his team tied the score in the bottom of the ninth and had the bases loaded and only one out. All they needed was a fly ball to bring a runner—and the pennant—home. But his last two batters couldn't do it.

A terrible footnote to this ill-fated afternoon was that the losing pitcher, Donnie Moore, was to take his own life less than three years later.

Gene will be 90 on Monday. A gala fund-raising dinner will be held at the Gene Autry Museum of Western Heritage that night. Eddy Arnold, Rosemary Clooney, Willie Nelson, Roy Clark and Glen Campbell are on the bill.

I went out to see Gene the other day. We go way back—to the days when I was a young magazine reporter and he was the king of Gower Gulch.

Gene is in the capable hands of his lovely wife, Jackie, who protects his sunset days.

He and I struggled through mists of memory to recall the magical days of yore. The casts of characters of Westerns are as long gone as silent pictures. Jimmy Stewart, Hank Fonda, Duke Wayne, Tom Mix and Gary Cooper have all headed for the last roundup. Only Gene remains.

He's still the Angels' Angel. Keeps 75% of the club but Disney runs it. He still thinks of the one pitch that got away.

Maybe it'll always be 1945 again and he'll be whistling for Champion after struggling out of the bonds the rustlers put on him. Maybe it'll be the ninth inning again and this time Doug DeCinces will hit that long fly to center with the pennant flying on it.

Did he have any regrets? I wondered.

"Not a one," smiled the last cowboy. "I'd like to do it all over again!"

••••••••••••••••••••

DECEMBER 11, 1997

Authority Has Become A Real Choke in Sports

In 1925, Babe Ruth, who was only the best baseball player there ever was, threatened to "punch the spit" out of his manager, Miller Huggins, called him a few obscenities, stalked out of the (St. Louis) locker room and didn't go back to New York with the team.

He was suspended from the team and fined (five grand was a lot in those days). He took the train to Chicago to protest to the commissioner of baseball, Judge Kenesaw Landis. And Landis told him to take a hike.

Then, in New York, at a banquet, the mayor of the city, Jimmy Walker, upbraided the Babe for his behavior and, in an emotional speech, begged him to stop letting down all the "dirty-faced" little kids who looked up to him. The Babe wept, history tells us.

In 1997, an all-star basketball player, Latrell Sprewell, also called his coach a few obscene names, then threatened to kill him and put his hands around his throat and tried to throttle him. Pulled off him, he later returned to throw a punch at him.

Then, in San Francisco, the mayor of the city, Willie Brown, cheered Sprewell to the echo and said the coach had it coming. It might be the first time in history a mayor of a city endorsed an aggravated assault, but it must have been a great comfort to city hall employees to know they could go in and choke their mayor whenever he did something that displeased them.

The lesson at work here is that constituted authority is in full, mindless retreat, not to say rout, these days. A wide receiver on the Oakland Raiders said the other day he is going to call his own plays on the line of scrimmage hereafter and ignore the coach's.

The inmates taking over the asylum? The elephants running the circus?

No. But disrespect for authority is at an all-time high in this country. In a recent interview with Ira Berkow in the New York Times, the basketball coach at Boston University who had his own star-player trouble noted, "Respect for authority has eroded. It's not just with coaches, it's with authority figures across the board. You tell a guy you want him to improve his free-throw shooting, he takes it that you don't like him. You know, 'You're dissing me!' A line I never thought guys would cross is crossed more easily every year."

Part of the problem, Coach Dennis Wolff told Berkow, is that players today have been "coddled" since they first demonstrated their jump shot or vertical leap. That's why some of them are a case of arrested development.

Sometimes, Wolff told Berkow, it's that the kid did not have a strong father figure in the home to lay down the law.

"Authority," of course, depends on the author. Authority gone mad as we have seen in Europe this century is an obscene horror that calls into question the whole concept. There are times it should have its throat strangled. Authority should always be questioned. The crew of the Bounty had good reason to mutiny. So did George Washington, you should excuse the expression.

But authority for the group good is another matter. Presumably, there was no authority in prehistoric times. Each man did what he wanted, the group be damned.

It was probably the Romans who created the modern notion of authority. They created the table of organization and built aqueducts and formed military chains of command and built a great civilization and brought discipline where there had been chaos. A blueprint for the world, even the Green Bay Packers, so to speak. They harnessed the human energy to work for a common good. Where once 10 guys might want to get together to build a bridge but the project would collapse when half of them stayed home, the Romans conscripted a whole society.

Their legions regularly defeated numerically superior forces with their organizational genius, their leadership. It has been noted by history that wherever the Roman legions went in the world, the civilization advanced. The areas the Romans bypassed remained backward.

What has this to do with athletes strangling their coaches? Just this: All sports, like Caesar's Gaul, are divided into three parts—players, coaches and owners. They have to work together. You render to Caesar (i.e., the coach) the things that are Caesar's.

It's the way things work. The legacy of western civilization, ever since we climbed out of the primordial ooze, is that man advances by teamwork and leadership. Otherwise you take on the world by your lonesome. Rugged individualism is overrated. No laws, no bosses, then no progress. Let me ask you: You want to see Latrell Sprewell take on the Chicago Bulls by himself? Even Michael Jordan needs a coach. If not for himself, at least for what he has called "my supporting cast."

We have all had our crosses to bear. I have had city editors I would like to introduce to Latrell Sprewell. Once I had a colleague, Will Fowler, who was so furious at our city editor, Jim Richardson, he ran screaming to his father, Gene Fowler, the great author. "Son," Gene said, "if he knows his business, you stand there and let him throw sockfuls of manure at you. So long as you learn."

Richardson's tantrums turned out some pretty good newspapermen. I don't doubt Carlesimo had some uncomplimentary things to say about his players. So did Vince Lombardi. Knute Rockne. Does that justify felonious assault?

Blaming the victim has become a national pastime anyway. If they ever caught Jack the Ripper, he would have been ready. The women asked for it, he would have contended. And called the mayor of San Francisco as a character witness.

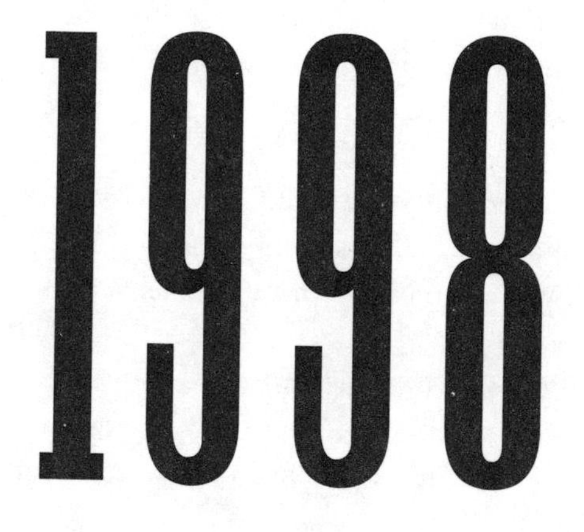
1998

JANUARY 2, 1998

Stars Get Eclipsed By the Rising Son

Washington State is in a rut. Every 67 years, regular as clockwork, the Cougars come to the Rose Bowl.

So, they have plenty of time to get it right.

Alas, it's back to the drawing board.

They missed the point again. They tried valiantly. They did manage to score in the Rose Bowl for the first time in 82 years.

They had the ball when the game ended and they had Michigan defenders trying to look over both shoulders at once. But time ran out.

As Rose Bowl games go, it was half-good. That is to say the second half was goose-pimple football. The first half was just more exciting than home movies, a 7-7 ho-hum, let-me-outta-here! What the fight mob calls an "agony fight."

Just as you were beginning to wonder if either one of them could win it, they took the gloves off. The final half was a slugfest, playground football. Dempsey-Firpo, Tommy Hearns and Marvin Hagler.

It was billed as Washington State quarterback Ryan Leaf vs. Michigan cornerback Charles Woodson, the Heisman Trophy winner. If so, it was a draw. In the first half, Leaf completed one pass to his end in the end zone and one to Woodson there.

In the second half, they were both upstaged by a guy who wasn't supposed to be a star, just a supporting player. Who found himself in the last place he wanted to be—the limelight.

Brian Griese's father could have told him. Dad had the same trouble back in 1967. He led Purdue to its only Rose Bowl appearance in history but the game-of-the-day award went to a defensive back even though Griese's passes were the difference.

His son, Brian, was supposed to be a chip off the old block, a similar non-factor Thursday. The word on Griese, the son, was for Washington State to ignore the passing. Michigan was supposed to run the ball down their throats. "Let him pass" was the watchword on him. Griese didn't have a gun for an arm.

The hell he didn't. Young Master Griese was only the player of the game. He's supposed to put passes in motion that are little more than complicated handoffs, but some of his throws looked like moon-shots. He's supposed to run only if a bear is chasing him, he's supposed to be just faster than fourth-class mail, but he scrambled for 28 yards.

He was only supposed to throw Texas Leaguer passes, but he completed three touchdown passes—for 58, 53 and 23 yards.

He was supposed to rely on an ingenious receiver but he completed 18 passes to eight different receivers.

Leaf, Griese's opposite on Washington State, was hardly disgraced. He was a natural with the football in his hand right up till the clock was reading 0:02.

Michigan finally figured a way to put the game in the hangar late in the game. They hit on the most basic of all strategies: Don't let the other guys have the ball, except on kickoffs.

They kept it for 6 minutes 47 seconds in the final quarter when they led, 21-16. It had been so long since Washington State had the ball, the Cougars almost forgot what it looked like.

They didn't have it much. But, turned out, they didn't need it much.

Michigan turned it over to Leaf and company on WSU's seven-yard line with only 29 seconds left to play.

Ten seconds later, Leaf, who has an intercontinental missile for an arm, had the Cougars near midfield, and, one pass-and-lateral later, had a first down on the Michigan 26. With two seconds left to play.

Michigan was ready to call 911. But then Leaf tried to spike a center snap onto the ground and leave himself one second for a last pass into the end zone. But two seconds in Rose Bowls are not like two seconds in an NBA game.

It was a sad way to end a game. The rest of his life, Leaf may see himself getting off a throw for the history books, the pass that won the Rose Bowl with zero seconds on the clock.

No one wants to take a called strike with the World Series on the line or blow Wimbledon on a double-fault. You don't like to be putting the ball on the ground when the clock strikes midnight for this Cinderella.

So, Brian Griese got the glass slipper, probably much to his annoyance.

He had come into the game just as he had wished—dismissed, neglected, unnoticed. A mole. A guy you don't pay attention to till too late.

"He's tremendously underrated, he's not supposed to be able to throw the football long or run downhill. He'll fool you," his coach, Lloyd Carr, explained afterward.

Griese himself explained, "I didn't want the limelight. I just want to be part of the team. I don't like to be singled out, get attention."

Too late, young Griese. In spite of your best efforts at camouflage, someone notices. "Hey! This guy is good!" You won the Rose Bowl—with a little help from your friends. You have blown your cover. You're famous. Like Dad.

Deal with it.

• • • • • • • • • • • • • • • • • • • •

JANUARY 11, 1998

He's the Mouth That Scored for Lakers

When they refer to a player as a "sixth man" in basketball, they usually mean a guy who comes off the bench when the team is in retreat, takes the ball, picks the team up again, turns the game around and rights the situation. John Havlicek of the old Boston Celtics comes to mind.

But the best sixth man I ever saw never made a basket, drew a foul, blocked a shot, inbounded a pass or grabbed a rebound for his team.

You know, the Lakers over the years have had some pretty valuable individuals—Elgin Baylor, Jerry West, Wilt Chamberlain, Kareem Abdul-Jabbar, Magic Johnson. A "Who's Who of Basketball."

But the best backcourt man they ever had was Chick Hearn.

You had to be there to know. I know. Because I was.

The Lakers picked up Chick Hearn for a song. He was no threat to any salary cap, but nobody with a basketball was any more valuable to the franchise than Chick with a microphone.

The Lakers had newly arrived from Minnesota, where they had been going broke, when Chick first joined them. Bob Short, the owner, was thinking of putting the team in a leaky boat in the Pacific at the time and cutting his losses when he approached Chick.

Chick knew basketball as few did. He had played in the AAU, the NBA of its time, and he had broadcast the frenetic high school tournaments in his native Illinois.

Short persuaded Chick to do the play-by-play of a playoff game the Lakers and St. Louis Hawks were contesting. The result, I can sum up in one anecdote:

The week before, the Lakers and Hawks drew 2,800 fans to the Sports Arena for a playoff game. Chick did the next game at St. Louis on radio. When the teams came back to Los Angeles, there were 15,000 in the seats. They have more or less been there for every game since.

Before Chick, basketball broadcasts were just more interesting than test patterns. Basketball was a stepchild of sports at the time anyway. The old-time columnists referred to it as "whistle ball" or "bounce ball," a game for guys who didn't like to get their hair mussed in a real game like football.

Chick Hearn made it seem like World War III. He almost reinvented the game, gave it a whole new language. "Give and go," "turnaround jumper," "dribble-drive to the basket," "going for the hole" came into the lexicon of the game, maybe even "slam dunk."

Guys didn't just bring the ball upcourt, they were "yo-yoing the ball to the top of the key." Players didn't just get fooled, they got "faked into the popcorn machine." "Airball" might have been a Hearnism. "Sky hook" definitely was.

Jerry West became "Mr. Clutch." The team of Johnson and Abdul-Jabbar became "Showtime." The game wasn't just iced when the lead got big, it was put "in the refrigerator."

Chick was no rah-rah boy, no cheerleader.

"Why doesn't he sleep on his own time?" he would complain on the air about a local player who seemed to have lost interest in the game.

Chick and the Lakers were a match made in heaven. Romeo-meets-Juliet stuff. Laurel and Hardy. Before Chick Hearn, the Lakers played at junior college gyms, on stage at the Shrine Auditorium, wherever they could light. Then, Jack Kent Cooke bought the team and built the Forum. Chick filled it. Cooke signed him to an exclusive contract.

He's still filling it. The game has gone through many changes, but the one constant was Francis Dayle Hearn.

You know, you hear about Cal Ripken Jr. And Lou Gehrig, the "Iron Horse." A.C. Green, who has played in 930 consecutive NBA games.

Wilt Chamberlain played in 1,205 games, 55,418 minutes. Abdul-Jabbar played 1,797 games, 66,297 minutes.

Great longevity? Magnificent dependability! Showing up for work and ready all those years.

But how about Chickie Baby? On Jan. 19 at the Great Western Forum, he will be working his 3,000th consecutive game for the Lakers. You don't even want to know how many minutes that comes to. And that's only since 1965. He had done five years of sporadic games before then.

Match that around the league.

There was almost no such game in L.A. till Chick came aboard. Tommy Hawkins, an original L.A. Laker, remembers riding around in a sound truck through the neighborhoods, ballyhooing the game: "Hi! I'm Tommy Hawkins of the Lakers. Why don't you come out and see us play the New York Knicks Saturday night? Plenty of good seats available."

The sound of Chick Hearn did more for the team. The Lakers prospered. And carried the pro game along with them.

Of all the minutes of all the nights he has broadcast, Chick says he remembers best the night in 1970 when West threw in a basket from his own backcourt at the buzzer against the Knicks in an NBA final. It only tied the game. Today, it would have been a three-point basket and won.

It was a fateful moment in Laker history. But I would opt for a different one. I would put in there the night Short turned to assistant Lou Mohs and said, "How about if we try to get this fellow Chick Hearn to broadcast our games? I like his flair."

That was 10 years before the guys on the team now were even born. They should get a nickname for Chick too. "Mr. Clutch" still has a nice ring to it.

• •

FEBRUARY 5, 1998

Golf's for Athletes—Sorry

OK, if they let Casey Martin play in golf tournaments in a cart, first of all, they have to let every player ride one.

You see, being able to ride is an incalculable advantage. The whole point of golf is being able to concentrate. Your ability to concentrate wanes the more tired you get. Anyone who thinks fatigue doesn't enter into golf doesn't know golf. Period.

Not muscle fatigue, mental fatigue.

The fourth major golf tournament, the PGA Championship, used to be match play. What you had to do was play 18 holes in the morning, then 18 in the afternoon, as many as six 18-hole matches with a 36-hole final.

You had to be an athlete to do that. As the rules-makers intended.

Perhaps you noticed in the recent tournament at Pebble Beach, Tom Lehman shot a 64 and was quick to acknowledge his 64 was in large part due to the fact he fashioned it playing 18 holes over two days, nine holes a day.

In 1953, Ben Hogan, still hobbled from a near-fatal accident four years before, had won three majors—the U.S. Open, British Open and the Masters. He could have achieved the only Grand Slam (all four majors in one year) in the history of golf had he been able to ride in a PGA. No one even considered allowing it.

I applaud society's tendencies to make life easier for those of us who are handicapped. I cheer for street-corner ramps, special sections for wheelchairs at sporting events, Braille on elevator buttons and so on.

And I agree golf has to obey the laws of the land. Who called more attention to the infamous "Caucasians Only" clause in the PGA charter than I did?

But I draw the line at the court's right to make playing rules for the game. I have long since resented the lawyers' intrusions in the games people play.

Congress didn't invent the game of golf and it has no business dictating how it should be played. The law should rule on the laws of the land, not the infield-fly rule. Or the out-of-bounds rule.

Let's take a ludicrous example. I admit, it's ludicrous but it's illustrative. Suppose I yearned for a big league baseball career. But I couldn't hit the curveball. Should I go get a lawyer to file suit, get an injunction against the pitchers throwing me a curveball? Say it interferes with my right to make a living?

Preposterous, I know. But don't bet me some lawyer isn't scratching his chin today and thinking, "Hmm?" Let me ask you: As my colleague Mike Downey has pointed out, shouldn't they have changed the rules and outlawed the bunt when the one-legged pitcher Monty Stratton took the mound? The only humane thing to do, right? But how would, say, a Maury Wills get on base?

They had a one-armed outfielder (Pete Gray) once (during World War II). But they didn't get a rule saying runners could not cop another base on him while he was changing the ball from glove to throwing hand. Some shyster with a slow day might have found a way to get his name in all the papers by filing suit on his behalf. No one takes a base because the right fielder is handicapped?

The fields of play, unfortunately, are for the fit. Infirmities block a lot of us from taking part in the games we love. Inferior eyesight, insufficient speed, poor center of gravity, too raw a nervous system.

You level the field socially, not physically. It was Jimmy Connors, the tennis player, who once sneered at golf, "How can it be a sport when nobody runs?" Well, how can it be a sport when nobody even walks?

In 1964, Ken Venturi won the U.S. Open, playing the last 36 holes on a day when the heat was so unbearable he played the last nine holes with a worried doctor trailing behind. He finished near delirium, dehydrated, hallucinatory, exhausted. But he won his Open.

Now, would it have been fair for him to have been overtaken on that last day by a golfer playing in a canvas-covered cart with maybe a fan on the steering column?

The rules require that a man be able to walk the five miles or so on a sometimes hilly golf course, week after week, round after round and have the stamina and strength to fend off fatigue for at least 18 holes and score. Only a handful of the millions of golfers the world over can do it at the professional level.

Walking is an integral part of the game. Golf is not bridge, poker, fishing. The center of golf is concentrating. Physical effort chips away at your ability to do that. I'll give you one personal example: I used to walk 36 holes a day covering a golf Open, 18 in the morning, 18 in the afternoon. Until one year at Winged Foot, I came back to the press room too exhausted to concentrate properly. I wrote a lousy column and I never walked a course like that again. I rode.

The Americans With Disabilities Act is meant to give the disabled an opportunity. It's not meant to give them an advantage.

If it is, it's unconstitutional.

•••••••••••••••••••

FEBRUARY 8, 1998

He Might Also Be A Legend as Coach

No one ever played the game of basketball any better than Larry Bird; not Michael Jordan, Oscar Robertson, Magic Johnson, Jerry West. Nobody.

The thing was, he was like DiMaggio in baseball. When the ball came down, Joe was under it. So was Bird. He was always in the right place at the right time. Never out of position. And when he had the ball, you had two—or three—points. When he was at the line, forget it. He made 319 of 343 free throws one season. In the playoffs one year, he made 101 of 109. Don't foul him. You might as well let him shoot. It's at least two any way you look at it.

He couldn't jump much. He didn't have to. He wasn't fast, but he was as quick as a Times Square pickpocket. He stole 1,556 balls in his career, all-time tops for a Boston Celtic.

So, you would know from all the foregoing that he couldn't possibly be a good coach. You know how that works. Great players have no patience to become great mentors. They can't deal with mediocrity.

Great managers and coaches know they have to. They come from the ranks of the less skilled themselves. They know what it takes to succeed when you don't have all that God-given talent. They're understanding, patient, sympathetic. Great generals know they don't have an army of superheroes.

A Babe Ruth could never be a manager, for instance. Because he'd be apt to say to a player, "Why don't you just go up there and hit a home run? That's what I'd do here."

Ted Williams tried managing but probably could never understand why his hitters swung at so many pitches that weren't strikes.

A Ben Hogan might say to a protege, "Why don't you hit your drive over there on the right 11 feet from that oleander. That's the short way to hole."

Great fighters never make great managers. The Four Horsemen tried coaching with only mediocre results.

So, when the Indiana Pacers hired Larry Bird before this season, it was assumed it was for his marquee value. Like a lightning rod, he would draw attention away from his underachieving squad, fill some seats from a sentimental point of view. He probably would run screaming for the exits before the year was out with this talent. Larry Bird wasn't coaching Larry Birds.

But this Bird is an eagle.

You see, Bird was used to being underrated. When he first came into the league, he was kind of this "Hick from French Lick." He was a guy who had tried going to Indiana University but couldn't stand crowds, so he enrolled at smaller, more bucolic Indiana State. He led the Sycamores to an undefeated regular season and a berth in the NCAA championship game.

The Celtics' general manager at the time, Red Auerbach, as good a judge of basketball talent as ever lived, drafted Bird a year early, then waited patiently till he played his final season at Indiana State.

Bird, at 6 feet 9, is what they call a small forward today, but he averaged 28 and 29 points a game his vintage years and he was devastating on the boards, pulling down more than 800 rebounds a season six times and 895 one season (up to 300 per annum more than Jordan).

But superstardom seemed to embarrass him. In interviews after games, he looked more like a murder suspect undergoing the third degree than the player of the game. He would hang his head, look around for an escape hatch.

Other players embellished their legends with postgame interviews. Bird just dressed quickly.

All of which seemed to add up to, no coach, he. The consensus was Larry Bird didn't have the background for the job. "Aw, shucks" would not make a postgame headline. And how do you teach people to do something you did instinctively?

The year before this Bird flew into the Celtics' nest, they were 29-53.

When Bird landed they were 61-21. He led them in points, rebounds, steals and scoring average.

But that was a Bird with the ball in the hand. What about the sideline Bird?

Well, if you looked in your paper this morning, perhaps you noticed the Indiana Pacers are in front of the Central Division with a 33-13 record. And guess who's coaching the East in today's All-Star game?

The Bird named Larry. It seems he's still finding a way to get open.

I went down to the locker room the other night after the Clippers' game to check on him.

Looked like the same old Larry Bird to me. As unpretentious as the Wabash but still in charge. Hogan hitting the ball where he wanted to. Williams picking out strikes.

How, he was asked, did he find coaching? Interesting, conceded Bird, grinning.

Is it fun? he was pressed. Bird grinned again. "I didn't say that. I said it was interesting."

Oh! Did he find it hard when some players did not play up to his level? He laughed. "Over the years, I've seen a lot of guys who didn't even play up to their own level."

Well, why did he get into coaching, asked his interrogator, thinking, perhaps, of the reported $4-million salary and a promise of ownership. Bird smiled. "I got bored. Boredom is the worst thing there is. Even getting beat is better than getting bored. I couldn't stand going around doing nothing."

Did he ever find himself wanting to dive on a loose ball out there or pull down a defensive rebound? Bird grinned. "Nope. I just hope my players will."

Well, did he expect to defy the odds and succeed? "I always expect to succeed," Bird said. "If you don't expect to succeed, you won't."

If I were the league, I'd circle the wagons, lock the shutters. This is a Bird of prey.

•••••••••••••••••••

MARCH 12, 1998

For Pete's Sake, Get in Trouble!

INDIAN WELLS, Calif.—Each year I come to the Newsweek tennis tournament here, I have this dream. In it, I see this headline: "Tennis Star Netted in Vice Raid."

Or, in my mind's eye, I read this story in which the world's best tennis player either a) fails to show up for a final and has to be disqualified; or b) refuses to take the court unless the promoter ups his appearance fee by a million or so; c) gets picked up for spousal or girlfriend abuse; d) kicks a photographer, chokes a coach; f) gives the finger to a booing crowd; g) robs a bank, hits a cop, leads a high-speed chase, or all three; and g) tries to argue his way out of it because he has this split personality and it was one of the other guys in his body who did it.

Alas! Pete Sampras has only one personality. He's the kind of guy who repairs divots, pays his taxes, is in bed by 11. He doesn't get into bar fights, throw anybody through plate-glass windows. He doesn't drink and drive, probably goes to church, takes his spoon out of his coffee before drinking it. He gets his hair cut and doesn't dye it purple. He wears white on the court. He doesn't even have an earring.

What he does do is play the best tennis day-in, day-out of anyone since Rod Laver. He has won Wimbledon four times. He has won 10 Grand Slam events. Only three men have won more and they're long gone. No active player is within five of him.

He smiles all the time. He's steak-and-potatoes, vanilla ice cream, white bread and probably puts sugar in his coffee. He doesn't even have a Roman numeral after his name.

He's not only the best player today, he could be the best player ever. A case could be made, given the competition today. I mean, nobody had to worry about the Swedes or Russians in Bill Tilden's day. Or Czechs. Just a few guys with "vons" in their names, and a lot of Brits named "Bunny."

He's as American as fudge. And if you think that isn't unusual today when a tennis cloakroom sounds like a UN meeting, you don't follow tennis.

So if Sampras has all this going for him, if he's, like, our last best hope in this ritualized sport, why does he get a sitting ovation? Why are the only ones asking for his autograph tax auditors? Why isn't he taking the court looking like a shoe billboard? Or on TV slobbering catsup all over his shirt?

What does he have to do?

Well, let's see. He can begin by calling Wimbledon officials "the pits." He can punch out a parking attendant. Bite his opponent in the ear. Argue line calls with four-letter words audible in the royal box.

I mean, what does he think this is—a game?! Get a life, Pete! Hit somebody! Stiff a White House invitation like Michael Jordan or Tiger Woods. That way you can snub a whole country.

Get sued for back taxes or back alimony. What? You're not married?! Well, get married! To some movie star so you can hit the tabloids regularly.

Why isn't he making movies like Shaquille O'Neal? He'd be perfect for Disney. As wholesome as Flubber. Bambi, for all of that.

But, no. That would be too much exposure for Sampras. This way, he has to carry his American Express card when he leaves home. No ticker-tape parades, no paparazzi staking out his London apartment.

Let's face it, we like our idols flawed in this country. Even Babe Ruth drank.

So what Pete needs is a make-over. A Latrell Sprewell goes to a public relations specialist for a make-over to show he's really a nice guy who tried to talk some sense to his coach and found the best way to do it was to begin by choking him.

Pete's P.R. is different. He needs a make-over in another direction. I mean, you can just hear the publicist telling him, "First, Pete, we gotta get you a beard. Get you to look less like an altar boy. Now, how do you go to work? By Beemer? No, Pete, you gotta get a motorcycle. Put your hat on backward and run over chickens. Snarl at autograph hounds, call head-linesmen 'chokers,' and maybe you could give some thought to spitting. Biting? Wear scruffy clothes and you might want to consider a ponytail. You know, just rub everybody's nose in it. You might want to scare up some scandal in your groupies. Look what it's done for the president of the U.S. People love it. I could get you on Letterman."

But Pete Sampras is down here for Charlie Pasarell's "Wimbledon West" at Grand Champions this week, where, for two years in a row, he has been knocked out of the tournament early.

So, the only part of his persona or apparel Pete's concerned with this week is his racket. He has gone to a thicker gut, he tells you, because he thinks the dry air added unexpected distance to his shots in past rounds here and cost him crucial points.

But never mind that. We're not interested in technical trivialities here. Does he plan to creep into the hearts of his countrymen by smashing his racket, cursing, vilifying, raging at authority and, in general, acting like your basic tennis spoiled brat?

Pete looks startled. "No," he said, "not my style. I don't like to lose control like that. That's not who I am. Sure, I get mad, but never to where I have to make a fool of myself."

As you can see, he's hopeless.

• • • • • • • • • • • • • • • • • • • •

MARCH 20, 1998

O'Malley Moved— Rest Is History

When Walter O'Malley moved the Dodgers out of Brooklyn, a lot of people there wanted to hang him in effigy. Others wanted to hang him in person.

But what he had done just might have saved baseball.

You don't think so? Think that might be a little hyperbolic?

Well, just ask any .248 hitter earning $3.1 million. He would have been lucky to get 35 grand back in the days when God was in Heaven and the Dodgers were still in Brooklyn.

O'Malley moved the game to a new level. TV was a catalyst, but there was TV in 1958 too.

The trouble was, baseball wasn't national till O'Malley came along. It was a pretty exclusive club, largely confined to the northeast section of the country.

The Boston Braves didn't upset the status quo much when they moved to Milwaukee in 1953. And in 1955, the Philadelphia Athletics moved only to the perimeter, Kansas City.

Baseball was so intermarrying, you're surprised it didn't get hemophilia. Thirteen times since 1921, the game's shining crown, the "World" Series, had been an all-New York affair, a so-called "Subway Series." The game was like a key club. Bring references. Wipe your feet. Anything west of the Hudson was Hicksville. West of the Mississippi, Indians.

When the Braves broke the mold and moved to Milwaukee, no one much cared. The Braves were the stepchild of Boston. The game there belonged to the Red Sox. The Braves used to play before crowds so small you could count them. And they had won only two pennants in their long history, both before World War I.

In Philadelphia, the A's had a long history of dismantling championship teams for money. This time, they sold everything—players, franchise, license to play, even home plate. They moved out of economic necessity.

But the world wasn't ready for O'Malley's shock. He not only moved the Dodgers, he took the Giants with him.

New Yorkers couldn't have been more outraged if he had jacked up the Empire State Building and moved it to Peoria. It was the biggest heist in sports history.

Actually, Giant owner Horace Stoneham wasn't much of a hard sell. He was going to move to Minneapolis anyway.

And the Dodgers in Brooklyn weren't really paupers in baseball terms. They were the most successful franchise in National League history. They had won six pennants in the 10 years before the move, had been in pennant playoffs twice. They had finished no worse than second over those years, drew a million customers a year, led the big leagues in net profit after taxes—$1,860,744—for the five-year period 1952-1956.

They were the darlings of every political activist in the country because they had integrated the sport a decade before.

O'Malley had acquired the club for an initial outlay of $720,000, after he had been sent by the Brooklyn Trust Co., executor for the estate that owned the club, to oversee its operation.

He oversaw it, but he didn't overlook it. He could see the club's value. It was a one-of-a-kind among only 16 in the world, rarer than diamonds, and he chafed under its penny-ante operation.

He wanted to build his own ballpark in downtown Brooklyn. He was playing in a rundown, cracker-box firetrap built in the early 1910s.

He wanted to move no farther than the intersection of Flatbush Avenue at Atlantic, but, even though the governor himself, Averell Harriman, came down to sign the enabling legislation, O'Malley got the runaround. The Sports Center Authority there, so to speak, died on third.

So O'Malley sang "California, Here I Come" and took his team to the airport.

Bill Veeck and his St. Louis Browns had tried to make this move a few years earlier, but Veeck was persona non grata with the execs of the game, notably Yankee owner Del Webb. O'Malley, on the other hand, was so powerful, it was said when Commissioner Ford Frick spoke, you could see O'Malley's lips move.

When O'Malley moved, he built his own ballpark in L.A., the last baseball executive to so do, but only after the city had deeded him 184.5 acres in Chavez Ravine and spent $4 million more grading and asphalting the property. O'Malley traded them the minor league ballpark, Wrigley Field, for the Chavez Ravine site, which was kind of laughable, since Wrigley Field was headed for the wreckers' ball anyway and, at 41st and Avalon, was hardly prime real estate. (In San Francisco, Stoneham got his city-built ballpark for a paltry $125,000 a year!)

The O'Malleys profited hugely from the transfer from Flatbush to Chavez Ravine. But how about the city of Los Angeles? How has it fared?

Well, compared to the blandishments other cities hold out to major league franchises from football to basketball, it may seem to some that the Dodgers came cheap.

How do you put a price on the benefit to the community of five World Series titles, nine National League pennants and nine division titles, plus other close title races?

How much business does that attract to a town? How much does the fact the city has a major league franchise in the first place play in attracting tourists, conventions, new businesses? The facts are, any city bids high for a Super Bowl, which comes with a high price tag affixed.

Even a World Cup with an alien sport commands spirited bidding.

The good to the game of baseball is incalculable. How much vitality does it attach to a sport to have out-of-town cadres hanging up "Beat L.A.!" signs? To have a franchise playing the bad guy in the melodramas of baseball? To move into an area where the rest of the country had already beaten them? The state is 32.6 million now. It was probably half that when the Dodgers came.

The Dodgers were the first team to attract more than 3 million fans in a single season, 3,347,845 in 1978, and they have done it 12 times. Before the Los Angeles Dodgers, not only had no team ever drawn 3 million, only one, the Cleveland Indians in 1948, had ever drawn 2 million.

There used to be a boast in Los Angeles, "No matter how hot it gets in the daytime, it's still cool at night." The puckish movie producer Bob Goldstein amended that once, observing wryly, "No matter how hot it gets in L.A. in the daytime, there's still nothing to do at night!"

The Dodgers gave L.A. something to do at night.

O'Malley had to survive a battle with J.A. "Black Jack" Smith, brother of San Diego's C. Arnholt Smith, who owned the minor league franchise, the Padres. Black Jack got a referendum put on the ballot that would have nullified the O'Malley deal with the city, and it failed to pass by only a few hundred votes.

One of Smith's charges was that O'Malley would build a papiermache ballpark in Chavez Ravine and, after a few perfunctory years, tear it down and put the land to more lucrative use.

Instead, O'Malley built the Taj Mahal of ballparks. It is as pristine today as it was 36 years ago, when it was built. It looks years younger than Eastern ballparks that were built years afterward. Part of that is climate. But part of it is Dodger care and maintenance. You can almost eat off the floors of Dodger Stadium. The O'Malleys treated their fans as guests, not intruders (try a Shea Stadium usher if you don't think the opposite can be true).

So, who got the better of the deal? I would say it's a wash. The

Dodgers have been good for L.A. And, of course, L.A. has been good for the Dodgers.

It's a different game today. I doubt if any Brooklyn Dodger ever got more than $100,000 a year. I doubt if any got that much. I know none got a million a year.

Today, you stay in contention extending multimillion-dollar contracts to 12-13 pitchers, .245 hitters, backup infielders. Baseball grew incrementally after the Dodger move. In real estate, the watchword is "Location! Location! Location!" O'Malley was far ahead of his fellow moguls in spotting that.

O'Malley and the Dodgers have been good neighbors. They maintained a franchise and an image remarkably free of controversy and scandal. They perpetuated a profile of a Dodger player who was a cross between Pee Wee Reese and Jackie Robinson, if not a model citizen at least a reasonable facsimile. Dodger players didn't hit night court. If they did, they were shortly no longer Dodger players. Not our kind, you see. Not Raiders, thank you.

If he did nothing else, O'Malley nationalized baseball. Before him, and except for St. Louis, it had never been west of the Mississippi River.

They didn't exactly run the business like a mom-and-pop store. But it was a family business, catering to moms and pops. And grandpops. I don't know of any sport you can bring a granddaughter to more comfortably and confidently than to Dodger baseball.

I would hope that doesn't change. Before the Dodgers, L.A.'s hometown heroes were Charlie Chaplin, Douglas Fairbanks, Mary Pickford, John Wayne, Clark Gable, James Stewart and Bob Hope, to name a few.

The Dodgers added Sandy Koufax, Don Drysdale, Jim Gilliam, Maury Wills, Fernando Valenzuela, Steve Garvey, Tommy Lasorda, Vin Scully and Mike Piazza, to name a few.

That's not a bad trade.

• •

APRIL 26, 1998

This Star Knows How to Produce

If I were Tim Salmon, I'd be a first-class jerk. A royal pain in the you-know-what. You know, come to the ballpark late...in a stretch limousine...in a bad mood...complaining about everything: "Can't somebody turn that music down! Who's the wise guy who took my hair dryer?"

That sort of thing. I'd throw my weight around. Brush past the autograph hounds: "Not now! Can't you see I'm busy?" Backbite the manager: "I can't do everything around here. What am I, Ty Cobb?" Skip batting practice: "I don't need it. Let the rest of those clowns who do take it." In other words, show 'em who the Star is. The one the people come to see.

Now, we switch to the real Tim Salmon. He is the Star of the Anaheim Angels, no question about that. But he shows up as if he came to pick up the towels. Or fix a shower leak.

He's as unassuming as a butler. He hustles. He works out. He takes outfield. You'd think he was trying to make the team, not lead it.

All he does is hit 30 or more home runs a year, drive in 100 or so runs, bat .290 to .300 and cross the plate 90 or more times.

If that doesn't entitle you to be insufferable, I don't know what does. If it were me I'd make Albert Belle look kindly. If Salmon did that in New York, they'd name a candy bar after him. He'd have a nickname. He'd be at least "King" Salmon.

He's the Anaheim Archangel. But you'd never know it. He's as taken for granted as the U.S. mail. You only notice it when it's not there.

He doesn't make waves. He's as dependable as the tides. He's polite to everyone. He's a church-going Christian. He arrives early, leaves late.

He loves the game and is grateful that he gets paid to play it. He's the Angels' quiet man.

When he got kicked out of a game last year, the whole league was in shock. It was the first time in six years and 700 games. He didn't curse the umpire, he just made a few suggestions about how the ump could be better. It was a rookie umpire and he had a strike zone the size of Texas. He struck Tim out on a ball so low, Salmon would have needed a nine-iron to hit it. Tim thought the ump ought to be made aware of that.

The league knows he's good, especially the pitchers. But a red light doesn't go on in the press boxes the way it does when Ken Griffey, Belle or Frank Thomas hits town. Oh, sure (yawn, yawn), Salmon is good. But who did he punch lately?

Tim accepts the second-banana role. He talks glowingly of Griffey—"I'm in envy of him. He bats the same way, the same stance he's always had. He's comfortable at the plate. Me, I change my stance to suit the pitcher. Griffey makes the pitcher change his." He also notes, "When compared to Griffey or (Mark) McGwire, I don't consider myself as that kind of player."

An interesting bit of modesty in a game where historically most ballplayers would demand to be traded if the manager had the nerve to replace them with Henry Aaron.

Salmon even admits to being overmatched by a pitcher.

"Oh, sure, it happens," he acknowledges. "Sometimes a pitcher like Randy Johnson is going to overpower you, no matter what you do."

Most big league ballplayers wouldn't admit they were overmatched by Nolan Ryan in his prime.

Last year, Salmon finished seventh in the American League MVP voting. Griffey hit 56 home runs and drove in a league-leading 147, so he got all 28 of the baseball writers' votes, for an aggregate 392 points. Fair enough.

But Tino Martinez of the Yankees, who hit .296, with 44 homers and 141 RBIs, was second with 248 points. Salmon also hit .296, with 33 home runs and 129 RBIs, but got only 84 points. Several players above him had lower batting averages, fewer homers or fewer RBIs, but more votes.

What should Tim do? Get a dangling earring? Miss the team bus? Become a jerk?

I bring all this up because we may get a redefinition of MVP. That's because Salmon is out of the lineup thanks to a strained ligament in his left foot that makes every step feel like walking on hot coals.

Even so, he came to bat, limping, the other night and promptly hit a massive home run, his seventh of the young season. But he had to leave the game when even a home run trot hurt.

It's hard to be a team leader from right field. But not impossible, Angel Manager Terry Collins says:

"His numbers dictate his importance to us. But you can't really appreciate Tim till you get to watch him every day and see his work habits. Whether he's hitting .175 or .375, Tim doesn't take anything for granted. He comes out, he hits early, he runs out every ball, he slides hard. He acts as if he has something to prove. If I'm a young player and I see that, I'm going to be impressed. He's our Star. And our leader."

So far as Collins is concerned, charisma is knocking in the winning run. Salmon does that. Quietly.

So, the archangel Tim is the leader of this heavenly chorus. If he can emulate another great leader, Joe DiMaggio, and manage to play despite a painful heel injury, he won't have to be rude and churlish to be recognized as a star. You'll be able to tell by the pennants.

MAY 28, 1998

McGwire Has Poetic License

There was ease in Casey's manner as he stepped up to his place;
There was pride in Casey's bearing and a smile on Casey's face,
And when, responding to the cheers, he lightly doffed his hat.
No stranger in the crowd could doubt 'twas Casey at the bat.
Ten thousand eyes were on him as he rubbed his hands with dirt;
Five thousand tongues applauded when he wiped them on his shirt.
Then, while the writhing pitcher ground the ball into his hip
Defiance gleamed in Casey's eye, a sneer curled Casey's lip.
....

It has been called "the grand old poem for the grand old game," baseball's signature muse.

It's as valid today as it was 110 years ago this month when it was first published in the San Francisco Examiner.

Today's Casey is the Rt. Honorable Mark David McGwire, resident first baseman and star slugger for the St. Louis Cardinals. And all of baseball.

He's the prototypal Casey, everything but the sneer upon his lip. If you sent to Central Casting for a Casey at the Bat, they would send you Mark McGwire. If you could build one from scratch, you would come up with Mark McGwire. He's that ever-lovin' cliche—what Baseball is all about.

He couldn't be anything else. Look at him: 6 feet 5, 250 pounds, big smile, python biceps, red hair, he radiates strength and power. Babe Ruth II.

The thing about this Casey is, he has the mythic presence. A lot of the record homer-hitters didn't. Roger Maris, for example. Maris hit more homers in a season, 61, than anyone, but he never really scared a pitcher. He never hit 40 homers in any other season and he hit more 315-foot home runs over Yankee Stadium's inviting 298-foot right-field fence than any slugger ever did.

Fame frightened Maris. Ruth dined on it. Oddly enough, the only slugger I ever saw who would have fit as comfortably in it as Ruth was the late amiable Luke Easter. But Luke got in the big leagues too late.

How many home runs will McGwire hit this year? Would you believe 70? More? He's on pace for 81.

Consider this: McGwire hit his 25th home run May 25. Do you know when Ruth hit his 25th the year he hit 60? June 30. Think about it. McGwire is one month ahead of the greatest cluster of home run-hitting in history (Maris played 10 more games than Ruth).

Do you know when Maris hit his 25th in the year he hit 61? June 19. Maris hit his 25th in his 63rd game. McGwire hit his in his 49th.

Nor is he aiming at a friendly defenseless fence. Busch Stadium is an adult, unforgiving complex—330 feet down the lines, 402 to dead center and a daunting 372 in the alleys. Of course, when a ball meets McGwire's bat, it will go not only out of Fenway Park, it will go out of Yellowstone.

McGwire's credentials are impeccable. He has hit more than 50 homers twice. Last year, he hit 58. Only four players in history have hit that many, Ruth (twice), Maris, Jimmie Foxx and Hank Greenberg.

Ironically, because he was traded, McGwire's 58 didn't win a league title. His 58 would have been an all-time best in the National League (where Hack Wilson's 56 in 1930 is the league's top mark). But he hit only 24 in the National League, the rest in the AL before he got traded.

But Casey is at the bat in the grand old game again. St. Louis is Mudville. All baseball is Mudville. Crowds come to watch batting practice when McGwire is in town.

There'll be joy in Mudville this year of Our Lord as the modern-day Casey breaks a hallowed record. There were frowns when Maris displaced Ruth. No one will mind if McGwire replaces Maris.

He won't need postseason awards. He already got one. The other day, the Cardinals were playing the Giants. Bottom of the 14th, two out, nobody on, score tied. The new Casey at the bat. Does this mighty Casey strike out? Naw. The Giant manager walks him intentionally.

Now, there is a hoary baseball adage adhered to by almost all managers: Never, ever, put the winning run on base.

Dusty Baker ignores it. Two innings later, he wins the game. His strategy works.

So, do we now rework the grand old poem ending? To make it read:

Oh! Somewhere in this favored land the sun is shining bright
The band is playing somewhere and somewhere crowds have
gawked
But there is no joy in Mudville, mighty Mac has just been walked!

• •

JULY 9, 1998

Budding Leader

Does baseball need a commissioner?

Does an airliner need a pilot? Does a symphony need a conductor? Does a prison need a warden? A lion act a tamer?

Baseball without a commissioner is—well, picture 30 passengers on a 747, each with a different destination and a different timetable insisting his needs be met first. And no one at the controls.

The office came into being in the first place because the owners couldn't control the players. Now, they can't control one another.

The game picked Judge Landis back in the '20s because the players, who didn't have a union, found another way to make more money: They fixed games.

Landis fixed them. Even though he was a celebrated jurist, he ignored the law and the verdict of the jury that acquitted the eight "Black Sox" players accused of throwing the World Series. Judge Landis threw all eight out of the game anyway. The judge had his own jury nullification.

I bring this up because a friend of mine, Jerome Holtzman, probably the premier baseball writer of his time, has written a book about the office, "The Commissioners—Baseball's Midlife Crisis."

It's timely, because today Bud Selig is expected to become the ninth full-time commissioner in the game's history.

Holtzman examines the office of the commissioner from the days when baseball didn't have one to the present time when it doesn't either.

Landis ruled baseball the way the pharaohs ruled Egypt. He threw guys out of the game almost for double-parking, 19 players in four years. He also boxed the owners' ears, once breaking up the Cardinals' so-called "chain gang" of minor league farm clubs and setting free dozens of indentured players.

When he died, the owners vowed never again to select such a dictatorial, curmudgeonly autocrat. They strove to find one who was as owner-friendly as their butler ever since.

Baseball's second commissioner was A.B. "Happy" Chandler, who had been governor and U.S. senator from Kentucky.

A warm and gregarious man, Chandler did one meritorious thing: He could have vetoed Jackie Robinson's severing of the color line. Holtzman quotes Chandler telling Branch Rickey, "I am the only man on earth who can approve the transfer of his contract from Montreal to Brooklyn." Then, he did it.

The owners refused to renew his contract.

He was succeeded by Ford Frick, a former newspaperman who was probably as close to the owners' ideal as they were likely to find. The perception was, every time Ford Frick said something, you could see Walter O'Malley's lips move.

Still, Frick lasted 14 years. He was a supporter of the Baseball Hall of Fame at Cooperstown, N.Y. He also put an asterisk after Roger Maris' name when Maris broke Babe Ruth's home run record but needed 10 extra games and 50 extra at-bats to do it.

"History has not been kind to Frick," Holtzman acknowledges. Frick presided over the first franchise switches in the modern history of the game, the Boston Braves moving to Milwaukee, the St. Louis Browns to Baltimore, the Philadelphia Athletics to Kansas City, Washingtons all over the place, and the Dodgers and Giants to California. Frick raised no objection.

He was succeeded by a military man so unfamiliar to the game and the public that the writer Larry Fox was moved to exclaim, "My God, they've picked the Unknown Soldier!"

Former Air Force Gen. Spike Eckert was as unsuited for the job as a nun, and the owners, in some embarrassment, fired him in midterm.

The owners picked a league lawyer, Bowie Kuhn, next. The trouble was, by the time he came along, baseball already had a commissioner: Marvin Miller. The head of the players' union, Miller was really in charge of the grand old game by then.

Miller vs. Kuhn was Koufax vs. Willie Miranda, Sampras vs. Agassi. A mismatch.

Kuhn presided over the most devastating swipes at the underpinning of the game in history—the demolition of the reserve clause, the admission of arbitration. He let the fox in the henhouse. He made some pawing efforts to preserve the traditions of the game, but Miller kept slipping a called third strike past him.

Free agency came into being. The multimillion-dollar ballplayer emerged. Kuhn was helpless. He could not restrain owners from throwing money off the back of trains.

Peter Ueberroth thought he could. Ueberroth could have been the best commissioner the game had. But he despised the owners.

He began by recommending they stop dumping truckloads of money on .240 hitters. He urged them not to enter the free-agency bidding. He pointed out that 26 clubs were on the hook for $40 million to players who were retired or otherwise no longer playing.

To Ueberroth's surprise and chagrin, the union seized on his advice as evidence of "collusion," a violation of the Basic Agreement. The arbitrator agreed with them. Baseball was fined $280 million, the "largest single penalty in the history of sports."

Bart Giamatti succeeded Ueberroth. Giamatti is remembered chiefly for banning Pete Rose from the game for life. Rose bet on baseball. Rose also bet on horses, cards and the color of the next car coming down the street. But he didn't fix games.

Fay Vincent was the last full-time commissioner the game had. The owners not only dismissed him, they abolished the office.

Oh, they finally picked an owner for the job. But "owner-commissioner" is an oxymoron of the first water. So is "acting commissioner."

As this is written, Bud Selig is on the point of accepting the full-time commissionership. He managed to get his Milwaukee club out of the American League on his (interim) watch. But he also managed to get a World Series canceled.

Before Judge Landis would have let that happen, he would have kicked 30 owners out of the game for life. Which might have saved the game at that.

••••••••••••••••••••

AUGUST 9, 1998

How Can NFL Not Miss Us?

I can't for the life of me understand the NFL.

You know, the population of California is about 33 million. It's bigger than some countries. Correction: It's bigger than most countries.

And more than 50% of the state's population lives south of the Tehachapi Mountains.

And Los Angeles doesn't have a pro football franchise.

Green Bay, Wis., does. Figure that one out. Population? Oh, say, 100,000.

Buffalo has one. Population, 400,000. Jacksonville has one. Population, 700,000.

What does the NFL have against crowds? I thought that was the whole idea. Put franchises where there are lots of customers.

Oh, pro football is a sport where you only have to fill your stadium about nine times a year. So, you can get away with a Green Bay. You couldn't put a major league baseball franchise there. You have half a 162-game season to try to sell out.

You can put the odd heavyweight championship fight in Goldfield, Nev. Or Shelby, Mont. But you can't run a weekly fight card in either and hope to draw.

And what of television? You want to sell your beer in a 15-million market or a 50,000 one? Let me guess.

You know, 50-odd years ago, when pro football first came to Los Angeles, it had to take its hat off, wipe its feet and beg for admittance. The colleges were outraged. Let a pro team into L.A.? In the Coliseum? I should say not! Let them play in the 12,000-seat Gilmore Stadium. Nobody was going to go to the games anyway.

Even when the Dodgers came here, they had to survive an ugly referendum election to get to stay.

But a case could be made that L.A. helped elevate pro football to the sports staple it has become. Before 1946, it was kind of a cultivated taste, like caviar or liver pate. People went to Army-Navy, Yale-Harvard, Notre Dame-USC for their football, not to the Pottstown Maroons versus the Decatur Staleys.

The blackest day in the pro game's history was the day Carroll Rosenbloom jerked the Rams out of the Coliseum and took them south. He skewed the picture permanently. It was the main step in a series of steps that left L.A. abandoned on the doorstep with a note pinned on it.

The symbiotic relationship between the Rams and the town was perfect. The Raiders never approached it.

A part of the problem was that the Coliseum was run by a joint commission. You know the old story: A camel is a horse put together by a commission.

The commission had a no-hitter going. Subconsciously, it achieved what USC wanted back in 1946—it ran the pros out. The commission ran the Rams, Raiders and Bruins out of the Coliseum. It ran the Lakers and the Kings out of the Sports Arena. Of course, Walter O'Malley took the Dodgers out of the Coliseum as soon as he could. O'Malley thought the Coliseum commissioners were really the Marx Brothers.

So, the NFL guys won't go near the Coliseum. They want the community to build them a new Taj Mahal to play in at no cost. And why not? About 20 other municipalities have done so.

The league has always been an amalgamation of musical chair franchises anyway. They used to fight you when you wanted to move. Now, they got a better idea: They charge you. About $1 million per 100 miles, I believe.

So, what does L.A. do? Punt? Probably.

Do we wait for the pie-in-the-sky stadium? Say "Pretty please!" to the league?

We're beyond that. Tell me they don't miss us around the league. I mean, they don't get to hang out those "Beat L.A.!" banners anymore. The town you love to hate.

So, why don't we just scrape out the insides of the Coliseum, put a new state-of-the-art facility in there with personal-seat licenses, luxury boxes, club levels and all the other sweet swindles on corporate America's expense accounts? Name the stadium after a weed killer for $100 mil or so.

That's what Ed Roski and his colleagues want to do.

Roski is the co-owner of the Kings and co-owner of the new $370-million Staples Center under construction downtown, new home of the NHL and NBA in L.A.

Roski holds that the Coliseum is a part of L.A. worth preserving as a historic artifact. That's all very well, but we're not into history in this town. Stop 10 people in L.A., ask them who Mary Pickford was and you'll get blank stares from all 10.

But Roski contends that the Coliseum is the only viable alternative. Zero acquisition costs, three-quarters of a billion in federal investments in the area, no environmental impact study. Get a team, lock the commission politicians' follies in a mountain cabin someplace and kick off.

And, do we get an expansion team or the—yeech!—Arizona Cardinals? Or do we get the Minnesota Vikings and thaw them out?

The mystery is, where are the TV networks in this picture? They have as much at stake as the league, the community.

Studies have shown the town greets the loss of the NFL with a shrug, even that some Southern Californians prefer no home team because they get more league telecasts, sans blackouts.

I doubt it. Gamblers and pro football junkies will watch any football game ever played, but you can't tell me a hometown honk will stay home from the beach or the golf course to watch the Jacksonville What's-Their-Names play the Carolina Whozits. Not in my house, they won't. And we're supposed to care about the San Diego Chargers? Get a life.

Anyway, you gonna sell more Toyotas in northeastern Wisconsin than in Southern California? If you think so, you haven't been on the Ventura Freeway lately.

L.A. doesn't need football so much as football needs L.A. You NFL guys need L.A. I would recommend you listen carefully to all proposals, including the Coliseum card. If you continue to worry more about Cleveland than L.A., well, I hate to sound threatening, but there's always soccer.

Jim Murray's First and Last Columns

• • • • • • • • • • • • • • • • • • • •

FEBRUARY 12, 1961

In This Corner, With the Pen, Is the New Guy

I have been urged by my friends—all of whom mean well—to begin writing in this space without introducing myself, as if I have been standing here all the while only you haven't noticed. But I don't think I'll do that. I think I'll start off by telling you a little about myself and what I believe in. That way, we can start to fight right away.

First off, I am against the bunt in baseball—unless they start batting against the ball John McGraw batted against. The last time the bunt won a game, Frank Chance was a rookie.

I think the eight-point touchdown has had it. It's added nothing to the game unless, of course, you count the extra bookkeeping.

I'm glad the Rams traded Billy Wade. I won't say Billy was clumsy, but on the way back from the line of scrimmage with the ball he bumped into more people than a New York pickpocket. I have seen blockers make ballcarriers look bad. Wade was the only ballcarrier I ever saw make the blockers look bad. Those poor guys were getting cross-eyed trying to look for him out of both corners of their eyes. They never knew which way he went.

The play usually ended up with some mastodon of a defensive end holding Billy upside down by the heels and shaking him, like a father with a kid who's just swallowed a quarter. Billy gave up more ground, faster, than Mussolini at the end of the war. The Chicago Bears better put his shoes on backward or he'll dance right out of that little ballpark of theirs. I expect him to be the only quarterback ever tackled for a loss in the seats.

I think Jim Brosnan is the best writer in baseball. I think Cincinnati would be gladder if he were the best pitcher.

I know what's wrong with Eisenhower's golf swing but I'll be cussed if I can figure out what to do with that spasm of mine. (Ike lifts his left leg; I think I leave my feet altogether).

I'd like once more (if Jimmy Cannon will pardon me) to see Elroy Hirsch and Tommy Fears going out on a pass pattern and looking back for a Waterfield pass. Throw in Jimmy David on defense and I'll pay double. David was the only guy I ever saw who could maim a guy while pretending to help him up.

I hope Steve Bilko has lost weight. The last time I saw him in the Coliseum, the front of him got to the batter's box full seconds before the rest of him. If he were batting left-handed, part of him would be halfway to first base before the pitch came in. Even then, the umpire could beat him down there.

I don't think anyone should be surprised at the disappointing showing of our Olympians in the '60 Games. There is an old adage, "When in Rome, do as the Romans do." So our boys did. The coaches didn't like it, but the girls did.

I think almost every pitcher in the big leagues has a good spitball but I prefer to see Lew Burdette load one up for the batter in a tight situation and then make believe he's only wiping his chin. The only way you can be sure the ball is wet is if the ump calls for it and Lew rolls it to him.

I think the Washington Huskies football players were more enterprising than a bunch of Dead-End Kids in an empty candy store. But I still think the guys who are beating Minnesota over the head for claiming (correctly) that it had an edge in the second half in the Rose Bowl are the same guys who would be crying "Washington was robbed" if the roles were reversed in that game.

I have been held up to you as somewhat of a joke athletically, but I want you to know I had one superlative as a college freshman baseball player. I was the most nervous right fielder our team ever had. Our coach, Ralph Erickson, had only four fingers on his right hand and the prevailing theory was he had the regulation five until he saw us and started biting his nails. I caught a fly once and got so carried away I almost decapitated our first baseman on the throw-in. As I remember the first baseman, it wouldn't have affected his play much. He didn't use his head a great deal.

I won't say the kids today are softies but I'd like to see them learn to play Little League with the ball I had to play with. This was a "dime rocket," the cover of which came off after the first solid hit and it had to be wrapped in thick friction tape. I'd like to see Duke Snider throw it out of the Coliseum. In fact, I'd like to see him hit it past the pitcher's mound on the fly. I have bowled with lighter balls.

I was gratified by the reaction to the announcement Jim Murray was to write a sports column, an immediate and interested "Who??!" Mel Durslag did throw a bouquet, though. I'll read the card as soon as I take the brick out.

I came to Los Angeles in 1944 (the smog and I hit town together and neither one of us has been run out, despite the best efforts of public-spirited citizens) and my biggest sports disappointment was the 1955 Swaps-Nashua race, which I helped arrange. I have never believed Bill Shoemaker was properly tied on his mount that day when they sprang the barrier. But I will ask Bill—and believe what he says because his next lie will be his first.

I really don't understand why the Angels haven't signed up Bob Kelley to do their broadcasts. He's the only guy in town who can prevent Vin Scully from throwing a shutout.

I hope Bill Hartack, the jockey, continues to take himself off sore horses. I know it irks the stewards but I'd rather have them sore than the horses—especially if I'm betting on the race because if there's one sore horse in the field, I'm usually on him, handicapping it all the way.

I couldn't tell from that letter of Billy Wade's whether Don Paul wanted Waterfield's job or just wanted him to eat in his restaurant.

Every sportswriter is expected to make a prediction and because I would like to leave the game ahead, I will predict the Angels will not win the pennant—this year, anyway. On the other hand, the way they have been messing around with baseball, they just might change the game to loball. Then, the Angels would be a threat. Just my luck.

• •

AUGUST 16, 1998

You Can Teach an Old Horse New Tricks

DEL MAR—Well, it was a slam dunk for Free House, a "Where is everybody?" win.

The bridesmaid finally caught the bouquet. The best friend got the girl in the Warner Bros. movie for a change. The sidekick saves the fort.

Free House just won't fold the hand. Three times last year, in the most publicized races in the sport, he chased his competition across the finish line in the Kentucky Derby, Preakness and Belmont. In the money in all of them, in the photo in one of them, he was the hard-luck champion of horse racing.

He was expected to go quietly into the sunset. A game effort but no cigar.

He got a measure of revenge Saturday in the Pacific Classic here. He ran away from Touch Gold, who beat him in the Belmont. The horse who beat him in all three Triple Crown races, Silver Charm, didn't make the dance or he might have gotten a different view of Free House too.

The Pacific Classic is not your Run for the Roses. No bands play Stephen Foster as the horses come on the track. But it's not your basic overnight allowance, either. It's a $1-million race, major on the schedule. It's a very big win for Free House. He's not What's-His-Name anymore. He's Who's Who.

You know, in most sports, the athlete gets a generation to prove himself. A Jack Nicklaus wins his first major at 22 and his last at 46. A

George Foreman wins Olympic boxing gold in 1968, and 30 years later he's still fighting. Babe Ruth hits his first home run in 1915 and his last in 1935.

But a racehorse has to act like he's double-parked. He gets only months to prove he has been here.

And if his prime coincides with that of Man O' War, Citation, Secretariat or even Count Fleet, he might as well have been born a plow horse.

What did Free House do that turned him into a star? Well, he got older.

You know, it's the public's notion that the racing begins and ends with the Kentucky Derby and its Triple Crown satellites. Everything else is New Haven.

Trainers know better. Every real horseman knows a colt's (or a filly's) 3-year-old season is not indicative of real prowess. I mean, a Kentucky Derby is not only too early in the career, it's too early in the year.

It has been won by a lot of horses who are just better than claiming horses. It has been lost by a lot of horses who were too good to have that fate. Native Dancer comes to mind. Gallant Man. Damascus. Bold Ruler.

Of course, a horse doesn't know whether he won the Kentucky Derby or not. But his owner does. His rider does. History does.

But trainers as a class manage to hold back their enthusiasm. There's even evidence a trainer resents a Triple Crown race.

That's where a Pacific Classic comes in. It's a trainer's race. A real test of his skill in bringing a horse up to a race. The real business of racing.

A Kentucky Derby can be a crapshoot. Not a Pacific Classic. You win a Pacific Classic because you're at the top of your game, not because eight other horses were still wet behind the ears. Many a Derby has been blown by an immature runner jumping shadows, spitting bits, lugging out, horsing around.

Not a Pacific Classic. Here, the horses are all grown up, professional. These are the true class of the sport, older horses. Dependable, crafty. Consistent. They don't beat themselves.

There probably has never been a good older horse who couldn't beat a good 3-year-old. It's so taken for granted, they have to give the kids weight. Handicap horses used to be the glamour stars of the track anyway. They made a movie about Seabiscuit, who never ran in the Triple Crown and never got good till he got middle-aged. They wrote poems about John Henry, who never did either, even though he ran in 83 other races. They used to call Equipoise "The Chocolate Soldier." Exterminator, called "Old Bones," ran 100 races.

They were the heart and soul of racing.

Free House bid fair to join them Saturday. He won so easily, jockey Chris McCarron should have brought a book. He rode him like the Wilshire bus. "You could have ridden him today!" he called out to Free House's co-owner Trudy McCaffery.

McCarron rode such a confident race, he remembers thinking, "If I were a cocky individual, I would have turned to the other riders and said 'Shame on you!'"

Added McCarron, "This horse is so generous with his speed, I knew if he ran the way he trained, these guys were beat."

He has one holdover from his misspent youth: He tends to kick out sideways and decelerate in the stretch, almost start to tap-dance. "He gets to wondering where everybody went and to want to slow down and wait for them," McCarron explained. McCarron hustled him across the finish line four lengths ahead of second-place Gentlemen on Saturday and about 16 lengths ahead of Touch Gold.

Ironically, McCarron rode Touch Gold to victory in the Belmont.

So, is he glad the order was reversed Saturday? Is yesterday's jinx horse today's king of the handicap division?

"Arguably," said McCarron, "a case could be made."

Anyway, it's nice to know getting older has its flip side.

Epilogue

On September 26, 1998, about 2,500 fans of Jim Murray attended a memorial tribute to him at Dodger Stadium hosted by the Los Angeles Times and its sports editor, Bill Dwyre. The featured speakers were Al Michaels, host of ABC's "Monday Night Football"; jockey Chris McCarron; Oakland Raiders managing partner Al Davis; Jerry West, executive vice president of the Los Angeles Lakers; Chick Hearn, broadcaster for the Lakers; Ann Meyers Drysdale, former UCLA All-American basketball player and network sports commentator; and Vin Scully, broadcaster for the Los Angeles Dodgers. Their comments follow.

AL MICHAELS: Do you know the way certain things just get burned into your brain and they never leave? In the mid-'60s, in high school here, I picked up a Jim Murray column and he was in Cincinnati and it was that famous line where he was at Crosley Field and the freeway, I-75, was being constructed outside the ballpark. And he had been going there for years, and they had completed about nine more feet. And Jim wrote, "It must be Kentucky's turn to use the cement mixer." So in 1971, I am offered the job as the broadcaster for the Cincinnati Reds. This is a dream come true and I can't believe it, and I go to Cincinnati and meet with the general manager of the team, and he calls me up and he says, "Al, we're honored to ask you to become the number one broadcaster for the Cincinnati Reds." And I swear to you, all I can think of saying, though I didn't, was "Where is the cement mixer?" He was right, and we moved there for three years and they finished only another nine feet. Jim was always ahead of the curve.

I think about a couple of signal moments in sports in the early '60s. One in television, I think, was the advent of a show called "Wide World of Sports," the brainchild of Roon Arledge. Where he not only brought into your living room sports from around the world that you really didn't know a great deal about, or thought you cared about, but widened the scope of it, and made it interesting for you. And I think of that in concert with what took place on February 12, 1961, when Jim Murray's column first appeared in the Los Angeles Times, and the signal moment that that was, not only for sports journalism in this area, but for the country, and what it did for the profession. And that's what Jim did. He didn't just write about the game, the dugout, the clubhouse, the press box. Jim saw a grander vision. And for Jim, he always took you on this grand tour, so you learned so much about so many other things and the peripheral things that you wouldn't even think about or thought that you cared about. And he was, I guess, like any great writer, he was a teacher, and he was an educator, and I think in growing up and beginning to read him, when he started, he brought to all of us knowledge of, for instance, he would write about an athlete and compare him to Caruso. Now, I thought at that point Caruso was Eileen Eaton's attorney at the Olympic Auditorium. But then you look up Caruso and find out, Italian tenor, one of the greats of all. And I started buying Caruso albums because of Jim Murray.

He was an original. And I don't have to tell you how he has spawned through the years dozens and dozens of imitators. But he really transcended the business of sports writing. He did it in a different way, and from that very first column on, when we picked it up that morning and thought we hadn't seen anything like this, he was able to do that for 37 more years. And when you think when Jim began, this stadium was still under construction, it would open up the next year. The Angels had just been born, and would start to play that year. The Rose Bowl was still the bowl game. John Mackay was beginning that incredible run with USC football. We were on the verge of watching John Wooden begin the most unbelievable run in terms of dynasties in the history of sport at UCLA. The Lakers had just come to town with a couple of guys named (Elgin) Baylor and (Jerry) West. Santa Anita and Hollywood Park were drawing 50,000 on a Saturday afternoon. The Rams were drawing 80, 90 and sometimes even a hundred thousand. Arnold Palmer and Jack Nicklaus would come to town for tournaments and they were transcending their sport. And Jim was here to chronicle all of it, to guide us through what was a very golden time.

And we had a golden man who did it. I know we all have our favorites in terms of what the best Jim Murray column was, but to me, as great as he was with baseball and basketball, and boxing, the way he wrote about golf and the way he wrote about horse racing, were unlike anybody's ever understood either of those games. He just had this innate incredible feel. And how he did it, day after day and year after year, I think astonishes all of us and I guess maybe the only way you could do it is with a lot of love in your heart....

You know, Jim Murray, let's face it, he made us laugh, he made us cry, he could make you glad, he could make you mad, he could make you sad. But I think most of all, Jim Murray made you think, he made you think, every day.... And into his life came Linda. And Linda, I think everyone knows what it did for Jim, but on behalf of all of us who are here, thank you for that gift. Thank you for that extra decade of Jim Murray because we might as well have won the lottery. Jim Murray wasn't on this earth long enough. But thank God we had him as long as we did.

Chris McCarron: First of all, I can't begin to tell you how flattered and privileged I am to be invited to participate in the celebration of the life of a true sports legend. And I want to think Linda and Mr. Dwyre for bestowing this honor upon me. I know it was pure coincidence, but how fortunate am I to be able to say that the final story written by the greatest sports journalist of all time was about me and a partner of mine called Free House. Free House had just won the Million Dollar Pacific Classic. And because I knew Jim was at the races that afternoon, I couldn't wait to read his column the next morning. He had the uncanny ability to draw analogies that would sometimes make you laugh, and other times make you cry. With Free House, he stated how racehorses only have a couple of years to prove their worth, whereas human athletes are afforded a generation of time to impress us. Like Jack Nicklaus. He won the Masters 24 years after he won his first major. Or George Foreman's career, spanning over 30 years.

Jim had a way of putting things in perspective that was so easy to understand. We all know how much he loved the game of golf, as do I. And, because he had the opportunity to play the game, we could easily understand how perfectly insightful he could be about a golfer's swing or about a particular course, because he probably played that course. However, Jim never rode a racehorse, at least not to my knowledge anyway. But the way he wrote about Bill Shoemaker's technique, you'd think that Jim was his teacher. I remember one column he wrote about Shoe after he won the '86 Derby on Ferdinand. Shoe was over 50 years old at the time. And Jim said that "Bill Shoemaker has the hands of a concert pianist. He doesn't ride a horse, he plays a horse." And knowing Shoe, and knowing the great talent that he possessed with those hands of his, it just put the biggest smile on my face, and just a warm feeling all over my body. Jim could paint a picture so vividly with his words for us to appreciate that he didn't even need, we didn't even need to attend the sporting event just to feel like we were there. We could imagine just being there, every, every single time he wrote about a particular event.

I loved the story that Jim wrote this year, the week of the British Open. It was about Jack Nicklaus, I think it was 1963 or 1964, I'm not sure of the year. But Jack, I think, was either tied for the lead or one shot in front with one hole left to play. And as he's standing on the 18th tee, he's waiting to hear the reaction from the crowd because the two competitors that he had to beat were on the 17th green. And he figured that if he didn't, he wasn't sure how to play the last hole, aggressively or conservatively. And he thought that he could determine how to play the hole by listening to the roar of the crowd. He didn't hear any roar at all, so he figured both players must've parred the hole. So he went in and played that final hole conservatively and he lost the match. Afterwards he finds out that they both had birdied the hole. When he asked how come there was no congratulatory roar from the crowd, he was told that the British crowd doesn't cheer luck, they only cheer a skill. Both players were lucky to make birdie. And it completely threw Jack a curve and he lost the tournament.

When Jim used to write about stuff like that, you could just feel that you were there at the tournament taking part in it. He was just so gifted at bringing that point across. And I had dinner with Jim and Linda just two weeks before he passed away. We were down at Rancho Santa Fe during the Del Mar meet. And I used to love to ask Jim questions about Ben Hogan and players like that. And he told me Hogan very seldom, almost rarely, asked any advice of his caddie about a particular shot. And one day at Riviera, Mr. Hogan looked at the caddie and said, uh, "What do you think we got here?" And the caddie says, "Mr. Hogan, I think it's 145, maybe 46 yards." Hogan looked at him and said, "Well, make up your mind." That I just love, love stories like that.

Anyway, as as an active participant in the sport of horse racing for over 24 years, I've had to deal with the media in many different forms and on many different levels. But let me tell you, it can become pretty trying at times. However, I can tell you, without reservation, that Jim Murray was the kindest, most considerate and conscientious individual I ever had the pleasure of dealing with. In closing, I would like to say that on behalf of thoroughbred racing, our industry has been blessed and privileged to have Jim Murray as a fan and a friend. And we miss him.

Al Davis: Jim Murray did not play for the Los Angeles Raiders, nor did he play for the Oakland Raiders, nor did he ever, in any way, wear the famed silver and black. But if he did, he would've worn it with pride, with poise, with class because he was a star amongst stars. With all his excellence, with all his artistic touch, with all his warm human compassion, the thing that captured my imagination most about Jim Murray was the fact that while the company man is a bad connotation, Jim Murray, to me, was an organization man. He played for the Los Angeles Times. His devotion, his dedication, his loyalty, his towering courage were the things that make great organizations great. He won for 40 years. Forty years as a columnist.

We believe that plain old-fashioned wholesomeness is not passe. When you talk about the team of the decades, and we're talking about the 1960s, the 1970s, the 1980s and the 1990s, Jim Murray was the sports columnist of the decades. If a great man is someone who inspires in others the will to be great, the testimonials that came from all over the country by his contemporaries, the people who are here today, certainly establish Jim as a great man.

I remember in the mid 1980s, the Raiders were in Los Angeles. We were hot. I certainly refrained from making speaking engagements. But one group came up with a great idea: They would get Jim Murray some kind of honor and they would ask me to present him. And both of us accepted, and I said to Jim before the presentation, "Is there anything you want me to say?" And he said, "Well, don't be too laudatory." And I said, "Don't worry, Jim, I won't be, there's not that much there." And he said, "Be humorous, and take us back to Hartford and back to Brooklyn where I had come as a kid from Massachusetts and played my high school baseball at Ebbets Field." And there were great memories between us because he reeked with tradition, which I loved. I love tradition, I love history.

But I want to tell you the story I told that night that he came up to me—it's a funny story—afterwards and said, "That's the best I've heard in a long time." And I said, "With that in mind, I'll use it in the future." I had gone to Baltimore at a young age to be a scout for the Baltimore Colts. A friend of mine in Brooklyn, New York, became the sales manager of a dog food company called Yum Yum dog food. And they sold

Yum Yum dog food all over the country. My friend asked me to come up and listen to him speak. They brought in all the sales managers from all over the country, they were before him as I am before you. And he said to them, "Ain't we got the best company in the whole world?" And they all were roaring, "Yum Yum, yes sir! Yes sir!" He said, "Ain't we got the best dog food in the whole world?" And they said, "Yes sir, the product is great!" And they were screaming. And then he said to them, "Aint' we got the best sales force in the whole world!" And boy, by that time they were standing in their chairs with their glasses. And they looked out at him and he said, "Then why in the hell ain't we sellin' any dog food?" Well, a little guy got up in the back of the room and he said, "It's the damn dogs! They don't like it!" There's a sequel to it, but not tonight, maybe we'll come back.

I was so distraught, and I really was, over the news of Jim's passing. I admired the guy. I'm glad I came here today to pay tribute and to see some of the legendary heroes. To see some of my friends out in the group who I worked with, who I fought with, who I competed with, who were great in their own right. And it brings a realization of the debt, the continuous debt that we all owe to each other. And I for one will never forget that debt to Linda McCoy and the Murray family. Our heart goes out to you, and I want you to know our love and our door is always open. And I hope you'll use it from time to time.

I can remember recently all the talk of all the teams moving, and there came a report out of Connecticut that Lowell Weicker, who had been a senator, was now the governor of Connecticut. He was intending to bring pro football to Connecticut, to Hartford. He was going to build a stadium there, he had the Indian Village, where they had all that money available. And they would put their name on the stadium. And he contacted the Raiders about moving the Raiders to Hartford, Connecticut.

Well, I had a call from, guess who. Jim Murray. "Jim," I said, "what is it you want to know?" He said, "I want to know if this is a true story. A pro football team in Connecticut." Now, Jim had a hobby of taking on all the cities in America. For Oakland, this was his prime statement: "You pay a dollar to go across the bridge to San Francisco, but you get a free ride going back to Oakland." And my friends in Oakland used to say to me, "Can't you get him to cut it out?' And I used to say to them, "Hell, you should see how he took on Los Angeles." But let me go further with you. He was really interested in Hartford, Connecticut, for pro football. So I told him, "Yep." And he said to me, "Where are they gonna build it?" I said, "Right down by the railroad tracks right in downtown Hartford." He said, "That's where I lived." I said, "I'll tell you what I'll do. If I go back there, we'll see to it that your house becomes a historic monument." He says, "You're not kidding me, building a stadium in Hartford? Who's gonna come there?" I said, "I'll tell you one better, Jim. The mayor of Brooklyn was out here last week. And he wants to bring the team back to Brooklyn." Jim said, "Listen, if this becomes reality, I've seen it and I've heard it all. Hartford, it's impossible." They're still working in Hartford to get a team and I'm sure now that they'll take that house, condemn it and keep it as a historic monument.

I'd like to finish by saying, I've said it before, and I wish you'd bear with me, that I wish that I had a stadium that had a million seats. Maybe a thousand luxury boxes, and that I could go down memory lane and bring back all the great and special people who contributed to the sports world in my time, 1950s, 1960s, 1970s, 1980s and 1990s. And picture it as an Olympic procession. That every group would be categorized and they could parade around the stadium as those million fans would roar the roar of the crowd would be deafening. And I can see the sportswriters, wearing their fedoras, the red, white and blue. And maybe not carrying the flag, but walking out in the front, leading the group of sportswriters, would be Jim Murray.

And so I end this little tribute with the hope that time never really passes for the great ones. It just gives them a cloak of immortality. We continue to remember him, we continue to love him, and we continue to say, "Godspeed, Jim Murray, I know you're up there with many great people and I know you'll do your part to make it easy for all of us to come visit you." Thank you very much.

Jerry West: Everyone here has talked about Jim's affinity for picking on cities. Well, I tell ya, he picked on the whole state of West Virginia, where I'm from. In 1961, we did, we traveled by covered wagon in professional basketball. And Jim was in that covered wagon going to an exhibition game in Morgantown, West Virginia, where I played my college basketball. When we left there, we played an exhibition game, a sellout crowd, people were just absolutely wonderful. And the people in West Virginia, I call them simple, simple in the most wonderful way. It's a place I love. I love to go home, I love the people there. They're wonderful, they're loyal. The very next day there was a newspaper article that he had written about the state of West Virginia. All of a sudden Jim Murray became public enemy number one. I was the butt of every joke, and still today am the butt of every joke about West Virginia. Everyone kids me about West Virginia. Well, I will tell you that if Jim Murray had made another trip back to West Virginia anytime within three years, uh, his life span would've been much shorter. I have never seen a man talk so badly about a state. I think he made a statement in his article, everyone had these satellite dishes and stuff around. He said it was the state flower of West Virginia. He talked about people's cars, he said, "People were sewing patches on their cars with needle and thread."

But traveling with him was truly unique. I didn't look at him as a sportswriter. Most sportswriters come into all of us after a particularly tough, tough loss or a tough game. And they'll come in and ask the obvious questions, "Why didn't you do this? Why didn't you do that? Boy, you were terrible." Well, I'll tell you what. Jim Murray never had a bad day as a writer. When almost each and every one of [us] athletes have failed, we failed in front of the whole world, it's not a very good feeling. This man did not fail. Heard Tommy Hawkins say Murray was the Babe Ruth of sportswriting. Well, since I'm a basketball person, I will tell you, he is the Michael Jordan of writers. I have watched everyone mimic or copy Jim Murray. Can't do it. Just can't do that. This man is truly a legend....

I had a chance to play golf with Jim early in my life. We were playing at Tamarisk Country Club in Palm Springs. I had turned into a pretty respectable golfer. And I asked Jim, I said, "What kind of golfer are you, Jim?" He said, "Well, I'm not exactly Ben Hogan." And he proceeded to prove it that day. When we got in, I said, "What'd you shoot?" He said, "I didn't, uh, keep my score, I just weighed the score."

I get up early in the morning. There used to be a rush for me to get the paper and Jim Murray's column. There's no rush today, I'll tell you that. His articles touched so many people, so many athletes. I think we all, in the recesses of our mind, wish that we could write something as poignant and lasting as he's done over the years....

I guess all of us would like to leave a legacy. And everyone asks, people that have been successful at least in the public's eyes, what legacy would they like to leave. And I think we all could leave a legacy like Jim Murray, his words, the incredible respect that he shared with all of us who read him so glowingly. I guess for me, the one thing I would say, I was more than someone who read him. I considered him a friend. All of us are going to miss this man. We missed him when he passed away. But he has left a void for all of us who rushed to pick our morning newspapers up. I'm really deeply appreciative that you would have me here today, you know, following some of the very eloquent people that you will hear today. I feel kind of in awe of those people. But I'm deeply appreciative that, uh, you would have me. Thank you very much.

CHICK HEARN: Thank you very, very much. I addressed a group earlier in the week in another city. And I said, "This'll be the most difficult speech I've ever been asked to make." But I want to say to those who preceded me on the microphone and those who'll follow, that they've loosened up the strings and done what Jim would've wanted, have a good laugh. West is talking about that wagon and the caravan going to West Virginia. I was in that wagon. Hell, it wasn't getting in, it was trying to get out of town. By that time they'd formed a posse.

There's an old adage used about sports that "Records are made to be broken." And I think in almost every instance, they are. But I'll tell you one thing, the records of Jim Murray's writings will never be equaled, let alone surpassed. He could write about a cockfight, he could write about an automobile race, he could write about anything, and find the heart and soul of the subject and put it into words. I called him a wordsmith. He, unbelievably, wrote columns that many mornings, I got up and ran over and got the Webster dictionary, brought it back, or I'd read a paragraph, or the whole column twice to make sure that I had the gist of what he was saying, he was so clever with words. That's something that is God given, but it has to be mastered by someone with unbelievable, unequaled ability. And that's what Jim had. He was just unbelievable. He could start your day with a smile.

I know a lot of people in the sporting world that he didn't think were doing the right thing, but he would never embarrass them by saying it. He would use innuendoes that you would get the drift. He had some devil in him. The last time I saw him was closing day of the Hollywood Park meet this year. Linda and Jim, Marge and I shared a table. And had a nice lunch, wonderful lunch. And I said to him very honestly as he was looking over the racing program I said, "Jim, I don't know anything about the racing. But I hear you're the best there is. What'll I do?" He said, "I don't know anything about racing either." So he said, "Just look over your program and take six bucks and bet in on some horse in every race, across the board." So at the end of the fifth race, I'm sitting there looking at my five losing tickets. He comes back to the table and he had his left hand full of bills, dollar bills, five-dollar bills, ten-dollar bills, twenty-dollar bills. And he put them down at the table and he started to countin' them, and he got to three hundred and I quit lookin'. I said, "You son of a gun. You said you didn't know anything about it." He just said, "Irishman's luck, Chick, just lucky." And he meant it....

They always say about us Irishmen that if you kiss the Blarney stone, you are endowed with the gift of eloquence. And I think Jimmy must've kissed it many times because certainly he was endowed with a gift of eloquence. Unbelievable. Last night I was thinking of Jim as I watched the home run derby. First I see Sammy Sosa hit one. Puts him ahead of Big Mac (Mark McGwire) and just what, less than an hour later, Mac comes back and knocks one out of the park down in St. Louis. And I thought to myself, and I said to Marge, "Golly, would Murray have had a great column tomorrow morning about this race!" About the twists and turns that has taken. We are deprived of that. And I am so sorry, so sorry about so many things because of the loss of Jim.

But right now, I'll betcha, betcha anything, he's sitting up in heaven with Don Drysdale, and Murray's asking him about some of the great records that he established here as a Dodger under Peter O'Malley. They're sitting under a tree, I guess they have trees in heaven, don't they? Anyway, if you have pearly gates, you gotta have trees. But you can well bet that Jim Murray and Don Drysdale and Walter Ralston and so many others have been reunited, and I hope to someday all of us can join them. It's not original, thank you. Not original, but there's a saying that I like, it says, "May the wind always be at your back, may the sun always shine upon your face." Jim, may God hold you in the palm of His hand for eternity.

Ann Meyers Drysdale: Well, I know if Donnie was pitching, I think McGwire and Sosa would probably have some high and inside pitches on him. And I know when they played in the old-timer games too, Pee Wee was always the first one to go down....

When I was in high school and college, I was like any other kid who would read the sports page and, like any other athlete, couldn't wait to see their name in the paper. And in March of '78 I was privileged enough to win the national championship at UCLA, and my name appeared in Jim Murray's column. So for me, that was probably one of the pinnacles as far as an athlete, to have my name with so many others in Jim Murray's column. So it was pretty neat.

But through the years, I got to know Jim after marrying Don. And the biggest thing that I really admired was the admiration and the friendship and the respect that Don had with Jim. And to see them together, the biggest thing is that they were both gentlemen. And all of us have stories on Jim and, and again, like everybody else, most mornings you get up and you'd go out and get your paper and you couldn't wait to see the sports page, and see what he had written and what kind of picture he was going to paint for you. And Don never missed a turn in his work, and Jim never missed a turn either. He was always capable of making us feel, as so many others have said, and you can look and see what most sportswriters write, but Jim could make you feel and think with your heart.

I saw Jim a few years ago down at the Bob Hope golf tournament. I was playing down there and I was waiting for my car, and, with my mom, we were waiting out in the parking lot. And Jim was there, and he came over and took the time to spend about five or ten minutes telling me stories about Don. The fact that he would, and my mom is Irish, so we had that thing going. And then just this past June, Linda had asked me to play in the Tom Sullivan Tournament up in Riviera. And, again, Jim took the time to come over before we got teed off and told me stories about Sandy (Koufax) and Don, and to me that was so special, that he would take the time, and he was always coming up to me and doing those things. And, for me, he was just that gentleman that was able to do that.

And he not only made my world a better place, he made so many other people's world a better place, and God blessed him with such a special gift, and he was able to share that gift with us. And I've known that he just enriched all of us, so I feel very fortunate to be in this, this world of sports. And to be here at Dodger Stadium and Don out on the wall. So I know Jim's looking down, and I really appreciate being here today.

Bill Dwyre: We have the world of golf represented by the following. It's a letter that was addressed to (Jim's widow) Linda Murray, but it was meant for all of us here today. It says, "I am sorry I cannot join you, your families, and all of Jim's friends and admirers who will gather today at Dodger Stadium. Barbara and I feel very fortunate to have been among Jim's friends, and we were certainly among his greatest admirers. Jim was a terrific friend. The mutual affection we shared grew with each year as we crossed paths on the professional tour and renewed the friendship.

"When I first joined the tour in 1962, Jim Murray was perhaps the biggest name in all of sportswriting circles. And I imagine that even when I won my first U.S. Open, more people recognized his name than recognized mine. He had a gift for capturing the excitement of sports and making it come alive through the words he put on a page. Jim's contributions to the game of golf and all of sport, for that matter, are immeasurable. The stories he crafted brought many into our game, and his unique and clever wit captured the essence of this gentleman's sport. His talent will never be duplicated, but his qualities as a person are ones which everyone would do well to emulate.

"I cannot begin to tell you how touched Barbara and I were to find that Jim had mentioned me in his August 16th column. It became his parting gift of friendship and I will always cherish knowing that I was in his thoughts his final day with us. While Jim had many kind words for me during my career, when it comes to defining greatness, there is no question in my mind that Jim Murray was the greatest sports writer of all time. We will miss him, but his trademark smile and unforgettable words will live on."

It's signed, Jack Nicklaus.

Vin Scully: This is not an overcast day, nor is it a gloomy day. The Irish would call it a soft day. And considering the man whose memory we honor today in this hardhearted world, it's a perfect day. A soft day. I wear a smile today like so many of us because I smiled whenever I saw Jim. I smiled whenever I talked to Jim. And I will smile whenever I think of him.

And yet for me this is a very precious and poignant moment. You know, for many of us, looking back over our lives, there is a period of time where it honestly took courage to live. Courage and strength and hope, and humor. But courage and strength and hope and humor have to be bought and paid for with pain and work and prayer and tears. Jim Murray had all of those virtues during his lifetime. And he also had those crosses to bear. There was a decency about him that was glorious to behold. There was an indomitable spirit. And he gazed upon life and the world with somewhat of a bemused sense of humor.

I once introduced Jim at a dinner, and I said this from the heart. I said that if I ever had to be stranded on a desert island with a man, he would be the man. And I meant it. He was a great raconteur, especially of Irish stories. He was literate and well read without being stuffy. He had a God-given talent that was out there for the world to enjoy, whether he was covering the fields of entertainment or sports. And yet, with all of the honors he received, he remained ever humble, somewhat shy and self deprecating.

Jim Murray was my dear friend, and I sincerely thank God for the gift of his friendship. You know, the great use of life is to spend it for something that will outlast it. And Jim Murray used his life to the extent that he has indeed outlasted it. Wherever and whenever there will be sporting events, and wherever and whenever the media will gather to cover those events, Jim will live on as an icon to emulate. About 35 years ago, Jim and I were playing golf at Riviera—it was his favorite golf course. And somehow we got on the subject, he had just been starting to write the column, and he was talking about mail that you receive. And I told him I would always remember the first letter I ever received, and it was addressed to Mr. Ben S. Kelly. From that moment on, I was always either Kell or Kelly. And to go along with that feeling, he then became Murph or Murphy. And we would meet in crowded pressrooms and press boxes at all-star games and World Series and a voice would cry out, "Kell!" And I would turn around and say, "Murph!" And everybody would look at each other as if to say,

"The poor devils don't even know their own last names." You know, Shakespeare said it best, as he usually did, and when he wrote it, he might very well have been writing about Jim Murray. He wrote, "His life was gentle, and the elements so mixed in him that nature might stand up and say to all the world, 'This was a man.'"

And in closing, I have one personal request and I hope you don't mind me doing it. "Hey, Murph! It's Kell! Save me a seat!"